Love and the Long Path

*a love story between
two humans and the natural world*

HEATHER A. HOUSKEEPER

"The Botanical Hiker"

Love and the Long Path

© 2021, Heather A. Houskeeper.

Betula Press

Print ISBN: 978-1-09837-5-751
eBook ISBN: 978-1-09837-5-768

Also by Heather A. Houskeeper

*A Guide to the Edible and Medicinal
Plants of the Mountains to Sea Trail*

*A Guide to the Edible and Medicinal
Plants of the Finger Lakes Trail*

This book is dedicated to the many people who work to support, maintain, and preserve the Long Path. Without you, a journey like this would not be possible.

CONTENTS

PROLOGUE

We stepped close to the cliff's edge, summoning the sweet smell of the firs as we brushed against their scratchy boughs, round cones crunching beneath our feet. We had climbed 1,500 feet through a dark forest to reach this vista. I could hear my own pulse in my ears, a rhythmic deep thud. But as we gazed upon the layers of mountains in the distance, I heard it slow and go quiet and, in its absence, I wondered if we really stood here at all. We'd dreamed of summiting Slide Mountain, the highest peak in the Catskills, since before we even began our journey. For days, we'd been hiking through this mountain range, passing vista after vista, however none had prepared us for the immensity that this one, still below its summit, spread before us. No longer did we feel as if we stood on a cliff composed of solid rock packed in dirt and woven tight with tree roots, but literally on the slippery shoulder of a giant. We teetered hand in hand. This mountain felt alive, and here, perched atop it, there was now no denying that so were we.

INTRODUCTION

It took me a decade to summon the courage to hike
the Long Path with Scott. In fact, it took five solo long-distance hikes before I
had the guts. I remember the first time I encountered the Long Path when I was
twenty-four years old and hiking the Appalachian Trail from Georgia to Maine.

Every step was hard. Every single one. I developed blisters the size of quar-
ters that morphed from liquid-filled balloons to bloody scabs. My shoulders
and back rubbed raw. Rectangular white blazes on furrowed bark passed like
reflectors on a highway, one after another after another. I wrestled with lone-
liness and with feelings of guilt for setting out to do this hike in the first place.
My then-longtime partner did not share my love of the natural world nor did
he understand my passion to hike long miles and perceived my desire to walk
thousands of miles from home as an act of abandonment. I had just shimmied
my way through a crevice between two house-sized boulders in New York's
Harriman State Park when I came to a trail junction that bore a wooden sign: The
Long Path. I stood frozen in dismay. I'd been certain *I* was on the *longest path*.

The Long Path stuck with me. The Appalachian Trail wasn't all there was?
The gods had played a cruel trick. Farther up the trail, somewhere in Connecticut,
I ran into an old man with a beard that hung down past his shirt collar, wearing
blue jeans and a weathered flannel. He asked me how old I was and when I told

him, he laughed so hard his big belly shook. "Oh! You'll be doing this the rest of your days! You'll never be normal!"

I didn't make it that year. I hiked from Georgia to Virginia, then drove north and hiked from New Jersey into New Hampshire, hiking a total of 1,000 miles. That wasn't good enough for me. The following year, I started all over again and hiked the whole trail, 2,175 miles from beginning to end, passing that darn sign for the Long Path again. When I reached the top of Mount Katahdin, the trail's northern terminus, I cried tears of joy that finally I could put my dream to rest.

Afterwards I dove into the world of plants. I wanted to know them by name and their value. Although I had deeply immersed myself in nature, I had walked atop the trail but not with it. When I had a blistering infection, I hiked as fast as I could to reach a town pharmacy and when I got low on food, I hiked even faster to the nearest grocery where I would gorge on fresh produce. I was needled by the feeling that the medicine and food I needed likely lay all around me, there on the trail. I attended herbal medicine school and learned how to identify the plants of Appalachia, how to forage, and how to prepare these foods and medicines at home.

Then three years later, the tiny pilot flame that had burned quietly but steadily in my heart lit fire beneath my feet. I had to walk. I said a final goodbye to my longtime partner. Upon returning from the Appalachian Trail, my love for the rugged mountains, tiny wildflowers and towering trees, and possibility of what next grew, and our relationship deteriorated. On a spring day I stood atop Clingman's Dome, the highest peak on the Appalachian Trail and the beginning of North Carolina's Mountains to Sea Trail. From there I would walk 1,000 miles to the Outer Banks, researching the edible and medicinal plants I encountered and foraging, incorporating the plants into my backcountry meals and medicines. I'd put theory into practice, further expand my relationship with the plants, and conduct research for a book that I would write upon completion.

The hike was a success. As I trekked over the tallest mountains east of the Mississippi, I blended wood nettle into noodle dishes and tucked stonecrop into sandwiches. I warmed my numbed extremities by ingesting yarrow tea and later used that same infusion to clean my wounds. In the undulating farmland of the Piedmont, I gorged on handfuls of blackberries and rolled the green juicy stalks of cleavers into balls, popping them into my mouth as I walked. Black birch came to the rescue more than once to reduce pain and swelling in my ankles. Finally, as I neared the sandy beaches of the Outer Banks, I slivered the round leaves of pennywort for salads with yucca petals and wild blueberries. Three years later, I did it again, hiking from the coast to the mountains, but this time to promote my newly published book, *A Guide to the Edible and Medicinal Plants of the Mountains to Sea Trail*. Along the way, I reconciled the loss of my relationship and wondered just what it might be like to share this strong and mysterious connection with the land with another, with someone who appreciated it as much as I did. What would it feel like to sit on a mountaintop, gaze at the landscape not yet explored and think *what next* together? At the same time, I feared any partner in the future might only serve to hold me back.

After the hike, I joined my family in my hometown at a restaurant for a celebratory dinner. While there, I asked about the specialty beers and the waitress called over the bartender, who had the kindest eyes I'd ever seen in my life. He returned several times to check on my beverage, and that evening on the ride home, my mother teased that the bartender might have been more interested in me than the beer.

That spring I set off on the nearly thousand-mile Finger Lakes Trail that runs along the Southern Tier of New York State. I was working on my second book about plants, and connecting to the natural world through hiking had become my life's passion, my driving force. I was content when alone in the woods and solitude was comfortable. But time and again, I wondered just how my journeys might be enhanced by sharing them with a like-hearted soul. More than once, the kind, strangely familiar eyes of that bartender flashed before my mind's eye. But that was silly. I knew nothing of him. Besides, entering another relationship would only complicate matters.

When I'd hiked my last mile on the Finger Lakes Trail and stood before a wooden sign marking the eastern terminus, it felt like someone walloped me upside the head. Beside that sign, at a fork in the trail, was another that read: The Long Path. I considered following it. I could just keep hiking. But there was somewhere I had to be.

I returned to that same restaurant on the country road outside of town, and again, I was met with *kind* eyes. This time around, he didn't waste any time and neither did I. By the end of the night, I learned that he too had a love for the natural world. In fact, he had hiked throughout the country with nothing more than a knapsack and a pair of moccasins and had studied plant medicine with Native American elders. That is, sandwiched between his time as a touring guitarist and later, as a Blues Hall of Fame musician. He was intriguing to say the least. And so, that winter I spent my time getting to know Scott with the kind eyes.

Over the next couple of years our love unfolded. Scott told me that if I would get on stage and sing with him, he would hike long-distance with me. So, I sang. A lot. I figured more songs equaled more miles. We tramped through the region's mountains every chance we got and for the first time I had a kindred spirit with whom I could sleep under the stars, marvel at the intricacies of the tiniest flower, and create stories and songs inspired by our excursions. We began to notice a recurrence. Often, to choose our next hike, we'd pick a random point on the map, based upon names of mountains that sounded interesting. Time and time again, this point landed us on or near an intersection with the aqua blazes of the Long Path. Even when we planned our first multiday hike together on the Shawangunk Ridge Trail, which runs seventy-one miles from the highest point in New Jersey to a country road outside Rosendale, New York, we learned that the Long Path ran concurrently with it for thirty miles.

I had long sensed the subtle call of the Long Path, but now that it beckoned not only to me, but us, its allure was irresistible. I had needed to hike those many miles by myself to prepare for this journey with a like-hearted soul on a trail less traveled.

Looking to the mountains...

PART ONE:

PLAN TO

SURRENDER

CHAPTER ONE

I sat on the floor, an island surrounded by a sea of Knorr Pasta Sides, Nature's Valley granola bars, tins of mixed nuts, packages of six-count English muffins, and jars of peanut butter. Once more I studied our itinerary counting, given our daily mileage, just how many breakfasts, lunches, dinners, and snacks to account for in each box. I ripped open the cardboard tops of Kraft mac and cheese boxes, pouring the spiral noodles into individual Ziploc bags, each with an accompanying packet of orange powder. On one side of me the mountain of cardboard packaging grew, while on my other side, a stack of bags became a sloppy mound. Empty boxes laid on the horizon, each with its own label: Goshen, Phoenicia, Palenville, Gilboa. This very act of organizing mail drops made my heart shine so bright I felt radiant. We were really doing it. We were really going to walk 358 miles from the paved streets of New York City to the edge of the Adirondacks in John Boyd Thacher State Park. These towns' names that meant nothing to me now would one day be vivid memories, trail towns, forever a part of my experience.

Mail drops are essentially packages of food that one prepares ahead of time, then mails to a town's post office by way of general delivery. It is of the utmost importance to know just how much you will need to sustain your energy on any given day and nothing more. Consider this—that the weight of any package you receive by mail must be carried on your back. Therefore, I try to avoid shipping as much as possible, instead resupplying as needed at local groceries and mini-marts when indicated that they're within walking distance of the trail. However, given the Long Path's remoteness as well as its lack of hiker-specific accommodations, this trail would require four mail drops, each containing three to seven days' worth of food. We planned on hiking for roughly thirty-five days, therefore these packages constituted a good percentage of our rations. Thru-hiking is just as much planning as it is throwing caution to the wind and walking for days, weeks, and months through the wilderness, the unknown.

This concept of planning is largely where Scott and I differed in our experience of walking long miles. In the beginning of our relationship, we spent hours beside a nearby lake late at night sharing stories. I'd felt more comfortable here than in the confines of four walls as I told him all about my last two months hiking the Finger Lakes Trail. And beneath the open sky where the stars shimmered and the light of the moon shone down upon us, he wooed me with his own tales of travel.

After over a decade in the music business, surrounded by bright lights, wealthy people, and a nightly schedule touring 200 days a year as a hired guitarist, the industry had almost consumed him. Although he played alongside his childhood idols and took the guidance of the music greats that had managed to retain their integrity, so many around him were misguided and lost in the tumultuous whirlwind of fame. He found himself aimless in the time he did have free from work and watched friends disintegrate into drugs and car wrecks. He held his girlfriend in his arms as she died of an overdose. And so, one night he piled all his precious musical instruments, sentimental tour passes, autographed photos, and various designer rock star garb in a heap in the street outside his Manhattan apartment and lit it aflame. He slid into his sportscar, called his agent to collect the rest of his things and sell them, and drove west. From there he wandered.

He sold his sportscar for a VW bus and took to driving into small towns, parking, and then walking for a week or two at a time through the Rocky Mountains. He sought to reclaim his simple persona as Scott and was doing good until one day a group of random hippies in a Montana town misheard him introduce himself as "Sky," and so the name stuck. He carried a knapsack with a journal, a tarp, a bag of trail mix, and a bottle of water and walked, stopping when he felt compelled to sit in one spot and meditate and sleeping beneath a rock overhang when he needed rest. He told me of encounters with mountain lions, isolation-induced visions, and the magic of walking unmoored from the rest of society. One evening, he and I studied a map, roughly retraced his route, and figured out that he must have walked over 500 miles during those couple of years of wandering. That same night, I fell even deeper in love.

So I knew the man was capable of walking and perhaps withstanding discomfort even better than myself—Lord knows I'd never start a multiday hike through the mountains with just a bag of trail mix and a tarp—but I didn't know just how he would fare with the structure of a planned thru-hike. His journeying had also taken place nearly twenty years previously and he was fifteen years my senior. However, if there is one thing I have learned, it is that long-distance hiking is more mental than it is physical.

Each and every day of our hike we would strive for a certain number of miles so that we could reach our next destination without depleting our allotted food or being *forced* to sleep under a rock. This hike would be very different from his wanderings.

Mail drops filled with heavily processed packaged foods may not seem the diet of a forager, but I'm obviously no purist and definitely no health-food zealot. I tried the health-food thing back on my first hike of the Appalachian Trail. I packed out a small head of broccoli, a bag of quinoa, palm-oil free peanut butter, dehydrated black beans, a host of spices, and even a little bottle of tamari. Yet on day one of the trail, after hiking what felt like the hardest seven miles of my life and faced with having to prepare a gourmet meal using a single aluminum pot, plastic spoon, and a half liter of water on my stove, which would burn out in roughly ten minutes . . . I opted for pita and peanut butter for dinner. On my third night, I met another female hiker about my age, Llama. While I laid out my fixings for yet another cold dinner, she, within minutes, whipped up a steaming pot of creamy noodles all from a single bag. She shared an extra bag with me and by the time I got to town the next day, I dropped my food in the trash and bought enough Knorr Pasta Sides to get me to the next town . . . where I did it again.

As for foraging, I've had a number of students in my naturalist classes ask with starry eyes if I ate only what I gathered. Quickly I shake them free of such lofty notions. Yes, it is entirely possible to live off foraged food, however there are several major complications in doing so on a thru-hike. Firstly, there are not enough hours in the day to gather adequate wild food and still hike ten to twenty miles a day. Secondly, without preservation, the range of nutrients wild foods offer is too limiting to sustain a healthy diet. Each season bears its own food: spring provides greens, summer supplies berries, autumn offers nuts and seeds, and winter roots. One would have to plan on hunting wild game as well to complete their diet. As a vegetarian, until I am forced to eat meat to survive, I've no intentions of consuming it. Thirdly, even if you wanted to spend your time hunting and gathering, I don't know of a long trail that would legally permit you to do so. The Long Path, like all other long-distance trails in the United States, is made up of land under state and private ownership, each with its own set of rules about hunting and gathering.

What I've done instead on my long-distance hikes is forage where appropriate and then incorporate these morsels of nutrition into my backcountry meals, providing fresh vegetables, seeds, and berries where I would otherwise have none. On this trail, given we'd be hiking in late summer and early autumn, our wild vegetables and fruits were limited, yet there would be a handful of hardy greens that persist into the cooler months and some fruits that ripen in fall. These would be particularly appreciated.

But really . . . how terrible is it to gobble a whole box of macaroni and cheese? Tell me you wouldn't want to if excused from calorie concerns and I'm sorry . . . I'd call you a liar.

Into each box of food went a bottle of HEET and small bottle of whiskey, one being a necessity and the other, well, a luxury . . . but that's debatable. HEET is a highly flammable fluid that is poured into a gas tank to remove water buildup but works fantastically well as a clean burning fuel for an alcohol stove. Just one ounce of the stuff creates a high heat flame that can boil a pot of water in seven minutes. The whiskey serves as a good nightcap when aching muscles against the hard ground threaten to keep you awake after a tough day of hiking. Here and there I scattered extra Ziploc bags, vials of water purification drops, wet wipes, and tubes of toothpaste, sundry items that would come in handy in a small town void of stores.

With a black permanent marker, on the top of each box I carefully penned the post office address and then, with an asterisk, scrawled "HOLD FOR THRU-HIKERS" with our projected date of arrival.

To plot one's mail drops, however, one must first plot the entire course of their journey. Resupply opportunities are the most important reason for this draft, but it also provides a glimpse into how many miles you'll have to hike between them, what streams offering water you'll cross, and the severity of high peaks you'll have to summit before reaching them. Other runner-ups are just how many showers you can expect to score along the trail, opportunities for nights in a bed at an inexpensive motel, or possible clever places to charge a cellphone. But these too are luxury items. Merely planning this hike would require its own figurative exploration.

Consider that, as of 2017, the Long Path had just 140 "end-to-enders." Of those 140 people, roughly twenty of them had thru-hiked the trail. To thru-hike a trail means to begin at one terminus and walk continuously to its other terminus. These statistics show that most people hike the Long Path in sections: they are called section-hikers. Sections can consist of a day's hike to several weeks of hiking. To hike sections certainly earns its due credit, given that it encompasses its own host of obstacles, but it is different. The one and only trail guide to the Long Path is written with the section-hiker in mind. Split up into forty sections, each consisting of roughly a day's hike, the guide offers mile-by-mile directions. Information is provided on where to park cars, complete with GPS coordinates. Details of the route abound with descriptions, from mountain views to opportunities for various side trails to the cultural history of an area. It is an invaluable resource painting an experience of the trail in words. But finding quickly and easily, as a *thru-hiker*, how to fulfill your needs required pouring over nearly 100 pages of information word by word.

For example, to find a good campsite other than a designated lean-to or campground, I searched for statements such as "a lovely place for a picnic" or "a good place for a lunch break." To find water sources I looked for key words like "cross a bridge" or "this area is often wet" or "restroom facilities available." As for finding resupply places in town, those that were obvious, like grocery stores, were listed, but mini-marts and vending machines were not, so I took to the internet, looking at Google Earth to see what businesses were within walking distance of a trailhead, then took to further investigating just what amenities each offered via numerous phone calls. I had learned from my previous long-distance hikes that, especially when it came to resupply, thinking outside the box was critical. A mini-mart could provide fuel for a stove whereas a grocery would not, and a vending machine could prove invaluable with days' worth of snacks or bottled water.

As for maps of the trail, those portions that traveled through state park or forest were accounted for. However, those which passed through private land or along roadways would require looking up county and town maps, then hunting out the route via landmarks and road crossings. This took more effort than it was worth and so I figured we would simply follow the blazes.

However, considering the initial concept of this trail, we still had it easy. Vincent J. Schaefer, a chemist and meteorologist with a lifelong passion for the outdoors, first conceived of the Long Path in 1931. Schaefer envisioned the Long Path as an unmarked path that would run through the woods from New York City to the northern Adirondacks, connecting scenic and historic points where one could "enjoy a sense of uncertainty, exploration, and achievement that reaches its highest level when the individual is dependent on the use of compass, marked map, and woods knowledge to reach an objective." We were lucky not only to have a detailed guidebook but also to have a blazed trail at all. We were also fortunate to have the acquaintance of Andy Garrison.

Andy is not only chair of the Long Path and chair of the New York/New Jersey Trail Conference Conservation Committee, but a tireless trail maintainer and an end-to-ender, having completed this trail in sections over a decade ago with his ten-year-old son, Andrew. We were already friendly with Andy, given his regular attendance at Scott's performances, and his son, now a young man, was quite the sax player and had on numerous occasions joined Scott on stage. When Andy learned we would be thru-hiking the trail, he was eager to lend a hand, but little did we know he was a living, breathing, guidebook to the trail that we'd been seeking.

I spoke at length about the route over the phone with Andy, who, while taking a rest on a day of trail work, was able to speak from memory about many of the places through which we would pass. He offered notes on where we might find resupply or camping to be tricky and noted reliable and unreliable water sources. I was thankful to learn before we left that one hotel listed in the guide had burned to the ground and another had long been boarded up. The fact that Andy could recall the entire route section by section without looking at a single map told me that this trail must surely be something special. I looked forward when these points on the map beside which I had scribbled notes were one day inscribed permanently upon our minds as well.

By the time we were ready to lock up our home and hit the trail, incorporating all this information like a patchwork, I had created a day-by-day itinerary. I knew the miles that seemed doable from the comforts of my desk would likely prove insurmountable after already walking ten miles on a rainy day or after sleeping poorly in frigid temperatures. But the inevitable surrender is part of the beauty and thrill of a thru-hike—ditching the plan, rolling with the punches, and standing with arms wide open at the top of a mountain you thought you might never reach.

Hitting the trail at the West 175th Street subway station.

PART TWO:

THE PALISADES

CHAPTER ONE

"I don't know why it's sending us this way!" I hollered from the back seat of my parents' sedan, clutching my cellphone and studying the GPS.

"What way?!" my father bellowed, his hands tight on the wheel. In appearance my father bears an uncanny resemblance to actor, Sam Elliot, in demeanor he's John Wayne, but when just the right factors align, he reminds me of Yosemite Sam. Beneath this tough exterior lies a big-hearted man on a constant quest for adventure. I wonder where I get it from.

"We have to make sure we don't go over the bridge!" my mother yelped for the fifth time. "Oh, I can't look!" Putting a hand over her brow, she sank deeper into the passenger seat. My mother on the other hand is polite as pie, Midwestern through and through, with a penchant for horses. She likes to plan and organize—sticky notes with lists speckle their home; these traits, too, I have inherited, and they have proved invaluable upon every journey I have embarked.

"We won't go over the bridge. Just stay straight," Scott stated calmly, trying to keep us all cool amidst the Labor Day traffic in Fort Lee, New Jersey.

This was li'l country meets big city. Finding our way to the start of the Long Path required parking in Fort Lee, New Jersey, where we would walk across the George Washington Bridge and into the Bronx to the West 175th Street subway station. My mother's greatest fear, and I must admit one of mine as well, is having to drive in New York City. Drivers who ditch turning signals, run yellow lights and make full use of their middle fingers being just a few of the reasons. Oh, and the tunnels—they freak me out, too. On occasion, I have done it, but each time have vowed never again, opting instead to take the train into the city. Scott, who had lived for twelve years in Manhattan, and my father, who had gone into the city periodically as young man for acting classes, found the driving far less frightening, but with the four of us packed into a tiny vehicle in search of a mysterious parking area the anxiety amped up.

We managed to find a parking spot on the side of a busy roadway and spilled out from the car in haste. My parents would walk with us to the southern terminus of the trail and then back over the George Washington Bridge, walking honorary miles on the Long Path. However, this wasn't the first trail my father had begun with me. In fact, every successful hike I had completed, my father had joined me for, if not the first mile, then the first few days, or in the case of the Appalachian Trail, the first several hundred miles.

Scott and I walked the curbside between a stone wall and parked cars, kicking empty bottles, wads of crumpled paper, and broken concrete aside. Never had I begun a thru-hike in such an environment. Normally the start of a thru-hike consists of a long drive down a seemingly never-ending winding country road ascending into the hills. But still the sun was shining, and the George Washington Bridge was in sight. The George Washington Bridge is perched 200 feet above the Hudson River, its steel towers reaching over 600 feet above the water. It is made up of an upper and lower level, each with multiple lanes, which make up 14 lanes that serve to transport vehicles in and out of New York City. This bridge sees over 103 million vehicles per year. I don't know how many were crossing the bridge on this day, but it sure seemed like a good portion of them. We were afforded a pedestrian and bicycle sidewalk although it seemed as if just as many people utilized feet and pedals as motorized transportation.

We walked single file as bicyclists dinged their bells and shouted, "On your left!" which was at least more polite than those that yelled, "Get out of the way!" as they whizzed by at full speed. Joggers, their ears plugged with headphones, and somehow with every hair in place in their high ponytails trotted by like ponies on parade. As a runner I couldn't imagine picking this busy route to clear my head, but when I looked out over the water to my right, the hustle and bustle faded into a background hum. Once halfway across the bridge, we were able to walk in pairs, and my parents took the lead. Seeing them walking hand in hand beneath the steel latticework of the bridge and the largest American flag I've ever seen, hung from between its spires, I felt privileged for the opportunity to take on this journey. To my left I could see the cliffs of the Palisades, where we'd be walking later in the day, trailing off into the distance. Looking down at Scott's hand in mine, I saw how we mirrored my parents, and I could feel his love and support pouring through me, a warm energy like liquid sunshine. I was lucky. So very lucky to have been graced with these people who had nurtured strength and stability in me, so much that I felt confident to take on yet another long journey by foot; to ultimately induce struggle and walk hundreds of miles simply for pleasure and wonder. And for the first time ever on a long walk, I wouldn't be alone.

Once across the mile-long bridge, we reached the winding ramp that led down to the sidewalk. My father held my mother close. "We're in the *city* now, stay close to me, keep your hand on your purse," he warned her. Scott, too, seemed to be scanning his surroundings for possible threats and told a story about how the last time he'd ventured this way, he'd encountered an overturned car aflame. However, none of this seemed in line with the well-polished cars parked *upright* against the curb, the nicely dressed passersby, and even the dear little tabby cat basking in the sunshine on a front stoop. Within just a couple city blocks, we reached the green rectangular sign for West 175th Street and the subway terminal.

While my parents snapped a few pictures of us, I whispered to Scott, "When you were a rock star living in Manhattan all those years ago, did you ever dream you'd set off across the city to hike for thirty days, shower for only five, and wallow in filth?"

"Um, no." He simply replied with a sideways glance and then leaped into my arms like a pretty lady on display for one last picture. To make this journey happen he would carry me and, yes, I would carry him.

Walking back across the bridge, now less distracted by the stream of people around us, we saw something we had not expected to see . . . the plants. A multitude of weeds sprung from the cracks and sediment that had collected on shallow shelves of the cliff face. Silvery mugwort leaves, yellow plumes of goldenrod, purple flowering faces of spiderwort and white star-shaped asters—all medicinal or edible plants—carving out a home wherever they could sprout a seed. I wondered if these plants had a consciousness, and if so, just what their impressions might be from their life-long perch along the busiest bridge in the world.

Once back at the car, Scott and I hoisted our heavy backpacks atop our shoulders. They seemed *far* too heavy for our having a resupply in two days. But this is the way a hiker begins no matter how many miles you have under your belt. Always with more stuff than you need. It is the sickness that befalls most all of us in modern-day society, but a long hike is the antidote. I knew over time we would lessen our load and shed the burden of weight . . . both physically and mentally. We said our goodbyes and I noticed that for the first time my parents didn't tear up. Perhaps they were comforted by the fact that tonight in the woods I would not be alone or if I fell and broke an ankle, Scott would be there to get help. But there was a levity in me, too. For the first time, I didn't feel like I was leaving someone or someone's memory behind. I had all that I needed.

It was one in the afternoon and we still had ten miles to hike through the Palisades Interstate Park. Walking the wooded trail through this slim corridor of forest that runs between the Palisades Interstate Parkway and the Hudson River, I felt as if my insides might implode from the churning of equal parts excitement and apprehension. This is usually how I feel at the start of a long trail.

Did I remember that extra bandana? How about the tent stakes? Do I have enough dinners to get to the next town? Are my shoes a half size too small? What's that weird twinge in my left knee? Here is my running list of concerns. Simply swap them out with different pieces of gear or body parts and it will fit any trail, or I imagine, any hiker.

Tonight I'll sleep to the sound of chirping crickets! No more buzzing cellphones! So much beauty! Imagine what I'll see tomorrow! All I must do now is hike! These are the highs . . . also interchangeable with any trail or likely any hiker.

I tried to describe my feelings to Scott and asked him if he felt the same.

"Yeah, I'm excited, but mostly very aware that we have a *long* way to go."

With temperatures in the eighties, it was far hotter than we had expected. We'd been concerned that, if anything, we'd face colder weather than we cared to endure. The last couple weeks had been chilly enough for sweaters and long pants. Knowing that we'd be climbing in elevation, heading northward, and walking into autumn, we'd brought thermal underlayers, knee-high socks, hats, gloves, and sleeping bags rated to withstand below freezing temperatures. Beads of sweat now dribbled down our temples. Perhaps we had overestimated. My backpack dug into my pelvic bone and lower back and tugged on my shoulders. Just five miles in and I already felt like I'd hiked ten. I was an ox in its yoke. But I didn't dare complain to Scott. And when I asked him how he felt, he didn't say a whole lot either. I could only assume that although he'd shrugged and said, "Good," he too was suffering the initial aches and pains but was also too proud to say so.

The trail was at least mostly level, winding us between red and white oaks, maples, and tulip trees. Periodically an old-growth tree would tower like a giant among them. It was a miracle that these trees had been spared amidst the heavy quarrying of the 1800s. Quarries had been big business back then, some blasting as much as 1,200 cubic yards daily. But rather than blasting, the insistent hum of traffic on the parkway, our soundtrack, mingled with the trill of birdsong. As the trail led us cliffside, pulling back the curtain of trees, we were afforded views of the Hudson River, where we collapsed and snacked, giving our muscles a moments time to rest. Repeatedly, we were sorely reminded of just how little we had traveled, the George Washington Bridge still looming, solid and constant, in the not-so-far distance. We passed numerous day hikers and each one avoided eye contact, a couple didn't even respond as we said hello, nearly brushing shoulders. This behavior, too, a reminder that we weren't all that far from where we had started in the city.

By dark we wandered down an overgrown gravel trail that branched off the Long Path and continued along the cliff's edge. In the black forest behind us, a barred owl hoo-hoo'd its shadowy call, *hoo, hoo, too-HOO, hoo hoo, too-HOO-aw,* when suddenly we were confronted by the most incredible view we had seen all day. We leaned our bellies against the metal cable of fencing held secure by steel pipes plunged into rock and gazed out at the Hudson's inky waters and the opposing shoreline. This cliff would make for an ideal stealth campsite. Stealth camping is not condoned by the New York–New Jersey Trail Conference, the organization that oversees the Long Path, but is practiced largely by hikers following the principles of Leave No Trace. Quite simply put, on an area that's not considered ecologically sensitive, a hiker can camp—using a free-standing tent, and without building a fire—and incur little damage. We'd do this several times along the Long Path given that legal and designated camping areas were not always readily available.

Within short order, we set up our tent and got to making dinner on our alcohol stoves. Tonight's meal would be hydrated instant Indian meals over Ramen noodles—a heavy dish in weight and therefore best to eat first. We arranged our sleeping pads atop a large flat rock surrounded by scratchy blueberry bushes and dry mosses and took a seat. As we spooned warm spicy mush into our mouths, the full moon lit up our dining area like candlelight and sent light streaking across the water below. With a strong breeze in the air, the bugs were nonexistent, all except for a few large red ants that wandered onto Scott's sleeping pad, which he promptly crushed with his thumb. We ate with the ferocity of seasoned thru-hikers and while gazing across the Hudson at the city's twinkling lights, shimmering fireworks suddenly exploded above the opposing ridgeline. Granted, it was Labor Day, but still they seemed a celebration just for us.

Once in our tent, settled atop our sleeping bags that were too warm to climb inside, a symphony arose. It gradually grew in volume until we were steeped in sound, the vibrational rhythms of crickets, katydids, and bullfrogs. Just before dozing off to sleep, I laid there thinking how every single aspect of this moment was perfect. This could be it and my life will have been complete.

We awoke in the morning to the same soft breeze that had lulled us to sleep. It was only 7 a.m. and I was out of the tent and making coffee. At home we are not early risers, but already it seemed our bodies were making the adjustment to the cycles of light and dark. Breakfast was warm oatmeal and black instant coffee. Folgers for me and Starbucks for Scott. He'd insisted upon it, even though each little packet weighed twice as much as mine and cost nearly a buck a serving. That's the cost of hiking with a rock star. Nonetheless within short order we were well fueled, packed up, and moving our muscles for another day of hiking.

Within just a few miles, the sun rising rapidly into the sky, it was apparent that today would be even hotter than yesterday. Temps were expected to reach ninety degrees at zenith. The terrain was also proving difficult, with numerous climbs up and down large slabs of stone, appropriately termed "Giant's Stairs." It was easy to see how these cliffs had been considered a wealthy resource of rock. However, we soon came upon a structure that resembled a miniature castle, two stories tall, complete with a stone spire and steel gate for a front door, and we learned just how these cliffs remained at all. This was a monument to the New Jersey State Federation of Women's

Clubs, which had battled fiercely against the quarrymen for the protection of the Palisades cliffs. These women had seen that the intrinsic beauty of these cliffs well outweighed their monetary value and had articulated their arguments to their government officials. By 1900, Governor Foster Voorhees of New Jersey and Governor Theodore Roosevelt of New York had created the Palisades Interstate Park Commission to acquire and protect these cliffs for public enjoyment. We would continue to see the importance of preservation efforts along the length of the Long Path. The successes of the Women's Federation and of the many others who came after them, had assured that this patchwork of land the trail utilizes would be available for public recreation. Without them we wouldn't be walking this trail at all.

Climbing down yet another stone staircase, we passed from New Jersey, through a swinging door in a crude chain-link fence, into New York State. This fence appeared to run through the width of the woods to the cliff's edge, and we wondered just which side was trying to keep the other out. This brazen imprint of man, marking a rather arbitrary boundary, seemed a sad mile marker to begin our 350-mile journey through the state of New York, but a mile marker nonetheless. Soon thereafter, we exited the Palisades and entered Tallman Mountain State Park. Here the trail traveled atop long mounds of earth that had initially been built to retain seepage for an oil storage facility. Thankfully that project never came to fruition, and so, with leafy oaks towering overhead and moss beneath our feet, it felt as if we were walking grand platforms constructed just for the hiker.

From atop a high knoll, through the thick humidity we glimpsed what looked like an expansive cornfield below us, ears of corn waving gently in the light breeze. However, as we descended, we soon realized that this wasn't corn at all, but rather *Phragmites communis*, commonly called giant reed, in the Piermont Marsh. Standing before it, we felt we might begin to sway with this wall of eight-foot-tall swamp grass. Although beautiful, I've since learned that there's a reason for its air of otherworldliness. This community of phragmites is likely made up of a variety that came from Europe. There are accounts of phragmites in the United States before the arrival of colonists, but our native subspecies is unlikely to create such sweeping monoculture. Such nonnative communities create a sort of blanket, crowding out other native plants such as cattails, wild rice, and wetland specific flowers.

However, like many of the nonnative plants that now call our land home, phragmites is well naturalized and nearly impossible to eradicate. Therefore, we may as well put it to use. Numerous parts of this lithe grass are edible such as its seeds and rootstocks, which can be ground into flour, as well as its young stems, which can be dried and pounded into a fine powder that can be moistened and roasted like a marshmallow. Reportedly it is also one of the best plants for purifying wastewater due to its web of super strong roots. Lastly, we could be using this reed for baskets, mats, and paper, as it was historically employed. This sea of phragmites before us would not be the last along the Long Path corridor.

We entered the small town of Piermont, hot and tired, with six and a half miles to go, Andy Garrison's words resounding through our heads: *Ah it'll be a breeze. The first twenty-two miles are all flat. I hiked those miles with Andrew in one day!* It seemed Andy must have a different definition of flat, and ten-year-old Andrew must have been made of tougher stuff than us.

We staggered down the sidewalk and stumbled into Bunbury's Coffee, which promised "Ice Cold Coffee and Lattes." Inside, the café looked less like a coffee shop and more like a small library with its walls of bookshelves. It was simply dreamy. We clumsily made our way to the counter past a handful of patrons that sat about at a couple of small tables and a sofa. Glancing up at us from their reading material, despite our large backpacks and trekking poles, which seemed mighty imposing in such a tight space, they smiled warmly, as if we were no intrusion at all. The barista whipped us up two iced lattes making sure we received every last drop from the pitcher, topping our drinks off after we'd sipped some room for more. We slid off our backpacks and eased into chairs at an empty table. Upon pulling out our map, we suddenly spied another route that we could take . . . an abandoned railroad track turned trail that ran from Piermont to Nyack, where we planned on stopping for the night. It was considered an *official* side trail, according to the guide.

"Well, let's take that one!" Scott said with eyes bright.

"I don't know hon, it's not the route laid out for the official Long Path."

"But it's an *official* side trail." He pointed out.

"Yeah, but what does that mean?"

"I don't know, but it's *official*." He liked to poke fun at my insistence on hiking the prescribed trail. Even on our day hikes he was usually keen to my desire to reach a trail's end or a particular spot on the map that I had declared our goal, whereas he would have been happy to just amble for the day. "Ah, whatever you want to do," he relented, resigning himself to my long-distance hiking ethos despite his wanting to follow the path less traveled.

I could not help but wonder if this was the route that the others who came before us had hiked. Walking six and a half miles along a graded tract certainly seemed easier than the route described, but we were not out here to hike easy. We were out here to hike the Long Path, whatever that entailed.

"Then let's take the route we had planned on taking. Anyway, it will be cooler in the woods than on a wide-open path," I said, in an effort to console him, but he only slouched further into his chair.

Apparently, our discussion had caught the ear of our fellow patrons because we were soon explaining the logistics of our long hike, including gear choices and how many miles we planned to do each day. Much to our surprise these folks actually knew of the Long Path. Before we had left, we'd mentioned our upcoming journey to so many, and no one had ever heard of it. It was refreshing to talk with people who were also enthusiastic about the trail, and they did well in snapping us out of our grumpy heat-induced haze. A half hour later, we left Bunbury's with well wishes following us out the door.

The *official* Long Path led us up a seemingly endless paved road through a cemetery, and then on a trail up and over viewless rocky knolls and wooded hilltops with a road crossing sliced between each one. These road crossings only served to infuriate Scott, who could plainly see that there was a more direct path on pavement. After crossing a residential street lined with pristine, luxurious homes, we entered Blauvelt State Park. What we found in the forest could not have been in starker contrast.

Trees were spray-painted with street tags, and broken bottles littered the trail. I imagined this was likely the work of the overprivileged neighborhood children. I guess it's hard to appreciate things when you have so much handed to you. On the other hand, could I blame them for running amuck in this forest? Before Blauvelt was a state park it was a National Guard rifle range and, at 335 acres in 1910, had been declared the largest rifle range in the country. But it didn't last long. The property was transferred to the Palisades Interstate Park Commission after concerns were voiced about the lead from the bullets periodically sprayed into the nearby residential area. Still-remaining underground tunnels and concrete walls allegedly crisscross this patch of woods like a maze. I'm sure the kids know just where to find them. As we wandered through the maze of defaced trees, Scott seemed to lag farther behind. I didn't want to hike too far ahead, so I asked him to take the lead, putting us as the same pace. But his wobbling could hardly be called hiking.

"Are you okay, hon? Do you need some water?" I wasn't sure if I should grow angry or alarmed. His footing seemed all off.

"Nah, I don't need water. I'm fine." He answered, his speech slurred.

"Honey, stop screwing around. Let's get to town. We're almost there," I told him sternly. This had to be an act. Surely, he was playing up his exhaustion to be a wise ass.

"What? We're going to town. I'm fine!" he said, still slurring and then chuckling. Unless he had chugged a found bottle of booze without my knowing it, something was definitely *not* fine with him. Though it was still hot and muggy out, I could see the sweat that had trickled down his face all day had dried, and his skin felt cool to the touch. I offered him water and snacks repeatedly, and each time he refused. Finally, I simply unwrapped a granola bar and shoved it at him.

CHAPTER TWO

We followed sidewalks lit by streetlamps into the town of Nyack. Our last few miles had taken far longer than we'd predicted. I regretted not taking the alternate trail Scott had wanted to take and for pushing him on such a hot, hot day. But now in the cool night air, Scott had sobered up. Both of us too tired to speak, we proceeded toward our lodging in a daze, fueled only by the prospect of a warm shower, something to eat besides camp food, and a bed.

The Time Hotel, almost mockingly, sat atop a *steep* hill on the edge of the commercial district of Nyack. From this distance it looked more like a factory than an inviting place of rest. Hand in hand, we trudged our way up to its front doors, which resembled those of the Women's Federation castle, except that they were painted crimson red. Using all my might, I swung one open and we stepped inside. Here in the foyer we were greeted by a ceiling-to-floor velvet wall-hanging of a colorful Day of the Dead skull. To the right, sat a white faux-fur couch. Hesitantly, we shuffled across the shining tiled floor and up to the long front desk where a woman stood behind its counter, her large bust strapped into a white button-down shirt and black vest, her hair a shoulder length wave of voluptuous curls. It took a moment before she acknowledged us but when she finally lifted her thick black eyelashes, she gave us a solemn inspection.

Frankly, I couldn't blame her. Only two days out, our hiker aroma was already beginning to ferment, and if I could smell it, it had to be bad. Dusty dirt coated our calves and our trekking poles clattered to the ground when we tried to lean them against the counter's smooth surface.

"Can I help you?" she asked coldly.

"We have a reservation?" I answered, half questioning if we indeed had the right place.

My experience of trailside motels are normally one level ma-and-pa establishments that look like they were built circa twenty-first century and *never* remodeled. But maybe this is what the Trail Gods deal you when you are traveling with a rock star. Maybe they had Starbucks here for him too.

We gave her Scott's name and learned that, sure enough, this was the place. I dove into my list of questions. Laundry? Ice machine? Vending?

She explained that there was a laundry *service* that could have our clothes returned to us by five o'clock tomorrow night. There was no ice machine, but she could have a bell boy bring us a bucket when we were settled into our room. Lastly, there was no vending, but a restaurant was conveniently located inside the hotel. I could feel the dollars in my pocket sprouting wings and taking flight, even if we had rented the room for a modest price, comparable to a night at the average Day's Inn.

We took our room keys and stepped inside an elevator with wall-to-wall mirrors and doors that opened on both sides. By the time we reached our floor, I was completely confused as to what side would open. Once inside our room, our phones began to buzz and vibrate from inside our backpacks as we fumbled for a solid five minutes, trying to figure out how to turn on the lights, a litany of curses spewing from my mouth. I had hoped only for a place of respite where I could kick up my smelly feet and gorge on food, not a five-star sensory experience.

Scott was the one to finally figure out that we had to slip our keycards into a plastic sleeve beside the door. The lights came on dimly, revealing a king-size bed and yet another floor-to-ceiling mirror. Sexy, if we had had the energy for such things. Wallpaper that resembled a Rorschach test enwrapped the room and an oriental rug with Day of the Dead skulls laid across the hardwood floor. The bathroom contained a square glass box that served as the shower, and on the backside of the door hung two cottony soft robes. When we finally pulled our phones out of our packs, we learned what all the buzzing had been about—notifications about an app we could download that would allow us to talk to "Alexa," the futuristic Amazon device that works through voice commands to turn lights off and on, change the thermostat, report the local forecast, play your favorite song, and order take out. Using it is kind of like stepping into an episode of the Jetsons. This was one giant leap from the woods.

We promptly stripped off our clothing for a shower and while standing in front of the mirror, saw raised pink bumps speckling our torsos. I had not as many as Scott, but apparently, although we hadn't felt a thing, we had made a good meal for some hungry insects. After a hot shower however, our bumps blossomed from pink to red, and we itched fiercely. I couldn't believe that we had been bitten by so many mosquitoes when we had barely spied one in the last two days.

We settled in with veggie burgers that cost as much as a steak dinner and the bellhop arrived with our ice bucket and equally pricey fountain sodas. Of course, he wanted a tip too. I resented the money that this place was sucking out of us on food that we could have gotten for half the price at a diner up the street, but as we laid in bed with the rain streaming down our giant windows, watching Hurricane Irma's path of destruction on the television, I was grateful for the plush accommodations. Our itching, too, eventually cooled. Thank God.

We awoke early, reorganized our gear, and met up with my father, who had faithfully kept his word to help us with anything we might need. On my second, and successful, thru-hike of the Appalachian Trail, my father, at the age of sixty-two, had joined me for large sections. Despite being a skilled outdoorsman, he had never backpacked long-distance. But thanks to this time on the trail, he knew that gear was crucial and that often on the first days of a hike it was necessary to dial in the few things that were essential and all those things that were not. He arrived with my lighter-weight sleeping bag rated to fifty degrees, exchanging it for my fifteen-degree-rated sleeping bag, lightening our load. We would use this sleeping bag along with our other, which was rated to thirty-two degrees, unzipped like quilts, and add on a silk sleep sack if we needed it to provide an additional ten degrees of warmth. From the forecast, it looked as if our temperatures would be staying unseasonably high.

It rained buckets throughout the morning, but by the afternoon the skies were merely overcast and drizzly. Scott and I set off walking roads and steep embankments through woods bordering residential areas, but eventually we paralleled the Hudson River shoreline, which we could glimpse through the trees.

Rounding a bend in the trail where the boughs of the trees overhead created a leafy archway, we were charged, well sort of, by two little dogs with tails wagging feverishly and tongues hanging out their mouths. We stopped in our tracks as they sniffed around our ankles.

"Hey! Get back here!" we heard a scolding voice holler through the brush.

Five more dogs appeared trotting and walking, with one pulled by his leash by a blonde-haired woman, who was still scolding. Upon seeing us, though, her eyes lit up.

"Where are *you* two going?" she demanded to know with a smile.

"The Adirondacks!" we proudly answered.

"Holy shit," she answered back dryly, her smile stretching wider.

This was Lisa, who had walked a gaggle of dogs daily on this portion of the trail for the last seven years and had *never* met anyone thru-hiking. While chatting, I put down my backpack to pull out our map and my pack of American Spirit cigarettes tumbled out. I hurriedly shoved them back in a pocket, hoping to avoid the conversation about the girl walking nearly 400 miles who also enjoys a smoke in the evening at camp.

"Oh my God. Do you have an extra one of those?" she said with a gasp.

Happily, I slid one from the pack, pleased that I wasn't about to receive a lecture.

"Can I smoke it with you?" she asked.

I hesitated as I prefer not to smoke while hiking, but Scott, who was more than happy to take a smoke break, pulled one promptly from the hip pocket of his backpack.

"I smoke one pack a year," she said lighting it up like a pro. "I don't want to be too healthy, ya know? Yoga, walking, meditation, all that stuff, I do it. It's the only thing that clears my head and keeps me truly calm but sometimes, ya know, I just want to push back, bang heroin, and listen to rock and roll," she took a drag. "So, I smoke a cigarette."

I loved Lisa already. Health had been a priority for me since my early twenties when I learned that I simply felt better when I ate real food, exercised when I felt bummed out, and got good sleep. I am all that healthy stuff—a practicing herbalist, certified yoga instructor, a long-distance hiker—but I also believe that all things should be practiced in moderation, including moderation. It's all too easy to become health obsessed and, really, happiness is most integral. If a pack a year makes you happy, smoke 'em.

Over a smoke, we learned that Lisa was the head of Free-Dog, a nonprofit that works to save the lives of dogs destined to be used in the trade of meat. These dogs of every color, size, and shape that she had with her on the trail were just a handful of those that she had rescued. I realized that although she was impressed with our venture, having never met anyone like us before, we had never met anyone quite like her either. These chance encounters are one of the primary reasons why long-distance trails that do not travel exclusively through remote wilderness are so special. In sharing the trail with local folks, essentially leaving the tiny subculture that is long-distance hiking, you meet people from all walks of life, people one may never have had the opportunity to cross paths with otherwise. It's hardly an adventure if you only interact with people just like yourself.

Wishing us good luck, she exchanged contact information with us, and we hiked onwards toward Hook Mountain. As we climbed through grassy, then rockier, woods nearing the summit, it began to drizzle. Low-lying clouds rolled in and drizzle turned to rain, so that we climbed through a mist punctuated by large raindrops.

When we finally summited the peak of Hook Mountain, although enshrouded in fog, we could still make out the elegant arches of the Tappan Zee Bridge in the distance, the Hudson River flowing strong below us and behind us, and the Palisades cliffs across which we had already walked. Silhouettes of mullein stood shadowy and surreal. Their stalks, dabbed with yellow flowers at the tips, glowed faintly through the mist. Mullein is a nonnative plant that can grow to six feet tall, and normally resides along railroads and roadways, but scarcely ever atop a mountain. These skeletal stalks offered a strange contrast to the native prickly pear at our feet. We had encountered this rare cactus on a couple exposed cliffs in marginal struggling communities in the northeast, but here we found plump spikey paddles clumped together on either side of the trail. These paddles provide a succulent vegetable after the spines and skins are removed, as do the fruits of prickly pear that develop after their large golden flowers are pollinated and fall away. Although we had found Hook Mountain in the gray, prickly pear was evidence that this rocky cliff oft experienced days of sun, providing a special microclimate for a plant more suited to the warm, sandy coast.

Descending from the cliffs and into the woods, we followed a steep zig-zagging trail between boulders and leaning trees, their roots precariously woven into the rocky soil. Dusk was coming soon and despite the wet day, we were low on water. With none in sight for the next several miles, when we reached the Knickerbocker Engine Company at a rural road crossing, we knocked on the door. And then knocked harder.

Finally, a man opened the door a crack and eyeballed us, especially Scott. It had never occurred to me how I might be approached differently on this hike given that I was not hiking solo. As a young white woman alone, I was typically presumed harmless and, I imagine, also in need of help. People were usually eager to lend a hand, whether that was in filling up a water bottle, offering me a ride, or a place to stay. I guess these had been circumstances in which the societal stereotype had served me.

"Hi there, we're hiking the Long Path and are out of water. Is there an outside spigot where we might be able to fill up?" Scott asked.

"You're hiking what?" The man asked gruffly.

"The Long Path, it goes right past your fire company here." I chimed in, pointing to the blaze on the telephone pole beside the building.

He craned his head and eyed us again. After a moment's hesitation, he opened the door.

"Come on in. You guys can fill up at the faucet," he said, making sure that we walked in front of him past the fire engine and into the kitchen area.

As we filled up our bottles and then our water bladders as well, preparing for the evening's camp, we chatted some about our hike, explaining that we had started at the George Washington Bridge and where the route would lead us.

"You guys are crazy. I like to walk from the couch to the fridge and back again," he said with a chuckle.

That evening we set up our tent in a grassy patch of forest. When the sky darkened and it started to sprinkle, we ended up cooking our dinner of dehydrated noodles under the vestibule. Later that night, we laid awake for some time laying shoulder to shoulder and listened to the rain pummeling our thin nylon roof. Intermittent flashes of lightning illuminated our tent, but instead of bemoaning the stormy night, all we felt was gratitude for our cozy shelter.

CHAPTER THREE

Birdsong trickled through the stillness—a sure sign
that the rains had passed. Unzipping the door revealed clear blue skies and
golden light spilling through the treetops. Beside me Scott rolled over with a
huff, scratching his back, and then rolled over yet again, scratching his belly and
around his shirt collar. Bright red bumps encircled his throat like a necklace.

"These bites itch like hell," he said, now sitting up in our sleeping bag,
still scratching.

"Oh, sweetie. Those look awful. Maybe I can find some chickweed or plantain we can use outside in the grass." Plantain is a common weed with leaves that
are highly mucilaginous. Chickweed, too, is a cooling anti-inflammatory weed,
with a succulent stem and leaves. When moistened, most easily with your own
saliva by chewing them up, these plants make an excellent poultice for quelling
itchy bites. I crawled from the tent onto a dewy carpet. "Here's some, love!" I
announced excitedly, seeing the broad spoon-shaped leaves of plantain with
their characteristic parallel veins. I plucked a couple and turned back for the
tent when I saw that Scott was sitting with his shirt off. He looked at me with
horror, his mouth agape.

"What the hell is this?!" Scott said, squeezing a fat red bump with his fingers.

"Oh my God, honey," I said with a gasp, trying my best not to sound alarmed.

Those little bug bites that we had seen two nights ago in the Time Hotel were now not only scarlet and angry but some the size of half dollars, each with a pus-filled pimple at its center. Closer inspection revealed more on his back and his arms, inside his armpits, up his neck, and even several on his nipples. I pulled up my shirt and saw that mine, too, had morphed into raised red bumps on my stomach and ribcage, but nowhere even close to the severity of his.

"Plantain is not going to do shit," he declared. "What the hell is this?!" He repeated, itching more.

"Try not to itch them."

"Well, they itch like hell!"

"Here, chew these up and put them on your bites," I ordered, passing the leaves to him. "You chew 'em!" he barked back.

I felt my face grow hot and I shot him a look that could burn all the plantain on the hillside.

"Look, I'm sorry. These are freaking me out! I haven't even had a cup of coffee yet and you're shoving leaves at me."

"I know they are. I get it. I'm just trying to help," I said, calming down. I knew he was miserable, and I, too, was freaked out. I had never seen anything like it.

"I know. I'm sorry," he repeated.

"We have to figure out what this is," I said, pulling out my smartphone to do some Google doctoring.

"Look, can you just make the coffee?" he asked, with a pleading look.

"Can you just chew the leaves?" I shot back.

"I'll chew the damn leaves."

"Deal," I said, passing him the leaves. "There's more outside."

So, while the water boiled, I got to work. Search after search revealed the same likely culprit.

"It's because I smooshed them," he said with remorse, now sipping his coffee.

He was right. Well, I don't know about the karma of smooshing them, but on the first night we camped on the Palisades cliffs, we had encountered red ants while cooking outside on the rocks. Likely, we carried them inside the tent on our sleeping pads and, as we laid blissfully sleeping, they dined on us like a buffet. Apparently, Scott had been tastier.

As we read more online, we learned that *some* people have severe allergic reactions to red ant bites, so much that they can become dizzy and delirious. I thought back on how frustrated I'd been with Scott for acting like a drunken fool in our last miles into Nyack. It all made sense. It was also not uncommon for the actual bites to appear twenty-four to forty-eight hours after contact.

Now we knew the cause, but as I continued to read about how easily they could become infected, my body tensed. I hated to say it, but we would need to take a couple days off the trail and give him some time to heal up. With the heat of his backpack and clothes rubbing against his skin, he would only aggravate the bites, and God forbid we didn't keep them clean enough. Out here on the trail I've seen wounds as common as a blister land people in the hospital. I suggested we call home and get picked up or at least hike into town and try to get to a doctor.

"Nope, not doing it," Scott said firmly.

"But hon, these could get worse," I said, inspecting one near his belly button.

"No," he said, shoving the leaves in his mouth and chewing. "If we go to a doctor, he's going to tell me not to hike and we're not stopping now, not even for a break. We'll just keep them clean. I'll be fine."

"Hon, I won't be upset. Taking a couple days off the trail is not the end of the world."

"No. I'll be fine. There's plenty more plantain out here." He spat the chewed leaves into the palm of his hand and placed the wad atop one of the worst-looking bites.

"Baby." I gave him a kiss on the forehead, one of the few parts of his body that didn't have a bite. I worried if hiking on was really the right decision or just plain foolishness. But, at the same time, my heart swelled. My pustule-covered baby was determined to hike this trail and whether it was for his sake or mine, it mattered not. I fell ever deeper in love while Scott went in search of more plantain leaves.

"Baby, wait. The plantain alone is not going to cut it. We'll use those but let's sanitize the hell out of those bites."

So, before leaving camp, I played nurse. We packed up the tent and I laid out on a flat rock a bottle of Purell hand sanitizer, a few Q-tips, and a handful of Band-Aids. Scott stripped down to his socks and I applied a dab of Purell to each and every one of his bites, covering the worst with crushed plantain and a Band-Aid to hold it in place. We counted roughly fifty bites. As miserable as we were, we laughed till we cried at the thought of someone coming upon us. What on earth would we say?

We got a late start hiking, but at least Scott's bites had cooled some, as had our tempers. As we padded down the trail, booms echoed through the open woods and resounded through the ground beneath our feet. At the next road crossing, we saw why. The tall cliffside across the road had been systematically sliced in horizontal layers, and the once-level ground scooped into a wide bowl. A steep bridge crossed part of the expanse using the edges of two inner cliffs. Before us was the largest quarry I had ever seen. Those booms had been the blasting of stone. A tall metal fence laced at its upper edge with barbed wire marked the perimeter. A truck groaned by burping smoke and kicking up dust in its wake. So, this could have been the fate of the Palisades cliffs had the Women's Federation not succeeded. The Earth, a living organism, animated and complete, had been gutted. No plants nor animals thrived in this crater, void of life.

We climbed the rocky, grass-covered cliffside of High Tor in the early afternoon sun. Here the rocks provided good handholds, but the blonde grass underfoot masked from our view the ankle-bending rocks. My hands grazed the button-like tops of hoary mountain mint, a native mint too precious to pick in this habitat, releasing its minty fragrance and invigorating my senses, propelling me upward. A particularly precious native mint—basil mountain mint—also calls High Tor home. Endangered in New York State and found in few other places in the world, it is considered globally rare. It was long labeled extirpated until it was rediscovered, first at Hook Mountain and then here. Considering how similar the two mints look to each other, it would be challenging to the most skilled botanist to tell them apart.

High Tor is the highest peak along the Palisades, reaching a relatively humble elevation of 832 feet, yet the trail wound us up steeply with only a few short switchbacks, so that we still felt accomplished upon reaching its summit. There, we were afforded a 360-degree view with the town of Haverstraw below and the blue bowl of Lake DeForest behind us. To the north, we spied a rolling blanket of green mountains and the next major point on our map—Harriman State Park. We spread out on a flat tan rock and had lunch as the hot sun beat down upon us.

From High Tor, we remained largely at elevation as we hiked onward over forking dirt forest roads, then up and over countless rocky and wooded knobs, and finally along a grassy ridge lined with cedar and hickory trees. Our steady stride faltered as we stopped repeatedly to inspect and gather the smooth-skinned green nuts that rolled like marbles beneath our feet. Each nut was about the size of a golf ball but split by four distinct seams, which informed us these were indeed hickory nuts. Seeing that the hickory trees' bark peeled away from their trunks in vertical strips told us that these were likely shagbark hickory. But really, as far as our late-night snack was concerned, we didn't care what species we had. Hickory nuts, although not commercially consumed, are related to pecans and just as tasty. We gathered our bounty in our hip pockets as we hiked. Periodically we rubbed shoulders with the branches of the cedar trees as we passed, and I couldn't help but think how these scaly needles could have worked as an insect repellent if we'd had them at our disposal just four days earlier. But these boughs, laden with blue-grey berries that when crushed emit the loveliest smell of juniper, provided their own aromatic medicine as we hiked along.

The edges of trail were also home to a number of nonnative plants, among them garlic mustard, peppermint, and cultivated grapes (easily discerned from wild grapes by their large fruits). These plants, normally found in civilization, along with the patches of perfectly level ground speckled with younger trees, indicated that this land was at one time likely a homesite. I knelt down and plucked a handful of heart-shaped, scallop-edged garlic mustard leaves for dinner later that night. Garlic mustard is one of my favorite greens. Every part of the plant is edible, from the roots to the flowers, and it can be found nearly year-round. Being invasive, its presence is a detriment to native plants and the insects that they host, and so by harvesting garlic mustard, one is essentially doing their bioregion a service. These leaves would provide a flavorful garlicky touch to our boring noodles. We followed a small side trail towards a clearing through the trees at the edge of the cliff. At first, we only spied the opposing ridge but then, as with one of those paintings you must stare at for a long time before the picture becomes evident, the real view came into focus. The rectangular shapes of the Manhattan skyline stood like a row of uneven blocks, far away and foggy in the distance. I squeezed a cedar berry between my fingers and held it to Scott's nose, then to mine. Perhaps the next time we smelled a cedar berry, we'd think of this moment, this feeling of accomplishment. Sure . . . we were only roughly forty miles in, but to see where we had begun, so far in the distance, we were instantly acutely aware of the many steps we had taken to get here.

After descending for a couple of miles, we reached the valley and a bustling road. We watched as cars zipped past at full speed heading for a light at a four-way intersection. I pulled out my notes and saw that a supermarket and a laundromat were allegedly a half mile from this crossing. We didn't need groceries or laundry done all that badly, though we couldn't help but wonder what treats lay in wait in town. Plus, we were running low on fuel for our stove, which we could usually find at a gas station. This area was worth a look around.

As walked a strip of sidewalk we soon realized there was about every business and service imaginable here, far more than the guidebook had listed. The first gem we spotted was a pharmacy. Once inside, we walked the aisles in search of Benadryl, hoping to quell Scott's allergic reaction. A young girl nervously asked from behind the counter if we needed help as we picked up this box and that one.

"Is there a pharmacist available? We have a bit of situation," I said to her as Scott wandered down another aisle, clearly avoiding a verdict.

A balding man in a white jacket came to the counter, and I began to explain our predicament.

"Hey, honey! Come here and show the man!" I called to Scott, who was now conveniently standing behind a rack of greeting cards.

Hesitantly he walked over and stood stone still, his gaze turned towards the floor. The pharmacist and I awaited the revealing.

"That's okay. You don't want to see this," Scott declared.

"See what?" the pharmacist asked, and I motioned to Scott to get on with it.

With a heavy sigh, he lifted his shirt, revealing the reddened spots that seemed more like he'd been struck with birdshot than ant bites.

We shared with him that we had been hiking for the last four days. Much to our relief, the pharmacist confirmed that these were indeed red ant bites and that it wasn't surprising we hadn't felt ourselves getting bitten.

"Oftentimes, people feel nothing until days later," he explained. "And some people will have worse reactions than others. Clearly you have an allergy," he said, turning his gaze to Scott.

"Clearly," Scott mumbled.

"What's this?" the pharmacist asked, leaning in for a closer look at the green glop squeezing out from beneath a Band-Aid.

"Those are plantain leaves," I said. "They are antimicrobial and have anti-inflammatory properties."

"I chewed 'em," Scott said smartly.

The pharmacist wrinkled his nose and leaned back. "Well, best to keep the area clean, but that's interesting. First I've heard of that." He scratched his head but seemed not to entirely discount the method.

We were instructed to keep the area clean with alcohol, then apply Benadryl and triple antibiotic ointment. They would heal just fine, the pharmacist said. This would become our regimen for the next week, morning and night. We made our purchase and headed back out into the land of commercial retail.

Scouring numerous gas stations, we found that not a single one had fuel. We did, however, pick up some ice-cold sodas in the process and hit up the liquor store for a bottle of whiskey. To avoid having to use more fuel on cooking that evening, we decided to grab dinner at a pizzeria. We set ourselves up for a long night as we shoved forkfuls of fried eggplant, cheese, sauce, and bread into our mouths. Likely we wouldn't resume hiking until sundown, but in the euphoria of fat- and carb-laden calorie bliss, it seemed worth it.

When we walked out the swinging glass door into the darkening blue night however, there was no denying our circumstances. We had two options. We could walk back up the road, roughly three-quarters of a mile, to the trailhead we had left and try to find a place to camp in the woods or we could hike northward one and a half miles to an area where we thought we could likely camp. There's just something that feels terribly wrong about retracing miles when long-distance hiking. Hikers will avoid it at all costs. So, strapping on headlamps, we chose to hike forward.

We left the roadside by clawing up an embankment alongside an overpass through shoulder-high weeds and pricker bushes. What we hadn't anticipated was just how little traveled these miles heading out of town were. Already we were having trouble discerning where the trail went, and darkness hadn't completely fallen yet. We crossed two more busy roads, dashing across them as fast as we could, and began walking along a wooded corridor sandwiched between the parkway and a chain-link fence. Now the night was black.

Although a bit nervous about what lay ahead, the darkness was exhilarating. Never had I felt comfortable enough to night-hike on my long-distance treks. Sure, I had come into camp countless times just as dark had fallen and one time on that first long hike along the Appalachian Trail found myself speed-hiking through the blackest black in a burned-out forest in the Tennessee mountains on a cold, star-studded night . . . but not because I had chosen to. With Scott by my side, I not only knew that I had someone who could help me if I tripped and fell, but also another set of eyes to search for blazes on the trees, as well as a defender against nocturnal wildlife.

We soon found that this wooded corridor was more ankle-twisting rock and root than it was woods, and the blazes sent us zigzagging across all of it.

"What drunken jackass painted these blazes?" Scott yelled out in anger. "They're winding us all over the place!"

"I don't know, honey. I imagine the route would be clearer if it was daylight," I said, trying to remain reasonable.

"Yeah, I doubt that. A blind man could do a better job."

"Hon, we just have to take our time."

"*Yeah*, I know. I just don't know why we can't go in a straight line."

We stumbled some yards and then stopped and searched by the light of our dim headlamps for yet another blaze, again and again and again. By now my exhilaration had vanished and our adventurous task seemed a dangerous one. If one of us broke an ankle, how would we ever get the other out of here? There was no way we could put a tent down in this terrain. So, we carried on and took turns taking the lead, so focused that we barely spoke.

The chain-link fence disappeared, replaced by a wide stream to our left. Suddenly, we reached what appeared to be a crossing, consisting of the stone ledge of a tunnel that ran beneath the parkway. The ledge was strangled by snaking roots and canopied by outreaching branches. I double-checked my directions. Sure enough, this was the route.

"This is bullshit!" Scott said, waving his hiking stick at the stone ledge.

"I know. Yes, it's bullshit," I said, just as unhappy as he was about the crossing but at the same time still trying to keep us cool. "I can go across first."

"No, I got it." He said with a huff, still wanting to be chivalrous even if he hated heights.

Climbing up some nearby rocks and tree roots, Scott led the way, clinging closely to the trees, whose branches scraped his arms and snagged his backpack. I followed suit but kept my distance so as not to get swatted in the face when the larger branches he passed snapped back. The black, frothy water flowed below. Reaching the other side, we hiked on in silence, wary of what was next. Until now it had seemed the trail was working with us rather than against us. We'd been betrayed.

We soon hit the wide dirt road of Cheesecote Mountain Town Park. We hiked uphill for what seemed like a very long time, growing farther from the Palisades and even farther from the pleasures of town that we had enjoyed not all that long ago. Finally, at a crest, we spied a level patch of land in the woods. Trying to figure out if there was room enough to throw down our five-by-seven-foot tent, we hastily searched out an agreeable patch on the forest floor. Good enough for a stealth site. Our standards weren't high.

Now nine-thirty at night, roughly two hours and five miles from town, we set up our tent and, inside, spread out our sleeping bags, atop solid rock and twining roots as they were, and called it a night. The blissfully good Italian food was long digested, but thank God we'd stopped at that liquor store. I nursed Scott's wounds yet again, this time as directed, with Benadryl and triple antibiotic cream. We followed this regimen with more than one long swig from that little bottle of whiskey, and finally, turning off our headlamps, allowed the darkness of the forest to encompass us. I laid there wondering what else this trail had in store for us.

Scott in Harriman State Park

PART THREE:

THE HUDSON

HIGHLANDS

Big Hill Shelter

CHAPTER ONE

Around noon we crossed into the cool shaded woods of Harriman State Park. One would never know, tromping through its 47,000 acres of protected land, that the park lies just fifty miles from New York City. We hiked uphill past towering oaks, maples, and birches. Boulders sat like giants watching, cool and calm in the long green grass that covered the forest floor. We felt like we were coming home. The very first place I had learned of the Long Path was here, while hiking the Appalachian Trail, and I had returned numerous times to explore other trails. For Scott, Harriman had been a regular stopover on his way home from work, a way to clear his head at the end of the day. And over the last two years we had returned together, sharing our favorite trails with each other. Of course, more than once we had stumbled onto the Long Path.

Up and up and up we went, then down, and up, and down, and up, over its rolling and sometimes steep knolls. We were grateful when we reached an inviting break spot. Leaning against a stone boulder we lunched near Big Hill Shelter which sat atop a rock cliff. Dotted along the Long Path are shelters, which may also be called lean-tos, that have been erected for passing hikers who wish to take cover or spend the night. These structures are made of three walls, a wooden floor, and a pitched roof. However only here in Harriman would we find them constructed out of the stone gathered from the surrounding soil. The Civilian

Conservation Corps built this handsome structure in the 1930s, complete with two fireplaces and chimneys, one on either end, making it accommodating even in winter. Although well weathered, its floor in need of new wooden slats and a thorough sweeping, it still resembled an inviting little home cradled in the forest. From this cliff, we could again see the faint outline of the Manhattan skyline, now even farther in the distance. The green mountains before us were smudged with yellow as if they'd been dabbed with a fat paintbrush. The sun shone bright and the air was crisp; the humidity we had battled since beginning our hike had dissolved. It felt like fall.

We packed up and reluctantly got moving again, our bellies full and our legs stiff from sitting. Just as we began to regain our pace, we spied frayed cable and chunks of steel protruding from the soil, shimmering in the sunlight that filtered through the canopy, and halted. This was the crash site of Northwest Orient Airlines Flight 6231. We had read about this deadly accident in the Long Path guidebook. On December 1, 1974, this Boeing 727 had been chartered to pick up the NFL's Baltimore Colts in Buffalo, New York. The craft never made it. After just twelve minutes in the air, the plane stalled and fell into a rapid descent, striking nose first into the earth. The three crew members on board were killed. We stood in silent horror before the remaining fragments of wreckage that had, over time, become a part of these woods and even this trail. We peered up at an opening in the treetops and could not resist imagining how that plane looked crashing through these trees and the terror of those on board. The crew had been experienced but had failed to turn on a heating unit at start of the flight, leading to icing and, in turn, incorrect airspeed readings and their resultant misjudgment.

From here we hiked northward, reaching the cove that had once served as the Hogencamp Mine. We wound through canyons formed by boulders and old stone foundations from the community that once surrounded the mine. The Hudson Highlands is a region rich in iron and for over a century, from the mid-1700s to the late 1800s, as many as twenty different mines were carved into these mountains. As we increased in elevation, the air smelled strong of sap and dirt and drying leaves. Periodically we caught the scent of sweet fern, which grew in leafy tuffs between the boulders, on the light breeze. Scott had introduced me to sweet fern on one of our first hikes together. Despite the fact I had been surrounded by it all my young life in the northeast, I had never noticed it. Now I cannot *not* see it. Although sweet fern's common name suggests it is a fern, it's actually a member of the wax myrtle family and, as many members of this family are, it is highly aromatic. Crush its fern-shaped leaves to emit its vanilla- and eucalyptus-like aroma and steep them in hot or cold water for a delicious beverage. I have found it is our native herb that most closely resembles the flavor of tea. Native Americans considered sweet fern a blood purifier—an herb that reduces stagnancy and enlivens the body—and a digestive aid. However, there would be no sweet fern tea today. Its green leaves were already beginning to darken, patchy with blackish-purple so that they took on a camouflage pattern, and were no longer prime for the picking.

We reached a three-way intersection with *Times Square*, painted in thick white paint on the face of a boulder. Perhaps this mile marker offered a bit of familiarity for the urban dweller amongst all these trees and rocks. However, judging by our achy legs, there was no denying we had walked a *long* way from that concrete jungle. Perfect place for a snack break.

I munched on a granola bar while Scott studied the guidebook. "You expect us to hike nearly seventeen miles today?" Scott asked, lifting his gaze and peering at me through narrowed eyes.

"What are you talking about? No, we're doing eleven."

"That's not what this says. Count 'em here. It's seventeen."

He passed me the guidebook and I began to check our directions yet another time today. It seemed every break we took required pouring over these notes. Again and again, I counted. Seventeen miles. Hastily I pulled out the map and measured and remeasured, using my finger to estimate each mile along our path.

"Shit." I'd done the math wrong. Somehow, in planning our itinerary, I'd omitted five miles. This late in the day, no way we'd make it to our destination for the night.

"Well here, we'll just go to this shelter instead of that one," I said, pointing to another shelter symbol on the map that was closer to where we were now.

"Nope, you want to go seventeen miles. We'll go seventeen miles," he said sternly. I couldn't tell if his tone was one of conviction or anger.

"We are *not* going seventeen miles," I assured him.

"Well could *you* go seventeen miles through here?" he asked me now, his eyes wide.

"No, I could *not* go seventeen miles, hon. I'm just as tired as you are. We'll just have to call it a day at Cohasset Shelter. It's closer."

"Look if you could hike it and you want to hike it, then you go right ahead, I don't want to slow you down," he snapped, digging through his backpack.

"I don't *want to* go seventeen miles! And I certainly don't want to hike on without you."

"Are you sure?" he asked.

"Yes, I'm sure! Hon, I made this itinerary while I was sitting on my ass at home. I made a miscalculation. I knew we'd chuck out this damn schedule sooner than later. It doesn't matter." I shot back sharply.

Clearly, we were both tired. We had hiked roughly fifty miles in the last five days. The night before we hadn't stopped for camp until nearly ten o'clock. He was covered in red ant bites that still itched and needed constant care. My lower back ached and my hip bones felt like they'd been beaten with a hammer. It'd been over two years since I'd carried a backpack for so many days straight.

"Whatever, let's just get going," Scott said, hoisting his pack.

We hiked through the woods in silence and then trudged alongside a massive mountaintop marsh obscured by vegetation for what seemed like an eternity, the croaking of frogs and chirping of crickets emanating from within its walls. The trail was eroded and thin as a ribbon, giving out beneath us, causing us time and again to nearly slide into the water. We cursed. We huffed. I wanted to enjoy the song, the smell of the marshland, the now golden dying light of dusk. But my heart felt like a paperweight and my fists clutched the handles of my trekking poles so tight that my palms felt like they were on fire. Damn him for being so sharp with me. Dammit to hell that we wouldn't reach our goal for the day and damn *me* for planning miles that were too much too soon. No, I hadn't planned to go seventeen miles, but even with lower mileage, each day it seemed we hit a wall a couple miles before camp. Our bodies were still acclimating to moving all day every day. I had known that the terrain was going to be challenging. I'd been foolish for planning such a long first day in Harriman.

Suddenly we reached an intersection marked by a stately wooden post bearing numerous signs, each engraved with trail names and the mileage to their corresponding destinations. I couldn't even remember when we'd left the marsh, I'd been so lost in my thoughts. But I knew, surely, where we were now. I peered with all my heart down the trail that crossed ours, letting my gaze settle on each white blaze that seemed to glow in the darkness of the forest. Each blaze spurred a longing, a love from deep within me. The Appalachian Trail.

"Look babe, the AT," I said with a gasp.

I turned to look at Scott and I noticed a slight grin cross his face like the cracking of an eggshell.

"We need a picture of us here," he said, pulling out his phone.

This was the very same sign that I had spied a decade before when hiking the AT. Now here I stood before it again . . . but this time with Scott by my side. My fists loosened their grip and a calming current flowed through me, from my head down to my toes. I felt my eyes start to well up.

"Holy shit," Scott said, staring coldly at the signage before him. I followed his gaze.

Long Path — John Boyd Thacher State Park.................291 miles.

"Yeah well at least we aren't going here," I countered, pointing to another line on the sign going the other direction:

Appalachian Trail — Katahdin.............................790 miles.

He rolled his eyes at me and snapped a couple of pictures.

"How much farther do we have to Cohasset Shelter?" Scott asked with a nod towards our path.

"About a mile."

"Okay, we can do that. Come on, this trail is not going to hike itself."

Scott took off down the trail and I followed close behind. So many memories began to percolate. I thought about how hard those miles on the AT had been and how wrought with physical and emotional pains, both big and small. Sure, my muscles hurt now, but nothing like they had back then. I thought of all the trails I had completed now. The Long Path would mark nearly 7,000 miles of thru-hiking. I thought about how separated I had felt from my partner then, how I had turned over in my head for miles on end the question of whether I or he was at fault for our crumbling relationship. No matter the answer I had chosen not to relinquish my dream. I lifted my gaze from the ground beneath my feet to Scott, who hiked steadily ahead of me. His calves flexed with each strong step and his arms struck his trekking poles into the dirt with such force that he seemed to accelerate along like a machine. He was working so hard to make our dream of hiking this trail together a reality. And it wasn't just for me. I knew by the way his face glowed at the sight of a vista or how he gasped at an owl hooting in the night or the way he'd comment on the beauty of a gnarled tree, that he too, wanted to be here. But most importantly, I knew by the way that he held me at night, our bodies wrapped tightly around each other and his breath on my skin, that he wanted to be here *with me*. Because I had persevered through that hike on the AT, I was *here with him*. Had I not, who knows where my path might have led and if we would have ever found each other. I wept as we walked.

By the light of the setting sun, we made it to Cohasset Shelter but found it dreary and dank at the bottom of a hollow. So instead we climbed to the nearby flat rock cliff and made camp atop a thick bed of soft moss. Here the wind blew hard and it wasn't long before we were bundling up, our body temperature cooling fast. For the first time on our journey we were thankful for the extra weight of winter clothing we'd been carrying as we slipped into long underwear, wrapped up in synthetic down jackets, and pulled on hats. But before dipping inside our tent to cook under the vestibule, we braved the cold to gaze over the darkening tree tops from a perch on the cliff. The waning moon shone bright above us and the stars studded the night sky, our breath now visible in the chill night air.

"I'm sorry for earlier, hon."

"There's nothing to be sorry for. I'm sorry," Scott replied, wrapping his arm around my shoulder, pulling me close.

"I just want you to know that I don't want to push you beyond your limits on this hike. I want us to enjoy it out here. This is not *my* adventure, but *our* adventure. I wouldn't want to hike this trail without you." I could feel the tears welling up again.

"You wouldn't?"

"No. This is ours," I said, now looking into his eyes.

"Well good. Because I wouldn't want to hike this trail without you. But remember—I *want* to hike this trail," he replied, maintaining my gaze.

I'd have to constantly remind myself of this fact on our hike. That Scott was not my past, was not the boyfriend who trudged along by my side only because he felt obligated. He hiked beside me, with me, with the same desires and goals, enlivened by the same beauty and sense of adventure that I felt.

That night, after a warm dinner and some swigs of whiskey, we nuzzled tightly together in our sleeping bag. It would be a chilly night. A gust of wind kicked up and in a nearby tree, an owl hooted. Scott gave a little chuckle. I soon heard his breath deepen and then felt mine begin to expand in unison. I was grateful. So very grateful for all the choices I had made that had led me to this point in time, to be sleeping atop this bed of moss wrapped in this man's arms on our *long path*.

CHAPTER TWO

Dawn swept through the forest bright and cool. I inhaled deeply, breathing in the smell of damp dirt and drying leaves. Today we would meet Star Left, who would join us for at least a day of hiking. Star Left was one of two long-distance hikers that I'd met while thru-hiking the Finger Lakes Trail. She and her hiking partner, Shepherd, had mapped out a route from Niagara Falls to the Gulf of Mexico, using the Finger Lakes Trail as a connecting link.

We had met roughly halfway through my journey in a patch of woods off a country road. Later that day, we all sat down to an exquisite backyard brunch prepared by a kind stranger. He'd been cleaning out his deceased father's house, which sat along the trail's route, when he'd met Star Left and Shepherd and offered them a place to camp. Arranged atop the glass face of an old door that had been laid atop two sawhorses to act as a table, he'd piled eggs, hash browns, and fresh fruit in overturned lids from metal pots, using them like plates. We saddled up to our banquet on milk crates and flimsy lawn chairs. In the hundreds of miles I'd walked on the Finger Lakes Trail, this was the first camaraderie I had experienced. Our conversation and laughter over a shared meal felt like Sunday brunch with friends, a small break from the trail, yet an instant bond that could only ever be had on the trail. The three of us teamed up, hiking for several days and nights, until our paths diverged with me going east toward the Catskills and them going south towards the Gulf.

I later learned after I'd finished that hike that Star Left and Shepherd had parted ways. Shepherd had headed northeast to hike the AT, but she'd continued along their planned route. This journey was Star Left's first long-distance hike but that mattered not. She hiked on by herself, totaling over 780 miles by the time she got off the trail and met up with her friend, George. While resting up at George's house, she got to better know his roommate, Ed. She and Ed fell head over heels in love and married several weeks later in Vegas. She and her husband now live Bergenfield, New Jersey, which just so happens to be close to the Long Path.

The day's hike began with a downhill slope through a rocky forest that turned to muck and marsh before reaching a road crossing. We took a short break here and, without any cell service to tell Star Left where we were in the day's hike, I scribbled a note on a piece a paper and left it atop a large boulder, held firm by a round stone. Hopefully she would find it. We climbed up and down numerous dry and grassy knolls in the brilliant morning sun, relishing in the movement that warmed our bones. From a level spot in the woods, we came face to face with a boulder the size of a two-story house, the aqua blazes of the Long Path clearly painted against its surface. Using our whole bodies, we were scaling it, clinging to tiny trees that had taken root in its cracks and using its stony lips as hand and foot holds, when over the sound of our own huffing and puffing, we heard voices in the distance. Still mid-climb, we paused looking to each other in confusion.

"What's that?" Scott asked, his hand wrapped around a leafy sapling.

"I don't know. It sounds like people." I said with a gasp.

"Maybe we should wait a minute."

"Yeah. Sounds good," I said, giving the whole weight of my body to the rock face now. This would be a fine place to rest. Better than having to communicate with what sounded like far too many voices.

We hadn't interacted with another person on the trail since Lisa of Free-Dog. It wasn't that we didn't want to see people. After all, those that we had met in towns had been so welcoming. Soon we'd be seeing a much-anticipated friend. But already, just the thought of having to interact with so many at once from the quietude of our path seemed overwhelming.

The voices sounded as if they were moving farther away now. Scott gave a quick nod, as if to say the coast is clear, and we continued our labored ascent. When we reached the boulder's summit, we saw another handsome lean-to, Stockbridge Shelter, and just beyond it, what looked like a school of neon fish swimming away towards a grassy vista 100 yards in the distance.

"Lunch break?" Scott asked.

We dropped our packs and spread out our pita and hard cheese while eye-balling the crowd of hikers adorned in their eye-popping colors, strapped into their small day packs, clicking and clacking their hiking sticks here and there, posing for pictures. It should have occurred to us sooner that when hiking in a park that's fifty miles from New York City on a Saturday, we'd find ourselves amongst others. But besides the assault of stimulus, neither of us could wrap our heads around wanting to hike in such a large group. How can one possibly absorb the subtleties of nature if one is constantly engaged in conversation? I found this a great deal on the AT. I knew hikers that traveled in packs, staying at the same shelters and hostels and hiking in single file. They could be heard coming from a half mile away. I enjoyed meeting new people along the way and would often hike with one person or another for a couple hours or a couple days sharing stories, just as I had with Star Left, but that's why I appreciated it. It was a sweet, compressed nugget of communication. Every word we shared had weight and meaning because neither of us had experienced such interaction in a long time. We got to know each other deeply and quickly because we had spent so much time in isolation, in the company of only the forest. We valued each other and then, when it returned, we valued the solitude.

By the time we were done lunching the school had luckily swam on, so we packed up and headed for the grassy clearing. From this vantage point we looked out over the mottled mountains that drew a sharp line against the clear blue sky. I thought about our first mile through the streets of New York City and over the George Washington Bridge.

"This is why no one looks at you in New York City."

"And why no one said hi to us on the trail through the Palisades," Scott seconded.

"Too many people. When you're so inundated by others, it's overstimulus. You have to simply block people out."

"At the same time, people don't know how to be alone. People are overstimulated to the point that they feel uncomfortable in the absence of stimulation."

"To be alone in the woods is a scary thing."

"Sad."

"I know. They don't know what they're missing. It's the most incredible feeling in the whole world. Sure, it's scary at first, but give your fears to the forest, feel that pulsing life all around you, and you know that you aren't really alone at all."

"Best therapy there is," Scott said, grabbing hold of my hand. "But I do like being out here with you." He gave my hand a little squeeze.

"I know, baby. I love being out here with you. It's kind of like being out here with myself."

We were descending a series of slanted stone steps when a woman in a blue t-shirt with dark brown hair appeared from around a bend below, hiking upward. She gave a little wave as she grew near and my heart jumped. It was Star Left. What a thrill it was to see this familiar face from a journey I had taken in what seemed like another lifetime. So much had happened since then, my life changing in so many ways, as I knew hers had too. Scott and I had gone to see her and her husband, Ed, perform at a little music venue in Piermont a year previous, so we had already met one another's companions but hadn't had much time to catch up. We hugged close and without a moment's pause continued hiking down the trail. We picked up talking as if no time had passed at all, and not so much about the milestones, but about our gear. She wanted to know if we were carrying a tent or a hammock, sleeping bags or down quilts. Hikers will be hikers. Scott let us jibber-jabber on and I guessed he never knew that two women could talk gear like two men talk cars, or in his case, musical equipment. We inadvertently caught up with the group, who barely noticed us coming through, and so we had to tap on shoulders and excuse ourselves to pass by.

We reached a road and hiked into a large parking lot packed with cars. This looked more like a commuter lot than it did a parking lot for the state park. This explained the school of neon fish. I saw Scott scanning the cars nervously, seemingly wondering where along the path the rest of the people might be hiding. We snacked by Star Left's car and she decided she would join us for not only the rest of the afternoon but for the night. It was already three o'clock as we sat with gear spread out on the pavement taking stock of what she had that we could use—bottled water, snacks, HEET for our camp stoves. She had come fully stocked with trail magic, now taking on the role of not only hiking companion but trail angel too. Trail magic is any act of generosity or kindness that a hiker receives—from a candy bar or a ride into town to a homecooked meal or a hot shower—and a trail angel is that person who provides trail magic. Looking at the map, we weighed our options and decided we'd hike five more miles through what the guide described as "by far the most rugged" portion of Harriman.

Onward and upward we went, climbing steeply up Long Mountain, where we found a metal plaque dedicated to Raymond H. Torrey affixed to the flat slab of stone that was its summit.

In Memory of
Raymond H. Torrey
A Great Disciple of
"The Long Brown Path"
1880–1938

Torrey was an influential journalist for the *New York Post*, famous for his column "The Long Brown Path", which paid homage to Walt Whitman's poem "Song of the Open Road." This same poem by Whitman later inspired Vincent J. Schaefer—the Long Path's originator—in his naming of the trail. Torrey embraced Shaefer's concept wholeheartedly and, through his column in 1933, announced Shaefer's plan for the Long Path. In the spring of 1934, Torrey publicized portions of the Long Path as they were scouted by Schaefer and his brother Paul, and an enthusiastic fellow named W.W. Cady. His column was also instrumental in the creation of the New York–New Jersey Trail Conference—the volunteer organization that now oversees an array of trails, including the Long Path. Staring down at his plaque, I imagined sitting at a street-side café, reading the descriptions of these tracts of wilderness, as of then little explored, with a cup of morning coffee, old-timey cars chugging by and kicking up dirt. However, Schaefer and Torrey's enthusiasm for an unblazed path was not immediately shared by the general public, and with the onslaught of World War II, the project gradually fell from view. It was not until 1960 that Robert Jessen of the Ramapo Ramblers hiking club and Michael Warren, a longtime volunteer with the New York–New Jersey Trail Conference, breathed new life into the project. By this time, given the impacts of ever-expanding suburbia, it became clear that Schaefer's concept had to be transformed—cleared and blazed with an official route—into the trail we know today. Although had it not been for Torrey, likely there would be no Long Path at all.

Lord knows we felt a sense of uncertainty, first, as we ascended loose dirt and rock- and root-strewn mountainsides, then achievement, as we summitted Howell Mountain, Brooks Mountain, and Blackcap Mountain. Atop nearly every mountain we walked long slabs of rock, which, though unforgiving on the soles of our feet, were at least level. It seemed that with each step we took another tree changed color, the autumn hues popping as if to purposely grab our attention and remind us of the beauty of the moment. In our last mile, however, Scott began to fall behind, and periodically I heard a "Goddammit!" or "Fucking hell!" He was ready to call it a day. Given that Star Left hiked with a lighter load, we were moving faster than usual, and with my being lost in conversation I knew I hadn't been as mindful to pacing ourselves. The miles had undeniably been hard and once again the sun was beginning to sink low. But we had just one more mountain and when we reached an open patch of grass just below the summit, Scott threw down his pack.

"Let's camp here," Scott said, rifling through his backpack now. He pulled out his pack of smokes.

"Yeah, I guess we could." I wanted to make it over this peak but at the same time the last thing I wanted to do today was push us over the edge.

"I thought you guys wanted to go a little farther?" Star Left said, clearly still feeling chipper, more chipper than us.

"Well, we were planning on it, but I don't know, it's getting late. I don't know what we'll find for camping up ahead." I was waffling. I less than loved having to be the one to call the shots here.

"It's going to be cold up here, probably a whole lot warmer down in the valley," Star Left countered.

She was right. The wind was already beginning to pick up. We'd definitely have another cold night's sleep if we stayed here. Plus, if we hiked a little farther, we could make up some of the mileage we'd lost the day before.

"What do you think, love?" I asked Scott, who was now focused only on his cigarette.

He shrugged his shoulders.

"I don't know, I think we might be getting a little tired," I told Star Left.

Star Left stared out into the woods. "You know, in hiking, one thing I've learned is that sometimes, if you push a little to get where you want to go, in the end you're happier that you did. The miles can be hard, but it's better to hike them when you can to stay on course."

Her words were spot on, but I knew they fell on deaf ears. She clearly wanted to get some miles in, and so did I, but more importantly I didn't want to sleep so near the mountain's summit in the cold.

"What do you think, love?" I asked him again, hoping to get a straight answer.

"Whatever you two want to do is fine with me," he said, snubbing out his cigarette and putting the butt in his pocket. His tone had been polite, but I could tell that he'd had his fill of Harriman's peaks for the day. If Raymond Torrey were to come walking around the bend, Scott might just pop him in the nose.

"Alright, let's go just a little farther, at least get down off the mountain," I compromised.

One more short steep push and thankfully the rest of our trek was downhill. The woods began to morph as we descended, the trees became thicker and grassy expanses turned to crunchy carpets of leaves. Birches and oaks persisted at great heights. We decided on a spot at the base of the mountain. As we explored the area, however, we found over a rise, the chain-link fence that lined West Point property, posted with ominous "No Trespassing" signs. Before us, just beyond a row of trees, was a powerline clearing, the lines slung loosely above the treetops, and over the wind we could hear passing cars on a busy road on the other side of the woods. Nonetheless, in our little patch of forest we were decidedly secure, and we quickly got to setting up camp and cooking dinner.

And there in our nest of the woods, once fed and warm, we passed around a bottle of whiskey and shared stories late into the night. Each one of us recounting years of past experiences that had formidably shaped us into the people we are now, wiser and happier. We learned more about the love that had hit both Star Left and Ed like a tidal wave and how they'd now settled into an ocean all their own, deep and calm. We shared our story of how we'd met and how different our experiences together were formed by those in our past and how we'd ended up here on the Long Path. With only our voices in the dark, and a barred owl hooting overhead, we listened and were heard without distraction and without façade.

CHAPTER THREE

We crossed busy Route 6 and turned onto an abandoned road. It was hard to imagine that this narrow tract of crumbling pavement that now served as trail had once been the primary route, before the new highway had been constructed. We'd said goodbye to Star Left. But earlier this morning, we'd awoken to find her basking in the sunlight on a large boulder at the edge of the powerline clearing. Cupping a tin mug in her hands, she looked as if she were soaking up every chirp of birdsong and ray of sun upon her skin before having to depart from the woods. After a little while, we'd joined her with a cup of coffee to warm our own bones beneath the open sky. We made a plan to meet in a week somewhere around Sam's Point. From here she would hike back to her car while we hiked onward. We lamented all the peaks that she'd have to climb for the *second* time. "Hey, I don't care, it's a day on the trail. Nowhere else I'd rather be," she assured us.

Again, it was just us. And on this easier terrain, we walked hand in hand, so grateful for the physical intimacy that can be forgotten when hiking hard miles. To either side of us grew walls of vine-wrapped trees, and wildflowers sprung forth from cracks in the pavement. Cultivated grape vines now gone wild hung heavy with ripe purplish-black fruits and twined around tall oaks. Nearby staghorn sumac sported its scarlet cones of fleshy seeds on velvety pedestals.

Periodically we stopped to do some gathering, rolling the grapes from their thin stalks between our fingers and into our mouths—these were some of the best we'd tasted, even if each contained several hard seeds we had to spit out. We snapped a single cone of sumac from a low-lying branch, shoving it in a water bottle to infuse while we hiked. The seeds of sumac in late summer and early fall provide an all-natural Vitamin C supplement and impart a lemon-like flavoring to water when submerged for a few hours. It would be tasty later in the day. Native goldenrod and white-petaled asters intermingled with arching plumes of nonnative mugwort and sunny-faced low-to-the-ground dandelions. All around us was evidence of nonnative plants growing alongside native and we were happy for both. At what point does a plant that has been here for centuries stop being considered a nonnative? Afterall, many of these plants casually considered weeds were initially planted here by the settlers for food and medicine. The leaves of mugwort may be steeped in hot water for a tea to aid in digestion and nearly every part of the dandelion is edible. We now followed in our ancestors' footsteps.

Our crumbling roadway led us through a clawing thicket and then popped us out amidst pristine homes in a well-manicured residential area.

"From wilderness to suburbia, just like that!" I declared, taking in our surroundings.

"You ain't kiddin'. There's got to be a mini-mart or something around here," Scott said, his voice full of hope. Scott was ever in search of a cold Gatorade.

"There's nothing in the guide."

"Yeah well, I don't buy it. There's have got to be amenities nearby with all these homes here."

He had a point. So, when we saw a man outside in his driveway, we decided we'd ask.

"You're hiking nearly 400 miles?" the man asked, turning on the tap.

This resident, George, ended up inviting us inside to fill up our water bottles at his sink. He'd received us cautiously at first. But upon learning that we were hiking the Long Path, he had quickly changed his demeanor. His mother however was now feeling wary, as she whispered to George through a cracked door.

"They're hikers, Mother," he assured her.

"Yes, we started in New York City," Scott answered, catching the clean running water that now streamed effortlessly into his bottle.

"New York City?" George echoed with a gasp.

"Yeah, we've been out here for almost a week now," I chimed in.

"What's this trail you're walking again?"

"The Long Path," we answered nearly in unison.

"I've never heard of it."

"It runs right in front of your house." Scott motioned with a nod towards the door.

Throughout our hike, this reaction would be the norm when talking to locals. There were folks who enjoyed a walk on a nearby trail but never knew its breadth, that it was a part of a larger trail system, and those who had only ever wondered at the aqua blazes painted on trees and road signs. There were those who had heard of the Long Path but never knew where it went, and *then*, there were those who, no matter how many times you told them you were hiking the Long Path, still referred to it as the Appalachian Trail. Nonetheless, to share that we were embarking on a journey of nearly 400 miles immediately garnered interest and graciousness. More importantly, what we'd repeatedly see was that when offered the opportunity, people wanted to help.

George ended up pointing us in the direction of a nearby deli called Danny's, which reportedly made some delicious sandwiches. Without a second thought, we thanked George, waved to Mom, and were on our way, our mouths watering at the mere thought of a sandwich. Within a couple of blocks we stood amidst a bustling town never mentioned in the guide. We asked a passerby on the sidewalk where we might find a bite to eat.

"Danny's, up there on the corner," the stranger said, pointing the way. Apparently, Danny's was the place to go.

We stood before a simple storefront, the name Danny's Market and Deli painted prominently above its awning, our spirits alighted by the decadent possibilities that might lie within its four walls. We swung open a glass door that gave a little jingle, but our spirits dropped when we stepped inside. It looked like this place had been here since the town was founded. The shelving consisted of metal racks, the lighting was dim, and the ceiling panels were stained and patchy. Was this really *the* place?

A slim Asian man appeared suddenly from behind the counter at the far end of the store. "Can I help you? Are you hiking? Do you want a sandwich?"

Yes, yes, and yes.

And so, despite the fact we had been about to turn 'round and head out the door, this man, who we presumed must be Danny himself, was so welcoming he lured us in for a closer look.

"Here, here!" he said, motioning for us to peer inside his glass display case. "I have egg salad. You can sample some first."

Before I knew it, he had a dollop on a little plastic spoon.

"Ladies first!" he said to Scott, pushing the spoon my direction.

"That's really good!" I exclaimed. In fact, it was the best egg salad I had ever tasted in my life.

"Of course it is!" Danny exclaimed and scooped up a sample for Scott to try.

"That *is* good!" Scott agreed, licking the spoon clean.

We ordered two egg salad sandwiches on hard rolls, grabbed a Gatorade and Dr. Pepper, and took a seat at the back of the deli in the one booth near an open sunny window. When Danny brought us our sandwiches, he told us to charge our phones if we needed and to feel free to get water from the tap or use the bathroom. Partway through our sandwiches he swung by again, asking if he had put too much lettuce on them or if they needed anything else. We told him they were perfect, the best we'd had yet, and got to talking about our long walk. We learned that he had served many a hiker in the twenty years that he'd owned the deli. He told us that he'd love to take a hike on this trail that inspires people but that he just didn't have the time. "Unless it's an emergency, I take no days off," he said. What we didn't tell him was how we couldn't imagine such a daily existence behind a counter inside these four walls. But it was obvious that here, in this present moment, even if it was also yesterday's and the day to come,

Danny was happy. His journey was this deli and we were glad that our path had intersected with his.

After idling away over an hour's time, happily sitting and not hiking, we moved to the outside front stoop to smoke a cigarette before hoisting packs and hitting pavement.

Danny pushed through the swinging glass door and stood before us. "Do you need a ride somewhere? Do you have everything you need?" He asked motioning to his car.

"Oh no, we're fine, but thank you," I said.

"Okay, well I'm heading out, there's a nice girl inside who can help you with anything you need. Good luck!" he said, and turned, jogging towards the parking lot across the street. Regretfully, we never did ascertain if his name was Danny, but one thing we knew, he was indeed a trail angel.

Walking through town we soon left the road through a thicket and emerged onto a gravel path that led along the course of a pipeline. Up a steep embankment to our right ran the commuter rail line that begins in Port Jervis, New York—the town in which I had lived for a couple years before meeting Scott and near to our home in Lackawaxen. We marveled at the thought of following that railway all the way back home. To our left ran Woodbury Creek. All was fine and good until we had to cross it.

At a bend, the blazes directed us left, underneath the stories-tall steel railroad bridge and through the creek's rushing waters that crashed over rocks below a slippery embankment. Across the expanse stood a wall of Japanese knotweed taller than us. Japanese knotweed is a highly invasive plant from Asia. It readily makes a home along waterways and roadsides, and although it is not one that we want to encourage, it is one we can eat. In the spring, its rhubarb-colored shoots may be snapped at their bases, stripped clean of leaves, and eaten raw or steamed. Lemony in flavor, they make a fine addition to salads and stir-fries. But it was not the season for harvest, nor the time. We had bigger things to worry about.

How could this be the way? We paced right then left trying in vain to find the best point in which to cross before finally deciding on a route and carefully, using our hiking sticks for balance, straddling its waters using a few exposed rock tops for steps. After clawing up the other side and through the jungle of bramble, we emerged on a paved road.

From here we resumed our walk alongside the active tracks, crisscrossing berms along our path. We spun round at the sound of a horn blasting in the distance to see a train growing larger on the horizon. The gravel rumbled beneath our feet. Last time that we rode this train we were en route from New York City, just as oblivious to our surroundings as today's passengers likely were. It seemed so long ago. Why not wake them up! Scott and I exchanged a mischievous look. We had a trademark photo we'd often take on mountain tops or sometimes at rushing waterfalls—our bare bums turned towards the camera, arms raised overhead in exaltation. Might it be appropriate here? Give them something to talk about. But our civilized selves chimed in and we decided instead to simply wave as it roared passed mere feet from us. We keeled over in laughter as it grew small in the distance. Modest or not, what a sight we must have been donning backpacks and big goofy smiles from the other side of those windows. However, as we began, now late in the afternoon, the most arduous leg of the day's hike with a climb up the side of Schunemunk Mountain, our laughter soon diminished.

We ascended for a long time through grassy rocky woods before first summiting High Knob, a rocky cliff that required scuffling along its edge and climbing boulders to its peak. Carefully, we craned our heads and behind us saw an expansive view of the town of Woodbury below. Rows of identical white houses with peaked roofs sat perfectly aligned with their tiny plots of lawn. Such organization already seemed so foreign to us with our spontaneous nightly campsites, each different from the night before. Scott, with his fear of heights, scrambled up the boulders fast, while I lingered and snapped a few pictures.

Beyond this vantage point we continued to climb, now shimmying and muscling between boulders shaped like cars tilted on their noses. Finally, we reached the exposed ridgetop and spied yellow blazes at a sharp turn in the trail. I checked my loose-leaf guidebook pages again. *The Long Path reaches the Jessup Trail (yellow) and the Highlands Trail (teal triangles) near the top of the ridge. The*

Long Path is co-aligned with the Jessup Trail to its end. Follow the yellow Jessup Trail blazes, as the Long Path and Highlands Trail are marked with their trail logos only at occasional intervals and at junctions.

Very well. We turned right and proceeded along the ridgeline. It felt so strange not to follow the rectangular aqua blazes of the Long Path that I checked our directions repeatedly, and each time I did, was reassured we were on course.

From Schunemunk's ridge the views were expansive. Behind us the tree-tops of Harriman State Park spread like a blanket and before us we could see the jagged peaks of the Catskills, far off and foggy. We glided across flat rock faces, climbed rock ledges, and hopped thin crevices. Large boulders, some perfectly round, sat perched atop the flat rock as if a giant had carefully placed them there, each with a purpose unknown to us. Megaliths to the mountain or perhaps the sky, the sun, or moon. Schunemunk is Lenape for "good fireplace," and long ago they had a village at the northern tip of this ridge. Surely they had understood this rock, having had a relationship with it, whereas we were just beginning to discover it; and its story was layered, literally.

Although the rock's surface at first appeared flat, it felt textured like antislip paper beneath our feet. Getting down on hands and knees we could see that it was comprised of many rocks, some pebble-sized, some as large as golf balls. Many shimmered like quartz, whereas others were a matte maroon or translucent pale pink. We wondered at the names of these fragments of hardened earth. Thousands of years ago, this ridge abutted the ocean; these pebbles were the result of waves crashing against its tall cliffs and rivers, depositing stones as they flowed back toward the sea.

In between these clasts resided an intricate patchwork of lichen, some gray and leafy, called foliose, others green and crustlike, aptly termed crustose. There were familiar wrinkled brown flaps of rock tripe, a foliose lichen that, true to form, looks like withering wet leaves stuck to the side of a rock. Lichen grow incredibly slow and are neither plant nor animal, but the organism resulting from a fungus and algae forming a symbiotic relationship. To think that they live merely on the fine sediment collected atop these rocks, moisture, and air . . . we were truly witness to an easily overlooked ecosystem at work.

Like the lichen, we too moved slow, and the sun was beginning to sink lower in the sky, casting a golden hue across our path, which was marked only sometimes with rock cairns. Cairns are piles of stacked stone—sometimes small and simple, sometimes tall and carefully balanced—left by hikers to aid others in finding their way. Looking at my watch, I realized that we had been on the ridge for well over an hour but had not yet begun to descend. The trail was only supposed to stretch three-quarters of a mile across the ridge before dropping us downward. Perhaps in our awe we had lost track of time. We had planned to camp in the woods below the summit, but with daylight quickly fading, when we spotted a small patch of dirt amidst the dwarfed pitch pines, slender oaks, and shrubby blueberry bushes that grew amongst the boulders, we decided to pitch our tent.

We set up camp in the dark and got to cooking under the vestibule considering there wasn't much room to sit elsewhere.

"This portion of trail is incredible. Beautiful and rugged," I said to Scott wistfully, carefully stirring our pot of noodles.

"Sure is," he replied. "But how come the guidebook didn't mention *anything* about all that climbing?" He questioned while unwrapping a package of pulverized cheese crackers.

"Good question! It seems an important detail. That was gorgeous, but it wasn't easy walking, the first of that kind we've encountered yet. I can't believe how slow we were moving." I placed the lid back on the pot half-cocked to let some steam escape.

"Yeah, I guess we were just soaking it up, but ya know, I wouldn't want to hike fast past all that anyway." Scott poured the cracker crumbs into his mouth from the wrapper.

"No, me either. I can't believe we didn't know about this place. It's really not that far from home." I brushed crumbs off Scott's shirt.

"We're definitely coming back here."

"Without a doubt. Perfect place for a day hike."

After a filling dinner of instant pasta alfredo, we laid nestled together inside our sleeping bag. Through the mesh screen of our tent we could see the night sky. It was brilliantly clear, speckled with stars, smudged with galaxies, and graced by a golden half-moon. And from here on the highest ridge in Orange County, it felt as if we were just a little bit closer to the moon. From a nearby tree, an owl hooted, *hoo, hoo, too-HOO, hoo hoo, too-HOO-aw,* a barred owl once again.

"You know, I think we've heard an owl nearly every night we've been out here," I said, turning my head to look at Scott now.

"We have. He's keeping an eye on us." Scott closed his eyes as if to listen more closely.

"You think so?"

"Definitely. The owl is my totem animal. They seem to show up wherever I am. I had a great horned owl that came to my window nightly and would just hoot away, *hoo-hoo hoooooo hoo-hoo!* For years, he came. Sometimes I'd spot him early in the morning up in a tree. There was one night when I was camping in West Virginia, I was dreaming about a pure white snowy owl, sitting atop my tent. I awoke in the night, crawled out of my tent to take a piss and there it was!"

"Nuh-uh. You don't typically see snowy owls that far south, do you?"

"Nope. They nest in the Arctic tundra. They do migrate south periodically, though usually no farther south than the Northeast. But there he was, white as snow, and just staring at me, unflinching. I've come to believe we have a kinship."

"What ever happened to the great horned owl?"

"I found him dead near the path that lead to my sweat lodge. And wouldn't you know it? He'd died right atop where I had buried the family dogs."

"Guess he *was* family."

"That's what I thought. So, I said a prayer and picked up a shovel."

We laid there a long while listening to, *hoo, hoo, too-HOO, hoo, hoo, too-HOO-aw,* call from the west of us and then the east. I imagined Scott's owl coming to his window and wondered about this one that we heard now, if he was as aware of us as we were of him. Suddenly, there was a high-pitched howling. Our eyelids flew open.

"Holy shit," I whispered loudly.

"They're really close." Scott was peering at the backside of the tent.

Coyotes. We smiled at their calls, our eyes wide with excitement, as they yipped and barked in the distance. Early on in our relationship, we'd heard them regularly near a lake that we'd frequently visit at night, and later, when we'd moved in together, we'd heard them call from the high cliff that towered above our house. It was a thrill still, though, to hear them out here, to share their mountaintop. Then just as abruptly as they had started, they fell silent. All the woods seemed hushed.

A single long sharp howl pierced the quiet of the night, tearing us from our trance. It sounded as if it'd come from the boulder right beside our tent. Looking at each other, we remained on our backs in silence but now only because we were too startled to speak. Scott grabbed the knife he always kept by his head and flicked it open.

Then, another howl. This time from the boulder to the other side of us.

"Shit, hon. What now?" I whispered in his ear as he still lay flat on his back, his knife atop his chest.

We heard a rustling in the leaf litter outside and then at the backside of our tent, near our heads, a shadow trotted by, the moonlight bright enough to illuminate the silhouette of a dog.

Still we didn't move a muscle. We laid there unmoving for what seemed an eternity, but was probably only a minute's passing, until we heard more howls. This time farther off.

"Did you see that hon?" I didn't know why I was still whispering, but it seemed like the smart thing to do.

"Hell yeah, I saw that." Scott was sitting up now, looking around the tent.

More howls went up in the distance, now even farther away, then yipping.

"They were checking us out." Scott said, closing his knife, placing it back by his head and laying down again.

"I guess they weren't interested." I felt I was more assuring myself than him.

"Nah. They don't want anything to do with us."

"Yeah, well that was a little close for comfort." I said letting out a big breath and curling up tight against him.

"Ya think?" Scott, too, gave a sigh of relief and wrapped his body around mine.

Faintly, in the distance, the hoots from the barred owl mingled now with the cries of the coyotes. Good thing that owl had had our backs.

We broke down camp and climbed out of our nook amidst the boulders to enjoy breakfast overlooking the Catskills. Scott seemed to smile more than usual this morning and I, too, felt bright. It was a town day and we had just eight easy miles until we reached Chester. In no time at all we'd descend from the ridge, hike along wooded trail, and reach the oh-so-easy paved Heritage Trail that we'd walk on into town. This time we'd reach our hotel in the early afternoon with time to run errands for resupply, catch up on journaling, and really truly enjoy some relaxation.

Onward we hiked, over a ridge that seemed to only get longer. We crawled up and over countless boulders and climbed up and down more ledges of fissured rock, all the while following the yellow and teal blazes for the Jessup and Highland Trails. None of it made any sense. After two hours, we finally began our descent.

"Oh, thank God!" I shook my hiking sticks at the sky. "This is it. We're going down!"

"About damn time."

With each descending step, my quads shook with fatigue and I could see Scott wincing now and again, our muscles depleted. Finally, we entered the woods. A steady stream flowed before us where the trail turned right. *But last night, we'd hauled liters of water up onto the ridge because we hadn't seen any mention in the guide of a reliable stream for miles. This wasn't right.* But, glad for refreshment, we stopped and filled up, proceeding down the steep trail that paralleled the stream, which dropped ever farther into a deepening ravine.

Before we'd gone very far, we reached a short side trail that we followed to a lookout over a cascading waterfall.

I'd seen a waterfall at Baby Brook on the map . . . In a flurry, I ripped the map from my pocket.

"Hon, this doesn't make sense." My lungs were tightening in my chest.

"But we're going down," Scott countered.

I studied the map hard, following the yellow dotted line of the Jessup Trail along with the blue triangles marking the Highland Trail. I retraced our route from camp repeatedly, then back to where we'd ascended from the roadway yesterday afternoon. *Oh shit.* At the top of the ridge, the Jessup and Highland Trails went right. But they also traveled left, and there they were marked with the Long Path emblem. Then I spotted Baby Brook.

"We're on the opposite end of the ridge," I declared to Scott calmly. Inside I was screaming.

"No," he said, his eyes unblinking, refusing to believe my words.

I suddenly had the notion that perhaps we, too, were mere playthings of the reigning giant of Schunemunk Mountain. Now he was squeezing all the air out of me between his thick tree-trunk fingers. I struggled for my breath and then managed, "Yes, hon. Yes." I came to stand beside him with the map.

"But we followed the blazes."

"We did. But we followed them the wrong direction. The trail came to a 'T,' and we went right, not left."

"I didn't see a trail to the left!" He was getting angry now and I remembered that he'd led the way onto the ridge.

"I didn't either. I should've at least *looked* at the map instead of just relying on the guide." I'd cost us so much time, so much energy. I should have questioned sooner when we just kept walking on the damn ridge.

We spread the map out between the two of us. *What if we just hiked farther down the mountain?* The trail might lead us to a road that we could walk into

Chester. But there was no way. To do that would only lengthen our day's miles even more, not to mention that we'd be skipping miles of the official Long Path, too, and that didn't sit well with me.

"We'll have to turn around," said Scott with resignation.

I took a deep breath and agreed. "Yeah. It's all we can do." I was working hard to mirror Scott's stoicism. His reservation was admirable. I'd expected him to lose it. Lord knows that I wanted to at this point.

"How far do you think we've come since our campsite?" Scott asked.

"About two and a half miles."

"Oh well, that's not too bad."

"Yeah, but we weren't even camped on the Long Path last night. We will have to go another one and a half beyond that just to get to the intersection."

He was definitely going to lose it now.

"Okay. Well, then that's what we do. It's all we can do." He said with a nod, starting back up the steep trail.

I was impressed to say the least. I knew it didn't pay to get angry, but didn't he want to pitch a fit? Yes, we'd both been at fault, but so easily he could've put it on me that I hadn't looked at the map, given that I was the one most often deciphering the directions. He could've demanded that we continue hiking down the trail and hitch our way into Chester. He also could've simply gotten so frustrated that it fed my frustration. But he didn't. Instead, we just turned around and hiked back the way we had come.

By two-thirty in the afternoon, we reached the junction. The heat of the day was upon us and our stomachs growled. We'd hiked hastily without stopping for a moment's break. At a curve in the trail ahead, we saw a yellow blaze, and continuing farther, hidden behind the bough of a pine tree, a circular metal disk that bore the Long Path emblem.

"Are you fucking kidding me?" Scott said with a huff, throwing down his sticks.

"No wonder we didn't see it." I let my sticks fall with a clatter.

"I'm taking a break."

"Ditto."

And so with that, we dropped our packs and pulled out a couple of granola bars. We'd hiked roughly seven hard miles this morning. Had we gone the right way, we could've nearly been to Chester . . . now we had still ten miles to go. It seemed hard to believe that twenty-four hours ago we'd been so enthralled with this ridge.

Within thirty-five minutes we had descended. Without boulders to climb and crevices to hop the walking was easy and we were quickly enlightened as to why the guide hadn't mentioned the severity of this section of trail. There was nothing spectacular about this *right way*. But when compared with this hum-drum scenery, some small part of me that I wasn't yet ready to listen to said that we'd been graced with the fortune of going the *wrong* way. We'd experienced the magnitude of the ridge. But it was impossible right now to be so optimistic. We were defeated.

We continued on a gradual decline, soon swooshing and scraping through brush so thick it was as if we passed through a miles-long car wash. Our ankles rolled as we stumbled over sharp rocks hidden beneath the tall grass. We might have been done with the boulder scaling, but here the trail offered its own kind of misery. The afternoon was hot and neither of us cared much for conversation. As various trails intersected with ours, we searched desperately for blazes through the trees, no longer trusting our judgement and more nervous than ever that we'd make a wrong turn. The hiker car wash transitioned to rolling ATV trails through open forest and then, sandwiched between busy road crossings, snippets of trail that wound through patches of woods littered with trash. Grumpy and near delirium, the trail seemed an awful place. Reaching Chester felt impossible.

The Heritage Trail

PART FOUR:

ORANGE

COUNTY

Witch hazel in flower

CHAPTER ONE

We hobbled into an enormous commuter parking lot in Monroe, our bodies bruised, and spirits broken. My feet throbbed and Scott's knees ached. This was the start of the Heritage Trail, an eleven-mile paved greenway, which we'd envisioned being a breeze, but now with four more miles to go on hard pavement, it seemed at best torturous. Screw that. We took a seat on a bench amidst a sea of parked cars and Googled a cab company. Instead, we'd take a taxi to a Holiday Inn Express and grab a cab in the morning back to this same location so we wouldn't skip any miles. Yes, it'd cost some money, but it was well worth it for the reprieve.

The taxi arrived within fifteen minutes and the driver opened the hatchback of his minivan so that we could stow our packs away. We climbed in, told him where we were headed, and with a nod, he proceeded. To share space so closely with someone yet not speak a word now felt strange, even if in our everyday life this would've been the norm. Soon the driver was speeding down the road, zipping around corners, the passing trees a blur outside my window. I grabbed hold of Scott's arm.

"He's going so fast," I whispered in Scott's ear.

"He's going forty-five miles per hour," Scott replied while looking at the speedometer.

When you're used to two miles an hour, I guess it's all relative.

The Holiday Inn Express appeared like an oasis. Once inside, we filled out the necessary paperwork and dragged our packs up to our room where we hastily stripped off our clothing and hopped in the shower. But we weren't done yet. It was time for an evening of resupply errands. Thankfully, the town of Chester proved to be hiker-friendly with all amenities within walking distance . . . short walking distance. We carried our one compact load of laundry in a stuff sack to the laundromat, stopped at the liquor store to grab another small plastic bottle of whisky, dropped into the CVS to get Scott more Band-Aids for his red ant bites that still needed care, and scarfed down three plates of food at the Chester Diner.

We awoke in the unnaturally black darkness of a hotel room, our mouths dry from the air conditioning that'd blown hard all night. I checked my phone and saw that I'd received a text message from our good friend, Alex, in Asheville, North Carolina. I'd lived for over a decade in Asheville—through my four years in college and then had remained there, making it home. I'd returned to the northeast in 2011, needing a change of scenery and ultimately a break from a place that would only remind me of my severed seven-year relationship. I wanted to be closer to family and feel the security of a home I had missed over the years. But a few years later, after my second hike on the Mountains to Sea Trail, I'd returned to Asheville to live, sharing a home with three of my closest friends. It was then that I'd made friends with Alex. I'd planned to return to Asheville after my hike on the Finger Lakes Trail. Instead, I fell in love with Scott and scratched those plans, but I had, as soon as possible, brought him down to Asheville to meet the sweet souls with whom I'd formed a deep connection over the years. Over the span of just two long visits, it was as if Scott had always been a part of the community. Their quick bond only reinforced that, this time, I'd indeed picked the right man. In particular, Alex and Scott had connected over music as she, too, was a musician. She was now traveling from a wedding in Boston to her grandmother's in Pennsylvania and wanted to drop in on our hike even if just for a few hours. My heart leaped at the chance to have with us a little piece of another place I considered home.

We left our heavy backpacks in the care of the front desk at the hotel and got walking from the commercial district of Chester through a quiet residential area and onto the Heritage Trail. Our bodies felt as if they were hovering just above the ground. What reason did we have to carry packs when we would have a friend to shuttle us to retrieve them? To be free of their weight—we felt we were floating! When we saw a restored old-fashioned train station, we knew we were in the right place. The Heritage Trail is the route of a once regularly traveled railway that's now been converted into a path, largely paved, for walkers and bicyclists. We'd decided, with Alex's help, we would start the day's miles here and hike back toward the parking lot in Monroe, where she would have parked and be walking toward us from. We were still doing the miles, simply in reverse.

We walked the Heritage Trail shrouded in the canopy of leafy oaks and maples beginning to change from green to reds, oranges, and yellows. Walking a wide corridor of pavement so flat and straight that it narrowed to a point on the horizon, between farm fields and well-maintained homes, it was as if we were in a picture book. A bicyclist periodically wheeled by lazily, giving a friendly smile or casual wave. These cyclists were void of the aggression of those we'd encountered on the George Washington Bridge. When afforded a little space, how much more courteous people can be to one another. Not to say that those people that had whizzed by us in New York City were brutish by nature, but when caged in, it seems humans sometimes lose their humanness.

When I spied a female figure walking towards us, a mess of blond dreads atop her head, blue jeans, and a purple Mr. T t-shirt, I knew it was Alex. She gave a little wave and we gave a great big holler. She replied with a whoop that resounded through the treetops. My feet suddenly took on such buoyancy, I had to resist sprinting towards her. In this moment I was blessed. Here on this piece of trail in New York, my worlds were colliding. I had it all. But we had only a mile and a half to hang before we'd reach her car back at the commuter parking lot.

As we walked, Scott and I rambled on as if we were a long-running album and she'd just pressed the play button. Sharing with her our story seemed to amplify all that we had experienced thus far. We'd walked just shy of 100 miles at this point, but we'd *lived* so much. We told her about the night hiking and the red ants and the coyotes and getting lost, when suddenly we appeared, as if we'd been transported, in that same commuter parking lot in Monroe. The one we had, weathered and weary, abandoned the day before. Her little sedan was laden with stuff, but we hopped in, pushing aside clothing, a sleeping bag, and a box of leftover takeout that I put in the back window. She put foot to pedal, rolled all of her windows down, and gave us a lift back to Chester where our packs awaited us at the hotel before finally returning us to the train station along the Heritage Trail. The three of us took a seat on a wrought-iron bench to have a snack and soak up our last few minutes together before she headed on her way. An elderly woman sat on the bench beside ours and I hoped that our colorful explanations and laughter weren't intruding upon her quiet time as Scott showed off his red ant bites and went into further detail about how they'd become oozing pustules and as I shared how good it'd felt to finally shower after days on the trail. We couldn't help it. We were two little kids bubbling over with excitement, the chance to tell our stories to a friend. Just then, the elderly woman rose from her seat with a wince.

"Those are some tales! I think I can manage to walk my small two miles back home now. Good luck on your long walk!" she said with a warm smile.

"Thank you! Two miles counts for a lot!" I told her, Scott and Alex agreeing.

"Nowhere near as far as you two have come," she answered and, with a little wave, stepped off the curb onto the paved trail.

Reluctantly, we said our goodbyes to Alex and then hiked on with full packs and full hearts, an easy trail before us. As predicted, the miles rolled by effortlessly. A lesson quickly learned on the trail: all miles are not created equal. Late in the afternoon we reached the village of Goshen, bustling with late afternoon traffic, and headed straight for the Post Office that sat on a corner. Inside, we retrieved our first maildrop and headed to the bench outside to dump out its contents and fill our packs that had for at least an afternoon, felt light. We sat there sorting out bags of oatmeal, organic Pop-Tarts, tuna packets, and instant noodles while a police car sat nearby. We were just packaging up the last of our goodies, when the officer stepped out of his vehicle.

He strolled up to us slowly. "So, I have to ask . . . " he said with a smirk, not exactly asking anything.

"We're hiking the Long Path. We're just organizing our food we picked up here at the post office," Scott explained.

"The Appalachian Trail? That's nowhere near here," he replied with a sideways look.

"No, not the AT, the Long Path. We started in New York City and we'll end up near the Adirondacks," I clarified.

"You guys walked from New York City?" he asked, his eyes wide. I wondered if he believed us. "That's amazing. You're just passing through?"

"Yes, headed onto a campsite for the night some miles away," Scott said, purposely being vague and I was glad. We were planning on stealth camping tonight in roadside woods.

"Wow. That's so cool. Do you need anything?"

"Nope, we have everything we need right here," I said, motioning to the box before us.

"Alright great! Well good luck you two." And with that he gave a warm nod and walked back to his car.

No matter how old I get, whenever a police officer approaches me, in my mind I'm that same trouble-making teenager and I'm sure I'm about to get busted . . . what for, I don't know. It's still a relief to be proven wrong. Not only had he believed us, but it even seemed he'd respected us for undertaking this journey.

The trail followed a sidewalk through town and despite our backpacks being full to the brim with food, we couldn't resist stopping in a little pizzeria along the way. We ordered two slices and two cold Dr. Peppers and answered question after question from the friendly employees and business owner. They'd never heard of the Long Path and asked if it was nearby. So, like we had with so many others, we pointed out the aqua blaze on the telephone pole just outside the front door.

"I always wondered what that was!" the delivery boy exclaimed. "That's so cool," he added, all of us now peering at the street through the large front window. It seemed everywhere we went, we spread the word of the Long Path. *Would any of these folks venture onto it in the future?*

With our bellies full, we waddled down the sidewalk until it disappeared, heading out of town on a country road. The sun was beginning to set low, blinding us as we walked and bathing everything in golden light. In my planning stages back home, knowing that we'd be sandwiched between town and state land here with no designated place to camp, I had, using Google's satellite images, discovered a large swath of green land with few residences in an area near Echo Lake. We figured we'd find a place to camp there, but as I watched the roadside vegetation grow taller and thicker, I began to worry. We passed some openings in the woods, but tree after tree was plastered with "No Trespassing" signs. We'd been walking for a little over a mile, when we reached a pond, with marshland surrounding it on either side like a horseshoe. *This* was Echo Lake? If so, then all this soggy, weed-stricken land was none other than the inviting green patch I'd seen on my computer screen.

"It's all marsh." Scott slouched his shoulders, his hiking sticks limp in his hands.

"I'm sorry, hon. I don't know what we'll do. We can't camp in this. We can't even *walk* across this." I was already beginning to blame myself, envisioning our miserable walk into the night down this long country road.

For a long while, we stood speechless, scanning the land before us. The lake was full of water-loving wildflowers. Floating on its surface in the center, were two white swans side by side. Tall grasses on its perimeter reached for the sky. It was undeniably beautiful, but for us, uninhabitable.

"We'll have to hike on." Scott broke our silence and started off down the road. I followed with my head hung low.

We passed the marshy area but now peered out over a forest full of trees and sharp rocks. There wasn't a single square foot of pure smooth soil. However, there weren't any private property postings, and with darkness quickly descending upon us, we left the road, ducking into the even greater darkness of the woods, and tiptoed our way in deeper.

"There's nowhere to put a tent here." This evening was beginning to look hopeless.

"Look, there," Scott said, "it looks like the land goes up. If we keep following it maybe it will flatten out on top." He pointed at the sloping side of a wooded hill where it looked like there were fewer rocks. We had no indication of what might be on top of that hill, but it was the best chance we had.

So, we carried on, stepping atop rocks that shifted beneath our weight and clawing through intricate spiderwebs that stretched between the trees, evidence that no one had been through these woods in a long time. We reached a narrow snaking inlet for the marsh and carefully crossed using a fat tree trunk as a bridge. From here we scrambled up the side of the leaf strewn hillside and reached its crest. To our luck, the ground was indeed flat and largely free of rocks, however, we stood beside what we could only guess was a road construction. Beside this swatch of cleared land piled with hay and gravel was our fated campsite, strewn with trash from whomever had once inhabited these woods. We tripped over rusty fencing and an old light fixture and stumbled over a downed telephone pole as we set up our tent amidst the debris in the dark. It was beyond primitive, but it would do.

Finally settled inside our tent, we'd just finished changing into sleep clothes and were sitting side by side, relieved at having made camp and enjoying a smoke, when suddenly, *KABOOM!* Something landed *hard* on the ground just outside the tent.

"What the hell was that?!" I whispered loudly to Scott who was now looking wide-eyed at me.

I scrambled for my headlamp and cautiously unzipped the door, only to see by the light of its dim beam, a dark four-legged creature waddling around about ten feet from the tent. I gasped loudly.

"What is it?" Scott demanded, his voice urgent.

"I—I don't know." I squinted, trying my best to keep tabs on it with my light. Scott leaned over my shoulder and peered out, flicking his headlamp on.

"What the hell is that?"

"I don't know. I don't think it's a bear," I said, relieved.

It continued to waddle around and headed toward a nearby tree.

"Should we get out and see?" I asked Scott.

"I don't know. I mean I guess so. We have to know what it is," he agreed, although he didn't sound eager.

Putting on our shoes, we quietly climbed out of the tent and both stepped closer to the creature, shining our headlamps.

"Shit. Is it a skunk?" Scott asked, taking a step back just as I, too, caught a flash of white.

"I can't tell. It could be a porcupine." I squinted. It was possible that the white we saw was from the needles of an illuminated porcupine.

Just then it waddled around to face us, its two glowing eyes reflecting our light.

"It's looking at us," I whispered loudly to Scott.

"*I see that,*" he whispered back sarcastically.

There we stood, the three of us, our eyes locked, unflinching. When I shuffled my feet in the leaf litter, it turned 'round and slowly waddled away, showing off a rounded back of needles shifting this way and that under its weight.

"It's a porcupine!" Scott whispered loudly.

"Thank God." I let out a deep sigh and watched as it nestled inside a large hole at the base of the tree, again staring straight at us.

"What now?" Scott asked.

"I don't know. I encountered a lot of them on the Finger Lakes Trail, the AT, too. They were never aggressive, but I don't know, this guy seems pissed. I think that's his home." I pointed to the tree.

"Well, let's give him some space," Scott suggested, motioning back to the tent.

Kicking off our shoes we climbed back inside, watching the porcupine from the security of our nylon home while he maintained our gaze just as steadily from his woody hole.

"As long as he stays over there," I said to Scott, keeping my eyes on the porcupine.

"Yeah, he better."

I wasn't thrilled with our neighbor but better a porcupine than a skunk. Likely we'd ruined this fat little fellow's night as well.

My eyelids thrust open and I laid perfectly still in the darkness. I'd heard a sound, kind of like the inadvertent sound one makes when sucking on a hard candy. *Nibbling. Our hiking sticks!* Dammit, that porcupine was making a meal—porcupines love salt and those handles were sweaty. I remembered the shelters in Vermont along the AT. The edges of the wooden floorboards had been gnawed to shreds by the porcupines, who relished the salty residue from hikers' sweaty legs. Some trail maintainers went so far as to seal these edges with sheet metal to discourage them. But I was too tired to move. He could have 'em.

When we finally climbed from our tent in the morning, our neighbor had apparently already left for the day. Our hiking sticks laid upon the ground, thankfully intact—but we did see that he'd dragged a long branch to his hole for a late-night snack.

We packed up camp, retraced our path back through the forest of hatchet-sharp rocks and onto the road. Today we would hike sixteen miles—our longest day yet—along country roads. But surely it'd be easy, right? After all, the Heritage Trail had been a breeze.

Remember what I said before? *Not all miles are created equal.* The temperatures were in the high eighties, and with little shade along the long stretches of pavement, the radiant heat was intense. Thanks to our five-day resupply in Goshen, our packs weighed heavily on our backs. We walked through the tiny towns of North Hampton and Waywayanda and it seemed every road took us steeply up while motorists zipped by in shiny cars without even a tap on their brakes. This corridor was a monotonous picture show of houses that looked better suited to cookie-cutter suburbia than the rural countryside. Why had these residents with considerable wealth chosen to build here? The country beauty, we supposed. But they had successfully squelched that.

That evening we stumbled back into the shaded woods by way of a steep gravel forest road. The air was moist with humidity, but the temperatures had lessened just enough that our sweat felt cool upon our skin. Although exhausted and quite literally dragging our feet, when the trail leveled out, we were gently embraced by the peacefulness of our surroundings. Stone walls lined our path and slender black birch trees towered beside us, their leaves yellowing like the now-fading sun.

The forest told a story of human presence. Long ago, stone walls—built with rock unearthed from surrounding land for the purpose of farming—provided property boundaries and natural borders for livestock. When a forest has been logged or otherwise disturbed, black birch seeds are quick to germinate. Couple this with the region's high deer population, which prefers other hardwood saplings and acorns, and birch quickly becomes a dominant tree. However, we humans have long had a relationship with this tree. Black birch, when tapped, provides a watery sap, which was boiled down into a syrup that was used as both flavoring and sweetener in our old-time birch beers. Its twigs and inner bark also contain methyl salicylate, which was extracted as a minty flavoring agent and used in medicines to reduce swelling and pain, and this tree nearly became endangered until the mid-twentieth century, when a synthetic form of the compound was created. Birch was also valued for its attractive hardwood and used in furniture and cabinetry, and is still used in this way today.

As we walked, we heard only the rustle of chipmunks and squirrels scurrying in the leaf litter and the periodic chirp of a bird singing its last notes before dark. We set up camp in the company of a witch hazel tree on a wide, level tract of land at the base of an embankment. Witch hazel, another tree valued for its medicinal properties, in this case its anti-inflammatory astringent bark, was also valued amongst pagans as a protector. Therefore, I have always considered a camp beneath its arching branches a fine place to sleep. Witch hazel is one of the few trees to bloom in the autumn. I imagined its spidery yellow blossoms soon to unfurl, the trees' gift to the forest when the other flowers have withered and gone to seed. Somehow we managed to cook dinner before the sun went down and soon relished the cool damp air befalling our little tent. Later that evening, an owl hooted overhead as we drifted off beneath the faintly glimmering stars. We slumbered safe in the forest's care.

Winding trail through berry bushes and
pitch pine in Minnewaska State Park Preserve

PART FIVE:

THE

SHAWANGUNKS

Star Left and Heather at Sam's Point

CHAPTER ONE

The early morning fog had settled heavy around our camp, enshrouding us in a cloud. I let Scott sleep and heated water as I listened to coyotes yip at a nearby pond. Whether we are there to bear witness or not, an entire world plays out, here in the wilderness. It considers us not, nor questions its own purpose; as life, it just carries on as it always has. In this moment, I was graced simply to be a part. Scott eventually stirred, and when he did, I presented him with a cup of instant coffee.

"I think it's going to be another hot one," Scott said as the sun gained height in the sky, shining down upon our little tent, dissolving the surrounding vapor.

"Yep. What were we ever thinking bringing that fifteen-degree sleeping bag?" I shook my head in disgust and pushed off our silk liner that was already too warm.

"It was cold when we left home, almost chilly enough for a frost," Scott reminded me.

Home. We'd only been hiking for roughly ten days, but already it seemed so far away. We were, however, camped just outside the town of Otisville and in fact closer than ever to our little house in Lackawaxen. This was the closest we'd be for the rest of our hike. Yesterday we'd spotted road signs pointing to towns we recognized and had seen with fresh eyes the woods and towns we had driven by for years but barely noticed. And later today, a face from home would join us for lunch—my mother.

We started off walking a rolling, rocky trail interspersed with patches of green moss so thick it felt like padded carpet beneath our feet—especially nice after a day of hard road walking. It wasn't long before we reached a junction with the Shawangunk Ridge Trail, the very trail on which we'd first become acquainted with the Long Path.

The Shawangunk Ridge Trail runs seventy-one miles from High Point State Park in New Jersey to Rosendale, New York, following the Shawangunk Ridge. This trail is considered part of the Long Path system and provides an official alternate route, using the Appalachian Trail as a connector from Harriman State Park to High Point State Park. At one time the route we had chosen to walk had offered little actual trail, consisting instead of long miles on roads. However, when land was acquired in Orange County, thanks to Andy Garrison, Jakob Franke, and the New York–New Jersey Trail Conference Conservation Committee, the route we walked was mapped out, allowing us to remain on the Long Path with less pavement. Franke, a dedicated trail builder, began his work with the Long Path in the early 1990s on the Shawangunk Ridge Trail, and in 2005 became Chair of the Long Path South until his passing in 2016. He and Andy were dear friends. The Conservation Committee—comprised of volunteers and NY–NJ Trail Conference staff—works to preserve and expand trail corridor, specifically that of long-distance trails, through the acquisition of land, easement rights, and right-of-way agreements. For the next thirty-four miles northward, the Long Path would run contiguously with the Shawangunk Ridge Trail, sharing the same trail.

We both stood gazing south down the Shawangunk Ridge Trail. If we hiked a few short miles we'd run into a section of the trail we'd hiked last year. We'd begun our day hike at High Point and had headed towards this very junction, dreaming up ideas of thru-hiking the Long Path. Now here we were, doing just that.

We reached the abandoned Erie Railroad line, which was now trail, but which had long been employed for freight. Just on the other side of a dirt embankment a train on the active New Jersey Transit line, which we had seen yesterday at Woodbury Creek, chugged by, and again, we gave a little wave. Perhaps it carried some of the same commuters. Good thing we hadn't mooned it. Unlike the Heritage Trail, however, this old railroad line was not paved. As we hiked, our ankles and knees rolled with every step atop sharp-cut stone that laid between black sooty soil and steel railroad ties. When the terrain beneath our feet shifted to fine gravel, we were relieved. That gravel then led us beneath some of the largest power lines we'd ever seen.

It started to drizzle, and overhead the lines buzzed with electricity. Although a far cry from picturesque wilderness, the beauty of this place was still outstanding. In the surrounding fields, the heavy moisture in the air enlivened the multitude of colorful wildflowers—yellow goldenrod, white and purple asters, and the pink pom-pom-like tops of clover. The leaves and flowers of goldenrod make a tasty allergy relieving tea, the flowers of clover activate the lymphatic system, and the asters—well, they provide their own aesthetic autumnal medicine. We were in a sea of plant life out of which steel spires rose like those of a magnificent castle. At our knees we shuffled through bush-like bunches of Saint John's wort whose once-yellow flowers had now gone to seed and whose leaves turned red with autumn. It seems appropriate that Saint John's wort, a plant known for its depression-relieving properties, would grow in a place intermingled with civilization, within our reach. I knelt, plucked a leaf and held it up to the sky to see its translucent glandular dots. These look like tiny pinpricks in the leaf and can only be seen when illuminated. I like to say that these serve as a reminder that Saint John's wort is the herb that "lets the light in."

Walking farther through this medicinal meadow, we brushed shoulders with six-foot-tall dried mullein stalks that we shook like rattles just for fun, their drying seeds shaking in their woody capsules. At our feet sat mullein's velvety first-year rosettes, their large leaves arranged circularly resembling actual roses.

Mullein, too, has a use. Its dried leaves can be infused in hot water, making a tea that moistens dry sinuses and provides expectorant properties.

"The Native Americans would smoke this leaf in a tobacco blend to open the bronchial passageways," Scott said, rubbing a moist leaf between his fingers.

Layers of colorful hillsides dotted with homes and a blue ridgeline on the horizon suddenly appeared to our left, framed by blond fields in the forefront and the gray sky above. This was the Neversink Valley, named for the river that meanders through it. Where one would least expect to find it, beneath omnipresent power lines, beauty continued to abound.

Eventually we re-entered the woods, resuming our walk atop the old railroad bed, and when we finally reached the road crossing, our calves were covered in black dust. Taking a seat atop our backpacks, Scott took out his phone and sent my mother a text that we'd be waiting here for her. Despite our looking like hobos, several people pulled over to ask us if we needed a ride. Maybe we didn't look as dirty and tired as we felt. When my mother pulled into the gravelly lot, scraping the underside of her Subaru sedan, I was again a child, filled with excitement and relief at the sight of her. Through the windshield, I saw a wide smile stretch across her face.

We shared stories at Nick's Pizzeria, one of the few establishments in the tiny town of Otisville. The burly guy behind the counter with a New York attitude—who I presumed to be the owner—didn't seem to have much time for Scott's and my hemming and hawing over his pizza selection oozing melty cheesy goodness. But, after we ordered a very hearty lunch for a mere three people and sat outside at his picnic table for nearly two hours, he softened up, came out and cracked some jokes, and even cut us a deal on the meal.

My mother told us about the routine happenings at home and filled us in on the activities of our cat, Fran, who she and my father were taking care of in our absence. Repeatedly, she asked us, "How are you guys doing?" Each time we replied, "Good." Until she finally just turned to Scott and asked him individually. Perhaps she wondered if she should rescue him from my crazy quest. But he, too, replied, "Really good, it's been beautiful," to which she nodded in resignation, as if to say, "Don't say I didn't try to give you an out."

But really, it was comforting just to be in her company, so normal, and I had the sense Scott felt that too. She offered to take us home for the night, but we refused, having already decided in advance we wouldn't return home unless it were an emergency. We'd long since finished our pizza and now we were dawdling. We hated to leave, but once again it was getting late in the day. After a few long hugs in which my mother again searched our faces for signs of pain and despair, we cruised back up the windy road to the trailhead and off she drove for home.

Far too full to walk, we reluctantly shouldered our packs and turned down the road which would lead us to the next trailhead in the woods, when a pick-up truck pulled up alongside us.

"Hey! Are you hiking the Long Path?" said a friendly voice.

It was none other than Andy Garrison.

"How did you know we were here?" Scott said with a chuckle.

"I didn't! Was just out doing some trail maintenance," he said, motioning to the back of his pickup truck. He pulled his truck over to the shoulder and hopped out.

"You two look great!" he said, with a smile beaming out from below his mustache.

"We *feel* great!" I replied, looking to Scott who nodded in agreement.

"Hey, you guys want to see my trail maintenance tools?" Andy said with a little sparkle in his eye.

We walked around to the back of his pickup truck and spied digging tools of various sorts, a hoe, chainsaw, and weed whacker.

"I was just working on knocking back some of the brush at the road crossings and along the tracks farther back on the trail. Those areas require a whole different batch of tools than I'd normally use due to the amount of weedy overgrowth."

If it weren't for people like Andy, we'd have no trail at all. The Long Path is built and maintained entirely by volunteers, people who love the trail so much they give their blood, sweat, and tears carving it through the woods. Many of these people will never have the opportunity to walk the trail end to end and some simply don't care to, for to walk the designated portion for which they are responsible is satisfaction enough.

There on the side of the road, we chatted with Andy for a good half hour, regaling him with our tales. Scott pointed out his red ant bites that were now beginning to heal on his arms and neck but still looked like birdshot scars. I told him about getting lost on Schunemunk and the close call with the coyotes. We rambled on about the beauty of this portion of trail through Orange County, reinforcing the work he had done in making it come to fruition. Having run into him here by chance was evidence of the serendipity inherent in any long-distance hike. I have always noticed after hiking long enough, after a string of days or weeks—sometimes it takes longer to fall into sync than other times—it seems that one will collide with just the right people at just the right time. I believe this synchronicity is something we could experience in our daily lives, too, if we only had the awareness, the presence of mind, to see the pieces falling into place or could get out of our own way and let them.

In his pickup, Andy went bumping down the winding road and when we turned and started up the steep trail to Gobbler's Knob, we heard him give a celebratory honk. We reached the small rock outcrop that is the summit in what seemed like no time. A year ago, we'd hiked this section and had struggled our way to the top, only to turn and hike back down, feeling accomplished. It seemed hard to believe that we'd found the walk so arduous and that now we'd just keep hiking northward.

We reached the Bashakill Wildlife Management Area in that magic hour of dusk. We remembered wearing hats and gloves and warm vests the last time we'd explored this portion of the trail on yet another day hike, the leaves every earthly color imaginable. Instead, on this early evening, we hiked in shorts and tank tops, and the foliage was still lush and mostly green. We'd talked about hiking the Long Path together and deep down I'd hoped against hope that we could really make it happen, that this man I loved so much would really want to do it. But it was our ability to dream and actually manifest those dreams, even in small ways, that played a great role in allowing myself to fall deeper and deeper in love with Scott. When we'd talked about finding a home to move into together, we did it, when we talked about performing music together, we did it, when we talked about traveling to a place we'd never been like Guatemala, we did it. These had been momentous occasions and I thought of the many smaller but still significant things we had sought and accomplished since we had met. Walking nearly 400 miles on a trail together, that, was by far the biggest and yet here we were—doing it.

The Long Path meanders through the 3,100-acre Bashakill Wildlife Management Area—home to the largest freshwater wetland in southeastern New York—on a grassy retired railroad bed through a narrow corridor of black and gray birch, oak, and maple. Beside us the expansive waters of the Basha Kill marsh reflected the last rays of the day's sun. As we strolled this seemingly endless tunnel of greenery and starkly contrasted pale and dark barks, the birds sang their evening songs and crickets pulsed with excitement for the coming darkness. After about a mile, the woods to the right of us began to open up and spread out, with ample space between tall slender trees. Stone walls wound like snakes through the forest harkening back to when this property was farmland abutting the Delaware and Hudson Canal. It'd be easy to set up camp here, we'd just have to be certain to wander deep enough into the woods that the early morning birdwatchers wouldn't spot us. So, when the trail bent left, we went right.

That night we laid in our tent, blissfully relaxed. What an easy evening. We were still so full from our meal at the pizzeria that there was no need to cook, nor were porcupines falling from trees or coyotes howling at our tent door. Instead we laid on our backs, looking up at the stars through our tent's mesh ceiling and listened to an owl hooting nearby.

I nestled my head inside the crook of Scott's arm, pressing close against his chest.

"So what trail are we going to do next?" Scott asked.

I laid there in silence, scared to breathe for it might wake me from this dream. *Surely, he hadn't just asked what long trail we might do after the Long Path.*

"Hey, did you hear me?" he asked again.

"*Yeah*, I heard you," I said, trying hard to contain my enthusiasm. "You mean what trail do we want to do after this one?" I needed to clarify.

"Yeah, which one?" he repeated. "There's so many." He seemed deep in thought.

I'd already thought this question numerous times since beginning our hike but hadn't dared say it aloud. I figured I should at least allow us to get through this one first before proposing yet another.

"I was thinking about the Florida Trail." I suggested. It would be flat—that would appeal to Scott—and it was a longer trail, measuring 1,100 miles—I'd like that.

"Yeah? Me too. But we'd have to hike that one in winter so that we wouldn't melt in the summer heat." *My God, he was serious. He was actually exploring the idea.*

"You're right. We could do it next winter," I replied, playing cool and calm.

"Next winter? Who says? We could do it this winter," he countered smartly.

"This winter? Wow. Well yes, I suppose we could." I wondered again if I were dreaming. "We'd just have to save up the money." I added, hoping the dose of reality didn't discourage his excitement.

"Hmph. True," he said, a little deflated. "Or what about the Continental Divide Trail? We could break it up into two or three sections, hike a different portion each spring and summer."

The Continental Divide Trail is 3,000 miles long. It seemed this boy had the bug! Just then, I swore I could hear the angels singing on high in the treetops above us.

"Sure could." I nuzzled my head deeper into his chest. "So, you really see yourself wanting to do more long trails?"

"Yeah. This experience has been so incredible already. I can only imagine what it'd be like to just keep on going after we're done. If it weren't for money, we could just hike the rest of our days."

I rolled over and gave him a long kiss, wishing to merge his very self into mine. I felt drunk—a warm wave of peace flooded my body while at the same time I felt like dancing beneath the stars, so excited for all the places we might go, all the mountaintops we might climb, all the beauty we might witness together.

From somewhere in the darkness, an owl hooted in approval, blessing our future journeys.

As long as all went according to plan, we'd reach Wurtsboro by late morning. Mist rose off the sky-blue waters of the Basha Kill, and spread out over the trail, giving it a dream-like quality. It was a rare opportunity to see this special place in the early morning light. Rarely at home did we ever manage to get such an early start on a day's hike. Each day off we either had a list of responsibilities to fulfill or we slept in late due to working late into the evening the night before. Here our internal clocks had grown accustomed to surrendering to sleep at a reasonable hour and awaking at first light, despite our being more physically active than ever. And out here, our only responsibility this morning was to hike five miles. So, we took our time, stopping to sit on the stone benches provided along the trail and snack on cheese crackers and trail mix. At a wooden plank bridge that stretched across a small inlet to the marsh, we discovered ripe autumn olives. These silver-speckled red fruits, each the size of a raisin, taste tart, like a cranberry. Autumn olive is a nonnative invasive shrub with origins in Eastern Asia that has naturalized throughout the eastern United States. Back in the 1950s, the U.S. Soil Conservation Service considered it a beneficial plant for reducing erosion, beautifying roadways, and attracting wildlife. The plant was highly recommended until its aggressive nature in outcompeting native plants was discovered. However, with its delicious and abundant fruit, the birds don't care if it belongs here or not and we didn't either. We reveled in rolling them from their equally silvery twigs, tossing them in our mouths, sucking off the flesh and spitting out the fibrous seeds. All the better to eat of its fruits with wild abandon.

Our fingers sticky and our bellies full, we were paying little mind to our path until a thick black ribbon slithered through the grass just before our feet. Instinctively, I yelped and leaped backwards, and Scott in turn turned and dashed ten feet back down the trail behind us. The only thing Scott likes less than heights is snakes. It was merely a northern black water snake, not venomous, but still, in their size, they can be intimidating. As the heat of the day increased, more snakes emerged from the cool grasses in search of a spot to sunbathe, and the mosquitoes, too, rose from their watery home in the marsh. I could handle the snakes, but the mosquitoes I loathed. Scott would have been happy without either.

We quickened our pace and in the last mile, the hum of teeny, winged bodies filled our ears, swarms of gnats encircling us. It was our last mile to the road when all of a sudden, I spotted a small, strange stone in the path. When I knelt to get a closer look, I could see this was no stone at all, but rather the tiniest black-dirt-covered snapping turtle I'd ever seen, no larger than a silver dollar. He looked as if he had been dipped in mud. Out came the camera, as I struggled to get a good shot of his little triangle-shaped face peeking out from beneath his shell. My calves burned from the mosquitoes that were taking full advantage of my stationary body. "Hey Bud. Watch out for these squeeters, they'll suck you dead," Scott told the little fellow and proceeded to hustle on down the trail, smacking his legs like he was doing a dance.

These wildlife sightings should've come as no surprise, given that the Basha Kill is home to over forty species of reptiles and amphibians. That's in addition to forty species of butterfly, thirty species of fish, 220 species of bird, and the largest number of dragonflies anywhere in New York State.

Our legs swept through tall grass, irritating our swollen, itchy legs, and the vegetation to either side of us grew thick. Did I mention that the Basha Kill is also home to over 200 plant species? But we were done, too agitated to botanize. Even as we climbed over and under numerous fallen trees across our path, we did our best to hurry along. It was high noon and the marsh was now thrumming with life. I had a feeling that here the slow did not survive. Once we could see a metal gate, we started to sprint. We hit pavement and emerged from the Basha Kill jungle covered in sweat, burning with bites, and relieved to stand where the light breeze could kiss our skin and blow away the bugs.

We continued to hike steadily until we finally reached Wurtsboro's main street and promptly collapsed on a bench. For a while we slugged water and gazed across the street at an eclectic shop that advertised gems and palm reading. When Scott mapped on his phone where our motel might be in relation to town's amenities, we swallowed the hard truth that our motel was one full mile outside of town. Not a big deal by car, but a very big deal by foot. Apparently, our miles weren't done. But first we'd do lunch.

From the corner of a four-way intersection and stoplight, we were pleased to see that in addition to fortune telling, the town center offered everything that we needed. There was a Stewart's gas station, a Chinese restaurant, a family restaurant and tavern called Danny's (go figure), a laundromat, and a liquor store. What more could we need? It was truly everything we could have hoped for. We ate lunch for $5 inside of Stewart's—a foot-long egg salad hoagie and two sodas—and took a short rest on two milk crates out back before again hoisting our packs and walking the long mile under the midday sun along the road to the Days Inn.

At the front desk, we stood before an Indian woman who eyeballed us warily. *Was it our appearance? Our smell?* Hard to say—I'd long since stopped smelling us and I hadn't looked in a mirror in days. I figured she'd be happy when we asked for a room in the building up on the hill that stood separate from the main hotel, but she appeared to only grow more suspicious. I wanted to assure her we weren't up to no good, but I didn't know how to explain the simple truth that it was about sex. When you only get so many nights a month to make love freshly showered, without the assistance of wet wipes and hand sanitizer, I am just sayin', you want your privacy. In some effort to assuage her fears, we told her that we were hiking the Long Path, but she didn't seem to know anything about the trail, nor was she interested. As she took my card, I felt like I could feel the sadness rolling off her in waves and by the light of the flickering florescent lights overhead, I could understand why. I wanted to grab her by the shoulders and proclaim to her the beauty that laid just down the road on the trail. *We had seen it. It was real!* But I knew I shouldn't, and besides, who was I to judge her unhappiness? Likely she worked this job out of necessity. Perhaps she had a child or an elderly parent to care for and support. Perhaps she feared the unknown because she'd already lived a life filled with uncertainty, whereas we had the ability, even if just for a month, to step off into the unknown, leaving the working world behind. We were privileged to explore and more importantly to have been brought up in a way that fostered in us the courage and confidence to explore. I would be a self-righteous ass to proselytize.

Our room was simple but clean and afforded all the luxuries such as a hot shower, running water, air conditioning, a bed, and lights that turned on with the flick of a switch . . . oh and a coffee maker, too. The trail makes you realize, real fast, just how luxurious all our everyday conveniences are.

After cleaning up and lounging about, then pouring over mileage for the next several days so that we could gather what we needed—no more, no less—from the grocery next door, we collected our laundry into a dry sack and walked the mile back into town to run errands. After dropping it at the laundromat, which was unbearably hot, so much that it appeared even the locals were forgoing laundry on this day, we went in search of dinner. We first stepped into Danny's Restaurant. Stationed at the four-way intersection, it appeared well established and well frequented.

A din of voices filled the dark space, so dark in fact that we could barely make out the patrons. We asked for a menu to look over and saw the usual fare of pastas and steaks, seafood, and chicken, then scanning the restaurant again, our eyes finally adjusted to the crowd around us. The place was packed. The bar had patrons two people deep. A woman cackled, flipping her hair over her shoulder at a man swilling a Budweiser. Beside us, an elderly-looking version of Axel Rose fed a jukebox, ACDC's "Back in Black" already blaring through its speakers. We looked at each other, thanked the hostess, and walked out.

"Oh, thank God!" I said upon stepping back into the sunlight.

"Screw that," Scott returned with a sneer.

"That place was just so enclosed, so crowded, so . . . " I trailed off, trying to think of how to properly describe what had bothered me so.

"So dark," Scott said, finishing my sentence.

"Yes!"

"And heavy," he added.

"Yes!"

We stood at the street corner now, where the cars seemed to come from all directions, waiting for a chance to cross the road. Suddenly, this little town center was overwhelming. I took a step out just as a car zipped across the intersection and Scott put his hand on my shoulder motioning to me to step back onto the curb. When the light turned red, we dashed across and jogged down the sidewalk, heading now for the Chinese restaurant we'd seen in a quaint shopping strip.

"But why?" I asked.

"Why what?"

"Why did it feel that way? I felt like I could hardly breathe in there," I explained, remarking again on the tavern. Back home, a place like that wouldn't phase me all that much. It was no different than the small New York bars I had frequented some years back when I lived in Port Jervis.

"I know, me too. The last place I'd want to eat," Scott said as we turned left into the parking lot and walked through the open glass front door of the Chinese restaurant. "I think we've adapted to the open space around us, the quiet, the solitude."

"You're right, babe. That's exactly what it is. It's just happened so quickly. I'd forgotten how your senses shift when spending every day in the woods. We're stimulated, but not bombarded. One thing happens at a time and mostly, we decide when and where."

I'd noticed this shift upon returning from every long walk, but I'd found it most difficult to handle after the Appalachian Trail. After spending six months in the quietude of the woods, the adjustment to the regular world was almost unbearable. Every time I stepped into a grocery store, I felt like I'd just thrown back two shots of espresso, my world swirling around me, the umpteen million choices of product on the shelf, the dinging of registers, the bright lights overhead. But it wasn't any one particular setting that was hard to handle, it was the overstimulus in general and the feeling I was trapped inside it, held captive by a building.

"It's just hard to believe that we feel this way so soon," I said to Scott.

"Well, I think the more that you return to the woods and the more time you spend there—remember we've spent a lot of time hiking and wandering the last couple of years—the more that existence feels *normal* and the rest just seems *abnormal*." Scott summed up our feelings succinctly while eyeing the backlit photos of plated food on the wall, both of us standing before a tall marble counter.

We ordered one dinner of broccoli and tofu in garlic sauce and sat down in one of the booths. When our food came, we also received two Styrofoam plates, plasticware, and a handful of little soy sauce packets. Our dining accommodations were meager, but at the same time, sitting in that restaurant sans AC with the front door propped open, sharing our one box of food, all felt right with the world. Less was more.

After dinner, we picked up our laundry and began our return, along the busy road by the light of passing headlights, to our hotel on the hill. As we walked, we pondered to each other why Wurtsboro had seemed so grim. It had provided us with all the supplies we needed, and it we'd enjoyed nearly a whole day of not hiking, but the town itself felt *hard*. We speculated if life here was raw. Perhaps folks didn't know what challenges they might face from day to day or on the flip side, maybe each day felt identical to the last. But life on the trail, too, could be raw, unpredictable, or even at times, *painfully* predictable. So really what was so different? Why was the brightness we felt in the woods not here in town?

We decided perhaps the greatest difference is that the day-to-day challenges aren't equally met with moments of beauty, or because a breath of fresh air is hard to find instead of it literally meeting you on a breeze, and because with all the work to be done, it was hard for those here to find stillness. And again, I had to wonder, did these folks know that all these things could be found through an opening in the thick vegetation on the edge of town? And they need not walk for days. All these needs—beauty, fresh air, stillness, and these were *needs*, the trail will teach you that—could be met in a short stroll.

But we managed to find the bright side of civilization back in our hotel room where we FaceTimed with friends, drinking many a plastic cup of whiskey and sprite, belly laughing and goofing off. Finally, we tumbled into bed, drunk in love and partly on booze, and cared not about disturbing our neighbors down the hill. We were happy as two pigs in mud or should I say . . . two hikers in a hotel room.

CHAPTER TWO

We hiked up the winding hill leaving Wurtsboro filled with intimidation. Nearly to the day, one year ago, we'd planned a four-day, three-night hike on the Shawangunk Ridge Trail and, by happenstance, the Long Path.

We'd started from out from Wurtsboro—with one vehicle parked at a VFW hall and the other at a hotel in New Paltz—with the hopes of hiking to the Mohonk Preserve, however, parking along the Shawangunk Ridge Trail had been just as hard as hiking it. Given the fact that designated camping was slim along this section, few areas permitted overnight parking. We'd tried a slew of locations, and after finally working out these logistics, we started our trip much later on the first day than planned. We did our best to make up the mileage, but the temps had been brutally hot and the terrain far more difficult than we had anticipated. Portions of the trail were closed in Minnewaska State Park Preserve due to a fire that had devastated the region, and we hadn't known about it until we were already en route. Our hike had ended in a phone call and a visit to my parents' residence from the New York State Police about my car, which was indeed parked legally at the VFW Hall but which they had deemed suspicious, and a long cab ride back to our vehicle in New Paltz, with a fraction of the miles that we had hoped to hike.

We were eager to see parts of the trail we had never reached last year, but well aware of the physical challenges the trail had in store for us before we got there. We reasoned that without vehicles we'd avoid at least one obstacle. We'd also double-checked before leaving for our thru-hike that the trail was most definitely open through Minnewaska State Park Preserve. However, none of this changed the fact that today we planned on hiking the same mileage that, last year, we'd done over the course of two days.

Just like the previous autumn, the temperature was unseasonably hot, nearing eighty degrees. Today our packs were laden with five days' worth of food. Scott seemed particularly quiet, which I knew was not a good sign. Likely he was recounting the strenuous initial miles up onto the Shawangunk Ridge. Cars accelerated by at full speed, careening around a bend in the road. But then, one slowed and did a quick U-turn. As it passed, it gave two quick beeps and we saw a smiling man waving through the window.

"What was that about?" I asked Scott.

"Who knows," he replied, uninterested.

We stopped and looked back down the road to see that the vehicle had pulled over onto the shoulder. Just then, a white-haired man wearing a button-down shirt threw open his car door and hollered out, "I've been reading your blog!" He waited as a couple more cars flew past and then hurried across the road, jogging toward us.

"Really?" I asked.

"Yes! I've been reading for a long time now. I was so excited to see that you guys were hiking the Long Path. I just think that's so cool," he explained, shaking our hands. "I saw on your blog last night that you two were going into the Shawangunks today. I thought maybe I might see you if I hopped on the trail, but I never thought I'd drive right past you as I was coming into town. I'm here to take a glider out for the day at the Wurtsboro airport with my son." He motioned back to his car and we saw a boy waving back at us.

I couldn't have been more pleased. Ever since my hike on the Mountains to Sea Trail I'd been blogging during my hikes, recording the trials and tribulations, great joys and unexpected encounters. I knew that I had readers, but I'd only met a handful of those who had found me purely through the web. Blogging throughout my journeys had significantly changed my hiking experience. No longer did I hike and disconnect from the rest of the world but rather I connected with my natural surroundings while maintaining and encouraging new connections in the civilized world. Doing so had provided me with support I'd never had on the AT as well as fostered new friendships. However, I couldn't help but question if it detracted from the wilderness immersion—if it was worth the trade. Here was evidence, in this man whose name, we learned, was John. My blogging also had the power to inspire others. That was pretty cool.

John offered to run to town and grab us some cold beverages and snacks. We had all that we needed on our backs, *more* than we needed in fact, but we appreciated the offer. We exchanged contact information and took a picture of the three of us to include on the next blog post. He even suggested that the next time we were in Manhattan we should give him a ring and he would take us for a ride over the cityscape in his glider. The mere thought frightened the hell out of me, as well as Scott, but still our fear did not diminish the scale of his offer.

"I was thinking that we'd drop in on the Shawangunk Ridge Trail Run too, and cheer on some of the runners as they cross the road," John added.

The run is an annual expedition that tests the limits of both amateur and professional runners and also works to promote this little-known trail. A fearless few sign up to run the entire length of the trail from end to end, running over its host of ankle-breaking rocks, bounding over jagged crevices, and straddling snaking roots, proceeding through the night with little food or water and without assistance. Typically, one to two extraordinary persons complete this feat. There are also shorter runs set up along the trail's route offering a half-marathon and a 30-mile route. We knew that throughout both today and tomorrow, we might have runners crashing past us, perhaps even with bobbing headlights, sweeping through our campsite in the evening.

"You should if you have time—I'm sure those runners could use all the encouragement they could get!" Scott said with a chuckle. "I have a hard enough time hiking this damn trail. You won't see me running through these woods!"

"Oh man, but you guys are hiking nearly 400 miles. That's just incredible. My girlfriend and I are working on the forty-one miles of trail in Steep Rock Nature Preserve in Connecticut, where we live. We've only done seventeen miles so far, but we're determined to do another small portion soon," John said, a big smile still stretched across his face.

"You two will do it, no doubt. It's just a matter of taking one step at a time. Last time we went through here, it took us two days to hike what we will hike just today. The more you hike, the stronger you get," Scott replied. John's enthusiasm had served to shake Scott from his daze. He was glowing. Less than two weeks in, he was already stronger than he knew. It's true that sometimes it takes sharing your story with others to realize just how far you have come.

We said our goodbyes and wished each other luck. I'd later learn from John through an online correspondence that just a couple months later he started a running streak, committing to running at least two miles every day. Three years later and he's still at it, having not missed a single day. Remarkable. To think of how many others he has inspired.

Scott and I resumed our climb up the long winding hill towards the trailhead. Rounding a bend, we turned right onto another road and arrived at that very same VFW hall. From here we followed the trail, marked by an aqua blaze and a blue Shawangunk Ridge Trail disc on a slender tree, into the woods.

We walked atop slippery rocks speckled with the first fallen leaves of autumn and tread over large flat-faced, pebble-covered boulders, conglomerate rock similar to that which we'd seen on Schunemunk's mountaintop. As we crested the ridge, we walked a narrow strip of trail alongside scratchy blueberry shrubs, brushed shoulders with scrub oak, and ducked beneath the branches of pitch pine short in stature. Pitch pine is eye-catching, as it looks dramatically different from white pine—a widespread evergreen and a common tree along the trail. Pitch Pine's bark is reddish and plated rather than gray and furrowed. It puts on needles not only on its limbs but along its trunk, too: spikes of green shoot from between its plated bark, oozing fragrant sap. The climb proved to be nearly as difficult as we remembered, but from the ridgetop, we reveled in views of the valley below and even spied an airplane hangar. At that very moment, a plane glided overhead. Could this be John, and if so, could he spy us down here waving up at him?

After what felt like an especially long time along the ridge, we descended to Roosa Gap and crossed paths with a group of four people section-hiking the Long Path for the afternoon. We chitchatted with Vic, Ben, Karen, and Jeff for a good while, and before we knew it, again we were exchanging contact information and snapping pictures. Long-distance hiking, whether it be thru-hiking or section-hiking, is such a small subculture that there's an instant connection amongst those who wish to spend their leisure time sweating up and down mountains, counting miles, and sleeping in dirt. Also, given that hiking requires the energy it does—both physical and logistical—there is almost always a given trust. To encounter another person on a trail, particularly a long way from a road crossing, means that this person went out of their way to get there. Your typical person of malicious intent is not going to go out of their way to hike miles into the woods in the hopes of taking advantage of someone.

After leaving our newfound friends, Scott and I began our ascent of the Wurtsboro Ridge, 800 feet over the course of the next mile, at times hand over hand, bouldering up slabs of Shawangunk white rock. This rock appears white due to the fact that is largely composed of quartz. Quartz is a hard rock, so hard that it's just a few grades below that of diamonds, making it incredibly resistant to erosion. Hence why this ridge juts out from the landscape like a long rocky spine. At two o'clock in the afternoon, the sun was high in the sky, with temperatures in the eighties and high humidity—the exact same conditions we'd endured when we'd section-hiked this portion. I remembered the last time we were here. Scott had proclaimed, "I'm never hiking to the top of this damn mountain again." Little had we known that we'd be thru-hiking the Long Path a year later. Scott climbed before me with strong legs and arms, yet I could see that sweat poured down his limbs, dripping onto the rocks below.

"Here we are again," Scott declared sarcastically.

"Yes, baby," I replied matter-of-factly.

"And it's fucking hot . . . again."

"Yes, it is, honey," I replied calmly again, then thought a moment and added, "Well, we'll never have to do this again."

"Damn right. You can hike this mountain 100 times if you want. I'll meet you on the other side with a cold beer," he said, still pushing his way to the top.

The trail took a wide turn, leaving the bouldering behind and now leading us into a burned-out mountaintop forest. For the next roughly five miles along this ridge, through the Roosa Gap and Shawangunk Ridge state forests, we'd walk woods that had burned due to a resident's brushfire gone awry two years previous, burning over 2,400 acres. However, the Shawangunk Mountains have long had a relationship with fire. Their very name suggests this relationship: Shawangunk derives from the Lenape language and literally means "in the smoky air."

Dating back to the first millennium BC, the Shawangunks have burned. It is believed that initially these fires were due to climatic change, specifically periods of drought, which increased incidents of fire. Whereas fire is normally destructive, it proved advantageous to certain plants that thrive amidst fire, such as pitch pine, the cones of which release seed in the presence of fire and then germinate readily in exposed nutrient-rich soil. Other fire-dependent or -tolerant plants include heaths such as blueberries, huckleberries, and wintergreen, as well as sassafras and oak. A fire-dependent ecosystem was established upon the Shawangunk Ridge and in turn bred more fire due to the easily flammable nature of such plants. The Native Americans were the first in this region to witness the benefits of periodic burning and began the practice of purposely setting the mountain forests aflame. Fires promoted the plants that bore them food, such as acorns from oaks, and encouraged the fruiting of blueberry and huckleberry bushes, while also providing ample food for the wild animals that they hunted. Although no hard evidence suggests that these mountains were named for the frequent burning, I have to suspect a link. European settlers took note and continued to burn the ridges, specifically to increase berry yield. Abundant berries provided not only food but, more importantly, income. Men and families took to living seasonally in shacks, tents, and cabins at the base of the ridge, and once a carriage road was built, in the Shawangunk forests to be ever closer to their crop, which they would then take by horse and buggy or by foot to markets and the nearby railway service that would deliver them into New York City. These folks came to be known as the "huckleberry pickers," huckleberry being the common name for noncultivated blueberries of the genus *Vaccinium.* Back when true huckleberries, of the genus *Gaylussacia,* were called crackerberries. The New York Department of Environmental Conservation began suppressing fires in the early to mid-1900s, however, controlled burns are now permitted by management along the Shawangunk Ridge, having since recognized the importance and safety of periodic burns. From where we stood, we had not yet reached the primary berry-picking "patch" which reportedly extended from Sam's Point to Lake Mohonk, but we would be trekking through it soon enough.

Suddenly we glimpsed it . . . the orange peaked roof of the fire tower that marked the summit. When we reached its base, without even dropping our packs, we collapsed atop the cold rock that laid in its shade.

Admittedly, I was as tired as he was. I believe the sun must always shine atop the Shawangunk Ridge. Feeling dehydrated and heady, we wished for nothing more than shade, of which we knew we'd be deprived for the next four miles. From our rock we took a thirty-minute lunch break of English muffins, peanut butter, and prized grape jelly, the packets of which I'd snuck into my pocket from the continental breakfast that morning at the hotel, both of us gazing at the trail ahead.

When we took stock of our water and found that we each had a little less than a liter, we realized we should've filled up back at the stream at Roosa Gap. Too late now. Reluctantly, we shouldered our packs for a hike across the scorching ridgetop. With each step I took, I did my best to meld into my surroundings. I focused on feeling the cool sweat against my hot skin, the heat spreading out atop my head, the feeling of solid ground beneath my feet and the sound of my steps crunching pine needles and crushing fine quartz sand. I gazed out at the skeletons of dead trees, their branches seared in midreach for the sky and parched white trunks stained black with soot. I looked at my own white flesh bright in the sunlight and smeared with dirt and I felt one and the same. Slabs of white rock crested the ridge, and stacks of white rocks—cairns to mark the way—rose from the ground like sculptures. I tried in vain to take pictures of Scott hiking ahead of me through this otherworldly landscape, but each photo appeared more washed out than the next, a bright square of sunlight and white with a dab of pine green for a tree and a dab of black for his tank-top and shorts. On a day such as this, the terrain was inhospitable to say the least, but it was also undeniably beautiful with a power to imprint us in this time and place. We were unable to be anywhere but here. But amidst all this white light the kaleidoscope colors of autumn periodically burst forth. We stopped more than once to admire the leaves of sassafras, which are already unique given that this tree produces three differently shaped leaves—one with three lobes, another shaped like a mitten, and one with smooth edges—but now they were green, painted with the most vibrant reds and oranges on which we'd ever laid eyes. Beside us, the green-leaved berry bushes also bled red, and at our feet, wintergreen plants were colored deep plum bearing scarlet berries that hung daintily on cane-shaped slender stems. Whereas at first this ridge had appeared barren, it was evident it bore an abundance of food and medicine. Sassafras roots may be simmered in water as a blood cleanser and provided a flavoring for our ol' time root beer. Its leaves, too, may be dried and pulverized. They can be used as a thickener in soups and convey a lemony flavoring. Blueberry bushes of course provide an edible fruit, but less appreciated are its leaves, which may be steeped in a tea beneficial for fighting off urinary tract infections and balancing blood sugar. If you've the patience to collect them, the fruits of wintergreen are minty fresh tasting, a delicious addition to oatmeal or yogurt, whereas its equally minty leaves contain methyl salicylate, like that of black birch, which acts as a muscular pain reliever. European settlers also collected wintergreen for profit, as it was valued for use in both medicine and flavoring.

We descended to a wooded col, a low point in the ridge, taking a short break on a lichen- and moss-covered rock, and then proceeded back up onto the ridge.

We sucked on our water hoses and Scott drenched his bandana with a splash from his water bottle, our once white skin now turning red like the leaves. By now we were both so dizzy that we took to making up silly songs to keep ourselves alert, and when finally we saw a peaked rock outcrop before us, white rocks shining on the opposite ridge, we fell silent with relief. The only way to go from here was down. Still without shade, we sat down on the edge of a rock, the late afternoon sun now at our backs, had a snack, and sucked our water bladders dry.

Following the steep and winding trail, we descended quickly, sliding this way and that on loose gravel, so grateful for the modest shade the pitch pines provided. When we began our descent into the forest, a leafy canopy graciously filtering that ever-present sun, we spied a familiar figure hiking uphill toward us.

"Don't worry, it's an easy one and a half miles from here to the road. Hmm, two miles tops," Star Left promptly declared. We must have looked a sight.

Scott rolled his eyes. No, that was not far in actuality, but right now the thought of two miles felt like ten. But instead of doing the same, I feigned chipper. "Okay great. Come on, babe. We got this."

Without our even asking, Star Left pulled from her pack two bottled waters. We guzzled them on the spot and then got walking before we lost our motivation. Continuing downhill, it wasn't long before we reached Old Route 52, which runs below present Route 52 at the base of a steep embankment. Despite our exhaustion, we chatted with Star Left a mile a minute about the last week and almost didn't notice the landscape of trash that litters this portion of the trail. Last time we'd hiked through here I'd half expected to get hit in the head with a Big Gulp tossed from a passing motorist above. The trail also passes several old stone foundations and a dilapidated trailer, its roof sagging from decay, and if it didn't feel so ominous, it would have been almost intriguing enough to explore.

When we passed a trickling waterfall that fell into a pool between a cluster of rocks, Star Left's voice faded into the background. Suddenly I remembered, in vivid clarity, sitting there at its base last year on our section-hike.

We'd both been exhausted, and Scott had been grumbling about the mileage. With each grumble, I grew more concerned that I'd done it again. I'd tried so hard to plan our mileage well, to not schedule too many miles each day, and to account for the terrain, but it was becoming glaringly obvious that I'd pushed us too hard. My mind raced with every other time I'd done this to men in my life.

Years back with my ex-partner, when our relationship was still new, we'd tried doing a couple of overnight backpacking trips together. Both had, however, ended in shouting matches and tears, cinching the deal that he'd never join me on another excursion. Then my father. He, who'd never been a backpacker, joined me for 600 remarkable miles on the Appalachian Trail, but I'd pushed him so hard on so many days. I never relented, although I could see him struggling, nor did he. Often a few miles before the day's end, he'd hike with grimacing determination, his presence void of pleasure, and mute, except for the periodic profanity he'd let slip.

And on that day by this waterfall with Scott, I had feared, with a deep-down, gut-wrenching pain, that I'd succeeded in destroying all hope of Scott ever wanting to hike with me again. This was our first multiday hike and he was miserable. This would be it. I had gone to the water to fill my bottle, but instead had dropped it at my feet, sat atop a large rock and cried. At first, I couldn't find the words to tell him what was wrong. That it was more than the heat, the dehydration, my aching feet. However, he cajoled me to talk and wrenched from me my concerns. His response was not at all what I expected.

"Am I tired? Hell yes. But I love being out here with you and I wouldn't trade this experience for anything else in the world," Scott had explained while squatting before me, his hands on my knees, looking me straight-on. "And, it wasn't *you* who picked the hardest portion of trail, it was *us*. I could've looked over the map better so that I knew what I was getting into. It's probably also the most beautiful part of the trail too—so whatever!" he added, now looking up at the slender stream of water pouring off the embankment. Then he turned his gaze back to me. "But mostly, I don't really care where we're hiking, as long as we're together. I love you and I love being here with you."

I knew he meant it, but still I had hoped that feeling wouldn't one day evaporate.

Now in the midst of a thru-hike with numerous multiday backpacking ventures under our belt, I knew that his love for me and his love for doing things *with* me would endure. My fears had been rooted only in my past experience, not the reality of *our* experience, one that was wholly new and different.

When we reached the trail crossing with present-day Route 52, we hoofed it another hundred yards down to Star Left's car, which she'd parked on private property by permission of the landowner. She too had been unable to find any other place to safely park overnight near the trail, so she'd simply knocked on the door of this home near the trailhead. While she proceeded to pull her gear out of her trunk, we finally dropped our packs and took a seat atop them. As we shoved her homemade cookies in our mouths and dropped crumbs all over ourselves, she presented the water and fuel she'd brought for us. And by the time we had filled our reserves, Scott and I could barely summon the energy to hoist our packs one more time. But camp laid just a half mile into the woods.

Crossing the road that marks the boundary of Minnewaska State Park Preserve, we slipped into a pristine patch of damp forest. We walked a winding trail, the moss so thick that it crept up the trunks of the tall trees lining it. The very forest itself seemed steeped in moisture and cool air and for this we were grateful. The trail wound us down closer to South Gully, a stream that rushes over smooth boulders, over and under fallen trees, and we spotted the campsite that we'd used the year before. A hurried hiker would never notice it, but we made quick note of the square of level ground and leaf-covered fire ring that had been there when we'd first discovered the site. The three of us shuffled and slid our way down the embankment to our nook for the night beside this gurgling stream.

The last time that we were here, Scott and I had sat leaning against trees that faced each other, talking by the light of the moon and observing a court-ship between two great horned owls nearby. One would call from the left of us and another would respond on our right. Suddenly, in a scuff, an owl landed on the embankment above us. But what came next was an even greater surprise. He spread his wings wide and promenaded to and fro, hooting as he strutted his stuff. His potential girlfriend responded, swooping down to perch on a tree branch overhead, hooting in return. And there she remained, playing hard to get. *Had this fella had ever landed his lady? If so, might we hear them or their yungins tonight?*

We set up our tent while Star Left hung her hammock, and then we all quickly got to cooking. For us, a pot of Knorr Pasta Sides and for her, instant rice and beans. After dinner, by the light of our headlamps and the myriad of stars shining through the treetops above, we passed around a bottle of Jim Beam. This time we shared stories not of our past, but of our hopes for the future. We talked about our dream of owning a travel trailer, living out of it fulltime and moving with the seasons. We'd spend the summers in Pennsylvania, the spring and fall in Asheville, and the winters in Florida, making a living through nature-based classes and musical performances. She shared that she and Ed also wished to expand upon their music. She was working hard on setting up some tour dates. "A travel trailer is a great idea! We could caravan together from gig to gig and from trail to trail!" she exclaimed. Chatting with her, our dreams did not seem so far out and we reveled in the companionship of a friend. From somewhere in the darkness, a *hoo-hoo hoooooo hoo-hoo* echoed, and we couldn't help but smile—proof that indeed our owl remained here. Hopefully he wasn't still single. We also stayed alert for the pounding feet of trail runners making their way steadily through the night, but we never did see one.

CHAPTER THREE

My head was heavy and my eyes crusty. Remnants of last night's Jim Beam, but this headache was likely nothing some coffee wouldn't fix. Good thing I could boil water in the vestibule of the tent, remaining in the comfort of my sleeping bag.

"Hey there!" I called to Star Left, who I could see was awake and reading in her hammock.

"Oh, good morning guys! Are you two coming to life in there? It took me awhile," she said with a chuckle.

"We're working on it. Check back with us after coffee."

But we couldn't dally long. Today would be a mile longer than the day before and by looking at the map, we knew that it'd be a challenging one. Before we knew it, we were stuffing our tent into its sack and talking logistics for the day. Star Left would hike south on the trail, back to her car, where she'd then drive ahead to meet us at Sam's Point Visitor's Center. We on the other hand, would shoulder packs to begin our 1,000-foot ascent over the next 2.5 miles to reach her.

Threads of fog twined through the towering trees, filtering the morning light in such a way that South Gully seemed still slumbering. The continuous uphill climb was proving to be a challenging way to start the day but at least the trail was soft dirt and well shaded. At a waterfall that cascaded over smooth rock ledges so level it looked as if someone had laid them there, we washed up, scrubbing the dirt off our calves and splashing our faces with ice-cold water. Never at home would I ever consider taking an icy bath such as this, but out here it was enlivening. To feel clean while hiking is a rarity. As we climbed higher and higher, South Gully dropped farther and farther below us into a great chasm of tall earthen walls. Eastern hemlock trees lined the edges of this ravine, their boughs of short blunt needles reaching out over the cliffs. Sometimes their roots could be seen dangling, exposed, from where chunks of soil and rock had loosened and tumbled into the water below. Eastern hemlock, like many members of the pine family, possesses medicinal properties that fit nicely in any hiker's wild first aid kid. Needles may be steeped in hot water for an infusion that is antibacterial, diaphoretic, and diuretic, and works well as both an expectorant and decongestant. The pliable needles of spring growth may be pinched from twig tips for a lemony trailside nibble, rich in vitamin C. I felt grateful to be amidst these trees and wondered how much longer we might be graced by their presence. A little critter from foreign lands called the woolly adelgid is steadily destroying eastern hemlocks. The forest and park services are hard at work combatting its destruction; however, each individual tree must be repeatedly treated. Therefore, unless we find another solution, it may be a losing battle.

Reaching a nearly level portion of trail, we passed remnants of huckleberry picker shacks. We had reached the edge of the famed huckleberry patch that would wind through the Shawangunks all the way to Lake Mohonk. Farming equipment, rusted and twisted, lay scattered amidst the ferns and grasses. This rubble gave us the eerie feeling that this land's inhabitants had one day just up and left. And perhaps they had. At the turn of the century there were estimated to be 10,000 people working the ridge for its abundant yield and those numbers continued to peak through the Great Depression. However, with the development of modern commercial agriculture and easy transportation, huckleberries fell out of favor. Huckleberry pickers faced the added challenge of New York State's forest management policy, which sought to suppress the forest fires set by pickers, and by the 1960s, the last pickers had abandoned their posts.

We left behind these pieces of the past by way of a pale dusty road and soon found ourselves face-to-face with modernity and the monstrosity that is the Sam's Point Visitor's Center. This is the very spot we'd made it to last year when our hike was so abruptly cut short. This portion of Minnewaska State Park Preserve is one of the most frequented spots along the Shawangunk Ridge, likely *because* of this visitor's center. The picturesque vista at the top of the nearby escarpment surely plays a role, but for some strange reason it seems a good number of we humans prefer to enjoy a day in the wilderness with the comfort of a vending machine, restroom, and spacious air-conditioned informational area nearby. The center is a multimillion-dollar beauty, however, if you ask me, an overindulgence. Let the natural scenery be the draw and instead put those funds into overnight parking areas and designated camping, paid ridge runners, and a crew of trail maintainers. The trails would likely suffer less abuse and degradation, given that fewer people would occupy them. And of those who did, a greater percentage would approach with reverence, with authenticity, and with the intentions to truly experience their surroundings rather than just snap a selfie. This doesn't mean we can't have an informational visitor's center, but why not use the restored farmhouse that sits locked up beside it?

The array of people mulling about the parking lot and picnic grounds was dizzying. Omitting the George Washington Bridge, this was the most people consolidated into one space we'd experience on the entire trail. To think, each vehicle pays $10 to park. I guess this visitor's center would eventually pay off . . . but at what expense? We managed to find Star Left, who was quietly reading a book atop a picnic table. Although we'd bathed some miles back, we were already drenched in sweat and I envied her clean attire. I reminded myself that she'd happily reverse roles, embrace the dirt to hike on farther today, tomorrow, and the day after that.

We started up the nicely graded gravel road, enjoying the easy terrain over this half mile to the overlook. At the top we veered from the road through a clearing in the stout pines and shrubs and found roughly twenty people enjoying the view. Had I been by myself, I might have just spun round and disappeared back into the shrubbery, but I knew it was silly to let my angst destroy the beauty of our surroundings, especially for Star Left and Scott. I took a deep breath and scanned the crowd. I noticed young and old alike, women in pointed flats as well as sensible hiking shoes, men in urban streetwear as well as quick dry shorts and t-shirts, children dashing back and forth across the flat surface of the rock to get different views. Suddenly I felt small. I had judged these people just as easily as I believed they'd judge me. And sure, were it not for the visitor's center, most of them wouldn't be here, but they had *chosen* today, of all the places to go, to go to this mountain top. Those who would otherwise not enter into our natural world due to any number of fears and felt safe here, and that was a good thing. Granted, there were a number of selfie sticks present and couples posing cheek to cheek at its edge, but sure enough, when a space opened up, we sidled up to do just the same.

From this enormous cliff of white Shawangunk slab rock, we gazed out over the bleached rocks of the ridge we had hiked the day before and farther off into the greenery of Harriman, splashed with rusty reds and golden yellows. I understood why the hoards flocked here. We'd all come, in a greater or lesser degree, to appreciate its grandeur. But there was still so much more to see, specifically Verkeerderkill Falls, another locale whose reputation precedes it and which we had been terribly disappointed to miss last year.

Hopping back onto the gravel road that runs along the top of the ridge, we walked easy mileage, passing the Ice Caves, a narrow corridor through a rock crevice that remains cold year-round. It was hard to believe that even now, with the sun shining bright and the temps in the eighties, that the mountain hid ice in its belly. However, when we'd visited last May, we'd found just that. In fact, there'd been so much ice on the path that loops through the cave that when we had come face-to-face with a solid wall of it; we'd had to double back.

But today the three of us hiked on speedily, no time for exploring an ice cave. Our feet pounded atop pale rock that jutted from the ground and our calves whisked us through berry bushes. We brushed shoulders with dwarfed pitch pine and sassafras. The same botanical inhabitants we had met the day before along the burned-out ridge, however, this ecosystem is uniquely classified as a dwarf pine ridge due to the predominance of pitch pine that stand no more than sixteen feet tall. It is the only dwarf pine ridge in the world and here we were traipsing through as quick as we could. The plight of a thru-hiker—never enough time. We passed a number of hikers going the opposite direction, back toward the parking lot, and each one seemed alien here, but then again, so did we. *Were we humans really meant to travel here, amidst the craggy pine, on this rugged ridge?*

The balls of our feet were sore by the time we reached the cliffs that overlook the falls, but it mattered not. We passed more and more people. Both children and adults waded in the shallow stream of water that ran towards the cliff's edge and we peered through the pines beside us for a rock outcrop that wasn't already occupied. Spotting a large boulder that had miraculously gone unnoticed, we hunched down low, ducked beneath boughs of an eastern hemlock, and halted at the edge of the dusty cliff. Before us flowed Verkeerderkill Falls, its waters streaming in narrow ribbons down sheer striated rock walls into what seemed like oblivion. These falls are over 180 feet tall, its base obscured by a pile of enormous sharp-edged boulders. Though I'd seen many photos of these falls rushing, despite the heavy rains that pummeled early in the summer, nature was in dry northeastern autumn here. As we dined on English muffins with peanut butter and Star Left chowed down on a granola bar, I pulled out the map outlining the rest of our mileage and was struck numb.

Since camp, we'd only hiked five and a half miles, which worse yet, meant we still had nearly ten miles to go. I wasn't so sure that we could make it to our goal near Berme Road but by God, we'd give it our best shot. Scott agreed. Afterall, according to the contour lines, the rest of the ridge looked largely level, so we could likely make some time. Within twenty minutes, we had packed up and parted ways with Star Left.

Well, there may not have been more than 200 feet of elevation change, but without a single strand of tree cover, the sun shone down upon us relentlessly, reflecting off the Shawangunks' white rock cliffs. Following faint red blazes, we moved slow and climbed, using our whole bodies, up and down stacked slab stone. The trail led us sometimes frightfully close to the cliff's edge, where beneath us was a sea of green smudged with islands of red and gold. Our packs heavy with plenty of water, we teetered and hoped we didn't lose balance.

When we finally scaled the ledges to High Point—an enormous slab of white rock that lays prostrate at the highest point on the ridge and affords panoramic views of the Mohonk Mountain House, Minnewaska, and those Catskill Mountains, which looked sharper and taller than ever—we felt like warriors. Even if it had taken us *two* hours to hike *two* miles. We raised our trekking poles to the sky victoriously, conquerors of the mighty white stone! We hollered across the mountaintops, although deep inside, we were humbled. One should never assume to make *time* in the Shawangunks. Then, collapsing in the bright sun, we sucked on our water hoses and felt our sweat evaporate in a strong breeze until it was time to start our descent, *slowly.*

The slab rock ledges continued until we encountered something called slickrock. Each time one of us tried to gain speed, our feet would slide out from beneath, landing us atop the hard rock in a clatter. The guidebook had described this portion as particularly "slippery", but we hadn't understood why, nor were we all that concerned given that we'd just traversed a ridge dry as bone. But it turns out they call it slick rock for a reason. Although at first grateful for the partial tree cover, the rock here was coated in moisture, providing a new but different challenge. It felt as if we walked on ice-covered ramps. Were it not for the patches of pale-green scruffy lichen and sponge-like black moss, which acted as treads, we would've slid our whole way down the trail.

On the map this portion of trail was labeled "Carriage Road" and the guidebook explained that this had been just that at one time, a corridor well traveled by the berry pickers. It was hard to imagine how they had ever traversed this path. In our minds we conjured visions of horse-drawn carriages led by men in threadbare clothing, hauling overflowing pails of huckleberries. We wondered how many buckets they'd spilled in the process.

After descending 1,600 feet over the course of three miles, when we were beginning to question if we'd ever reach the bottom of this ridge, we were enveloped by a green deciduous forest. Our feet throbbed from pounding rock and our joints ached from not only climbing but falling. Remarkably, neither of us had suffered any injuries. We'd nearly reached Berme Road, our goal for the day, and good thing, because we were *done*.

"Where the hell are we going to camp tonight?" Scott asked wearily.

"I don't know, it's so thick in here. I'll settle for a hole in a log tonight if we have to."

We scanned the edges of trail, but it seemed where there wasn't rock there was shrub.

"There!" I called out suddenly. Beneath a thick-trunked tree lay a patch of leaf-covered turf. It was perfect. We trampled down the bare branches of dead scratchy undergrowth, moving in a circular fashion like two dogs getting ready to bed down, and pulled out our tent. As darkness fell, we cooked up two pots of dehydrated cheesy scalloped potatoes, a meal we had much anticipated. However, when we scooped them into our mouths, we found them still hard and gelatinous rather than creamy. Ah, well. Food was food and we still gladly ate a whole pouch each. Afterwards, we laid on our backs in our tent, bellies full and swaddled in the black of the night, staring up at the few stars that shone through the branches overhead. From those very branches, a barred owl hooted, *hoo, hoo, too-HOO, hoo hoo, too-HOO-aw!*

CHAPTER FOUR

We walked along the narrow roadside, squeezed
between the guardrail and the rushing morning commute. Today we'd hike twelve
and a half miles of official trail, all mostly road, and we'd also walk an additional
three miles to resupply at a Walmart. Though we weren't thrilled about the miles
of pavement, nor the *extra* miles of pavement, in comparison to those drivers,
each face more grim than the next, we considered ourselves lucky to be out here
walking free of anyone else's dictates and with no other task but to acquire food
and keep on walking. Steam rose from the slick pavement, wet with dew. It would
be another hot one. I thought again of the hats and gloves and woolen vests we
carried. *Were we crazy to carry all this cold weather clothing?* It seemed it, but the
Catskills, known for their cooler weather, were not far off.

Reaching Walmart, we crossed its expansive parking lot, and at its
entrance, shrugged off our backpacks, dropping them in a cart along with our
hiking sticks. *No point in carrying those things if we didn't have to!* Wheeling our
packs like small children through the store, we barely received a second glance.
The customers here walked in a daze, mindlessly wandering up and down the
aisles without any awareness to their surroundings. But it wasn't long before we,
too, stood dazed and confused, overwhelmed at the myriad of choices before

us—chewy granola bars or crunchy, peaches-and-cream oatmeal or cinnamon swirl, butter noodles or parmesan, whole wheat tortillas or white—the options were endless. Here in this florescent warehouse was everything a person could ever want and acquired with only the effort it took to push a shopping cart and swipe a card. This reality seemed grotesque, how readily one could gratify their cravings. But I won't lie, when we hit the produce aisle, it seemed kind of wonderful. We grabbed up a couple of seeded bagels, a tub of hummus, two packaged hard-boiled eggs, a red pepper, and an avocado. This morning we would feast. Excitedly passing through the checkout lane, we headed outside to a bench, dropped our bags and got to preparing our breakfast. As we sat there on its cool metal slats, swilling down frosty juices and eating fresh foods, all was right with the world. Then I looked at our multitude of plastic bags sloppily laid before us.

Perhaps we had more than we needed.

"Oh my God honey, look at this," I said, holding my half-eaten bagel.

"What?" Scott said with a mumble, his mouth still full.

"*This.*" I motioned to the bags.

"What? Did we forget something?" Scott asked, still chewing.

"No, hon, I think we got it *all.*" I couldn't believe all of this was going to fit inside our backpacks. You see, no matter how many miles one has under their belt, it is never possible to go into a store such as Walmart and purchase *only* what one needs. The hiker appetite is always bigger than the backpack should really be.

Before long, we got to ripping open cardboard boxes, pouring noodles and powders into Ziplocs and tossing oatmeal packets and granola bars in our food-bags. Snacks for the day went into pockets on the outside of our packs, to be grabbed at the ready, and our block of cheese and extra hummus went into their own respective Ziploc bags so that they wouldn't ooze oil all over our gear. Before we knew it, we had two grocery bags filled with the remaining cardboard packaging and plastic wrap and our food bags were cinched shut. We had done alright. Turns out we had purchased just as much excess packaging as we had food—unnecessary not only for its weight, but for its waste.

Finally, it was time to leave the land o' plenty—err, too much—and hit the trail. As we retraced our steps along the busy and now-hot road, we hoped that the rest of our day's trek would not be as mundane as our last road walk had been. When we reached a double aqua blaze, marking a turn in the trail, we faced a shaded gravel road just beyond a steel gate. Sweet reprieve from the hot pavement.

We walked for hours down winding wooded roads beside stone walls and then along a seemingly endless towering wooden fence plastered with "No Trespassing" signs. Something seemed ominous about this property. *Just what were these people hiding on this clearly little traveled gravel road?* When I saw an opening in the slats, I peered through to see only a wide expanse of green and a perfectly round pond. As we walked on farther, we came to a looming gate with a telecom. Behind it stood an enormous modern house and beside it, an equally impressive garage. An Escalade was parked in the drive. *What on earth did these people do here?* The mob—there was no other explanation. They probably fitted their enemies with cement shoes and sunk 'em in the pond.

"Come on, babe, let's keep walking," Scott said to me as I stood gaping before the estate. It looked like he was scanning the treetops above us.

"What are you looking for?"

"Cameras."

"Don't be silly."

"I'm not. I'm serious," he said, tugging me along.

The fencing eventually ended and that's when we heard a car slowly rolling up behind us, the gravel crunching beneath its tires. We turned 'round to see a beat-up Mercury sedan, creeping in our direction. We kept walking, but when it pulled up alongside us, a skinny, scruffy man leaned his head out the window. A man with a belly so large it spilled over his seat belt sat beside him, a rifle across his lap.

"I'd watch out if I were you guys," said the skinny man.

Scott and I kept walking as the car crept along slowly.

"It's bear season here in New York. Better be careful," he said, eyeing us up and down.

"Okay, thanks," Scott said unflinchingly, holding eye contact with the skinny one.

Just then, the driver accelerated, spitting gravel out from beneath his tires and sped down the road.

"That doesn't make any sense. I thought hunting season started next month," I said.

"Me too. Bear season or not, that guy was sketchy."

"Yeah, he was," I seconded, squinting at the car, now in the distance.

The fact that this man might be a hunter wasn't what disturbed me. My father was an avid hunter; I had grown up around guns. It was nothing unusual to come home to a deer hanging up by its hind legs in the garage. We had a rifle that hung above the doorway in the living room. But the hunters I knew, especially those looking for bear, typically drove pickup trucks, not retired police cars. Shortly thereafter we passed a snake—the fattest and longest I've ever seen—squashed in the middle of the road, its thick meat burst from its skin and covered in dusty gravel. *Had the hunters purposely run right over it?* A half hour later, we spied their car again, now parked on the side of the road, the passenger side door slung open. Stopping, we gazed out towards the woods on either side of us—the men nowhere to be seen. We felt exposed. *Were we the ones being hunted?* For the next half mile, we hiked fast, keenly aware of just how vulnerable we were, our forest road so quickly transformed from welcoming to dark. When we reached an intersection with a paved road, we couldn't have been more relieved. In exchange for the darkness of our wooded track, we started uphill on a wide, open road, steamy in the afternoon sun. And it continued up. The distinct outline of the jagged Catskill Mountains came into view and we walked beside swaths of green farmland, meadows of wildflowers, and one quaint cottage after another, each more unique than the next. Upper Cherrytown Road seemed a lovely place to live. And as the road carried us uphill for the entirety of the afternoon, it was as if we were watching a moving picture reel to either side of us, we a part of the show.

Surveying the tremendous Catskill Mountains

PART SIX:

THE CATSKILLS

Balsam fir

CHAPTER ONE

When we could climb no higher, we left pavement and followed aqua blazes into Sundown Wild Forest. The cool of the forest embraced us and we walked the wide trail, marveling at the woods, which seemed wild indeed. Everywhere we looked were fallen trees, their trunks crisscrossing each other, some exposing intricately woven rootstocks. Green moss–covered rocks were dotted throughout the leaf litter, which appeared deep, and less matted than that of the other forests through which we had walked. The sun, now setting, sent a wide ray of golden light through the low treetops. Some trees were nothing more than standing trunks with broken, bare limbs. This seemed strange until we came to a rushing stream; likely, this area flooded from time to time, making it hard for many of these trees to sustain themselves.

We filled up our water bottles and then went wandering through this moist forest looking for a place to set up our tent. But it seemed each potential spot we found was either laden with rocks, riddled with holes hiding critters we didn't want to meet, or barred by a fallen tree. Finally, we decided on a little circular area and did our best to drive our tent stakes into the loose soil. Grateful to finally have found a spot, we began unpacking our gear and were just about to start changing clothes when I heard a rustle in the woods.

"What's that?" I asked, peering from my door at a pile of shifting leaves no more than twenty feet from our tent. Scott craned his head over my shoulder.

"Holy shit. What the—" Scott started.

My breath caught in my throat as I tried to make sense of what I was seeing. An arm, then another arm, and then a head emerged from the leaf litter and up popped a man donning camouflage from head to toe. A forest creature birthed from the bowels of Sundown Wild Forest. With a rifle in the crook of his arm, pointed toward the ground, he stood staring at us, clearly as confused at the sight of us as we were of him. After a pregnant moment, he spoke.

"Hi," he said quietly, and gave a little wave with his free hand.

"Hi there," Scott said back, plainly.

"You guys hiking?"

"Yeah," Scott answered, adding, "The Long Path."

"Be careful. I just saw a mother bear and two cubs go through here an hour ago. It's bear season but can't take a female. Have a good night," he said, walking on past our tent and onto the forest path that led back to the parking area.

"Holy shit. I never would've saw that guy," I said to Scott, dumbfounded.

"I guess it's hunting season after all."

We watched as the man continued down the road, soon disappearing into his surroundings as seamlessly as he had been hidden before.

"Great," I said, his parting words, *I just saw a mother bear and two cubs,* now echoing through my head.

"We'll definitely hang our food tonight," Scott said with a heavy sigh.

I've gradually grown more accustomed to sharing the woods with my bruin sisters and brothers, although it's been a long trying path to reach this level of comfort. I was nineteen years old when I set out on my first overnights on the Appalachian Trail, already training for hiking the whole trail someday. Naturally I'd gone to Sussex County, New Jersey, the section closest to my home in Milford, Pennsylvania. At this time, New Jersey was known for its large bear population, and bears regularly had run-ins with their human neighbors, or shall I say intruders. Partly because of the land's fragmentation due to development, as well as carelessness in safely disposing of food trash at home and in campgrounds, bears had not only grown comfortable with human presence but also with feasting on their scraps. They had come to associate people with food. Given the fact that bear hunting had long been banned in the area, bears had nothing to fear. And it seemed every venture I took led to an encounter with a bear.

On my first overnight, I nearly stumbled over a large male black bear making a hearty dinner of the abundant wild blueberries along the trail. I'd been trained in how to deal with black bears. I was, after all, what the staff at the state forest where I worked affectionately called me—the Bear Girl. My job was to tell visitors how to deter a bear should one wander into camp. So, I followed protocol. I clapped my hands, blew my trusty whistle, and waved my arms—only to have him stare back at me, less than fazed. I hemmed and hawed as to what to do next and then resigned to hiking a half mile back to the road. There, I met a thru-hiker who offered, courageously, to lead the way. By then, of course, the bear had vanished.

The next time I was out for my first multi-night trek, I'd decided I'd build my own shelter using a tarp and rope and had spent a solid hour in a wooded clearing doing so. Proud of my work, I settled down with my enormous food bag for dinner. There I sat with jelly dripping off my fingers as three bears wandered into camp. They nosed around my tarp and wandered about turning over rocks, likely looking for grubs, while I sat in terror. I remained sitting still as stone for what felt like an eternity and then jumped up and started hoofing it back to the road, at which point I found myself walking side by side with a very large bear just off the trail in the woods. When I reached the main road, I bravely called my parents to come save me. The next day my father helped me to retrieve my gear and food bag that I'd abandoned. We found it untouched. I tried to take this as a lesson that, although intimidating, bears were not to be feared. I desperately wanted to be fearless when it came to the wilderness.

Years later when I thru-hiked the AT, countless hikers I met complained of hiking day after day and not once spotting a bear. I, on the other hand, encountered bears in North Carolina, Virginia, New Jersey, New York, Connecticut, and Massachusetts. Due to these encounters and subsequent ones in which I was not eaten alive, I gradually *learned* that bears are nothing to fear. I now enjoy seeing a bear when out for a day hike, but that doesn't mean I want to sleep with 'em. So, on this night with our food hanging high in a tree far, far away from our tent, the crickets chirped rhythmically and the woods were so still that we barely heard a rustle in the deep leaves around us. We drifted off to sleep, but still, I slept with one eye open.

I awoke in the predawn light and nuzzled ever closer to Scott. In this moment, while the birds chirped high and bright, my world was perfection. I buried my head against his neck that smelled of sweat and dirt and counted the miles in my head that we had to do today. Only nine and a half—it'd be an easy day—the first easy day in what seemed a very long time. When the sun had fully risen, I climbed out of the tent and over to our bear bag, which still hung undisturbed in a tree a good thirty feet away.

After a leisurely breakfast of instant coffee and oatmeal, we filled up on water at the nearby stream and then packed up camp. It was time to hike. The morning was cooler than the last few, but the air still felt heavy with humidity. We started uphill on a gentle ascent along a trail thick with vegetation. If it hadn't been for the flowering goldenrod and purple-topped asters, I would've hardly believed it was just a day away from autumn. While climbing over a downed tree, the broad spoon-shaped leaves of stoneroot caught my eye. I stopped and broke a leaf in my hands, releasing its fragrant, lemony aroma.

I got to know stoneroot well in North Carolina, where it grew in abundance along damp trails. Here in the northeast, I'm all the more likely to encounter its lookalike, wood nettle. From a distance, the two appear nearly identical. However, upon closer inspection, stoneroot has fleshier leaves and is void of stinging hairs. The underground rhizome of stoneroot is considered a vascular tonic, beneficial in toning the venous system. Its name also provides a window into its traditional use as an antilithic, or in other words, to reduce or dissolve kidney stones. I can rarely resist crushing just a small portion of a leaf, its citrusy aroma is so intoxicating.

When we crested the hill, we passed several spacious level areas that would have, with little effort, provided a lovely campsite if only we could've summoned yet another mile or two from our legs the day before. The trail widened and we soon found ourselves in an open clearing standing before a thundering waterfall. The waters of Voornoy Kill Falls pummeled over a rocky ledge into a pristine pool lined with stone. Here smooth boulders, perfectly angled, created a flat shore for sitting. A sturdy wooden bridge proceeded across its expanse, but we had little interest in crossing and much more interest in a snack. We took a seat and, while munching on pistachios that were terribly laborious to break open, contemplated going for a dip. By the time we'd cracked twenty or thirty of those suckers, the morning's humidity had dissolved, revealing a clear blue sky. A crisp breeze blew over us, cooling our sweat dappled skin, and suddenly it seemed too chilly for a dip. Perhaps autumn temperatures would manifest on the Long Path after all.

We did some calculations and realized that we had a mere seven miles left to do. It was only midmorning. The miles had rolled by so easily! At this rate, could we attempt the mighty Peekamoose Mountain? Doing so would put us back on track with that silly little itinerary I'd composed from the comforts of my writing desk. But to ascend Peekamoose would cap our day with a 2,500-foot climb over the course of four miles. Then, once atop Peekamoose, to find a suitable place to camp, we'd have to also summit nearby Table Mountain before finally descending to a lean-to. Therefore, we were looking at an additional six miles leading us into the first of the Catskill High Peaks. It seemed daunting and frankly unlikely.

We carried on, hiking down wide woods roads and over the occasional hill. We crossed stream after stream. At one point we encountered a dark eastern hemlock grove, where tree trunks stood partially submerged in black water, the tops of moss-covered rocks peeking like stepping-stones just above the surface. Looking downstream, we spied the reason for this swamp in a large pile of branches damming a small creek. Beavers, apparently, hard at work. Finally leaving the woods roads behind, we began to ascend on an actual trail but found it littered with blowdowns. We later learned from Andy that this portion of trail regularly requires laborious trail work due to fallen trees. Dead trees lay like pickup sticks, which we were forced to duck beneath and clamber over. However, compared to the Shawangunk cliffs, this route was a walk in the park.

After thirty minutes, and for the first time since we'd hit trail, I raised my gaze and saw a cleared path before us. Scott was gaining speed. To keep up, I quickened my pace, happy to enjoy a steady stride once again.

"Screw it," Scott suddenly proclaimed.

"*Screw what?* This is the best trail we've had in days!" I countered.

"No. *Screw it.* Let's do it. Let's go to Peekamoose," he shot back.

"For real? It's going to be one hell of a climb, hon." I could barely believe my ears.

"Yeah so? We're feeling good and nine miles is too soon to stop for the day," he replied, still hiking full speed ahead.

And just like that, Scott had his trail legs.

Trail legs come at a cost. They require days and days of hiking when in fact the last thing you feel like doing is hiking. They require hiking through tight muscles, sore joints, a backpack that feels like a leaden weight pressing atop you, and feet that feel like someone took a meat tenderizer to them. People often ask me just what I do to get in shape for a long-distance hike. My answer is, not much. No training can truly prepare you for consecutive days of hiking with a thirty-pound pack, over rocks and roots, up and over mountains, along sun-soaked cliffs, and, in the case of the Long Path, over black-soot railroad tracks. Just get out there and do it.

When exactly *does* a person start to enjoy the long miles and the physical sensation of propelling one's self down a trail? It varies. My first hike on the AT, it was a solid month before one day—like magic—my body stopped fighting. However, with every subsequent long hike, I transitioned from normal human being to hiking machine more quickly. One of my greatest concerns before leaving for this trek was that Scott might not acquire his trail legs until we were nearly at the end of the trail. He'd never experience the joy of the miles and maybe never want to take on another long hike again. But here he was! Just two weeks into our journey and already acclimated. *"Nine miles is too soon to stop,"* he'd said. Me, I fell ever deeper in love.

We reached a small boulder that sat lonely in the woods. According to the map, it likely marked the summit of Bangle Hill, which, to us, appeared like a wooded knoll, with no impression of height and hardly worthy of an "x" to mark its summit on the map. We were reaching summits without even trying! However, as we broke for lunch, diving into a bag of crunchy cheese doodles and smearing hummus atop English muffins—delicious treats acquired from Walmart's land o' plenty—we studied the map some more. If we carried on, we wouldn't reach Peekamoose until three o'clock in the afternoon, which would make it near impossible to reach the lean-to two mountaintops away by dark. But there, alongside the dashed line of the trail, was a little black dot labeled *Reconnoiter Rock*. Given the contour lines, it looked like a level point in the long ascension to the summit of Peekamoose. We'd make camp there.

Our descent down the backside of Bangle Hill was steep and long, made even more painful in the knowledge that, once at its base, we'd then climb every single foot of elevation that we'd lost. I considered writing Andy a letter that he might consider installing some cable cars between these peaks. Over an hour later, we completed our descent and reached the base of Peekamoose Mountain, only to find a perfectly comfortable campsite beside a rushing creek. *Was it really wise to take on this mammoth mountain at the end of our day?* But Peekamoose beckoned, and so we started up the mountain.

Within a short distance we came to a large, flat-topped boulder with a multitude of cairns, intricate and simple, set atop it. A rustic altar to the mountain.

"Perhaps we should make an offering to Peekamoose in the hopes that he be merciful," I suggested.

Scott knelt and picked up an unassuming stone from the leaf litter and I did the same. Thoughtfully we placed them atop the boulder's surface and continued our ascent.

As we climbed, thankfully the steep grades were interspersed with level areas. *Our offering must have appeased God Peekamoose*, I thought to myself. Rather than a rock scramble, we tread upon real, true trail and found it wide enough at times to even hike side by side. The ascent would've been easier if our packs hadn't been laden with three liters of water each, but without these, we'd be without water at camp.

With each large boulder we saw ahead in our path, we hoped it might be Reconnoiter Rock. But as we reached them, one after another after another, none suggested the grandeur of a rock with its own name. Then . . . ninety minutes since we first began our climb we reached a jumble of enormous boulders adorned by a forest of wildflowers. White wood asters, blue-stemmed and zigzag goldenrod, Virginia waterleaf, pale jewelweed, and blackberries grew at the base of the topsy-turvy, heavy boulders, between them, and even in thick tufts atop them. We dropped our packs and climbed amongst the rocks like children. Reaching the top-most ledge, a car-sized hunk of stone, we walked out to its edge, the wildflowers grazing our calves, and saw through the leafy trees only an obscured view of mountains in the distance. Still, it seemed this could not be Reconnoiter Rock, but it would be *our* rock tonight and a fine base camp from which to ascend to the summit tomorrow.

From the boulders' base I plucked a few waterleaf leaves to add to our dinner that night. Stewed up with our noodles, these leaves would provide a morsel of nutrition. Waterleaf is a completely unassuming green leafy plant when not in flower, its flimsy leaves resembling those of oak or maple, depending upon the species. It earns its name from the white "water marks" that sometimes highlight its lobes, which look as if they were lightly stroked by a paintbrush and water-colored. In early spring, the flowers are much more likely to catch your eye than its leaves. It bears on slender cane-shaped stems, nodding bell-shaped flowers, white to purple in color, with protruding stamens that look almost too large for its cup-like petals.

Easily, we set up camp amidst the spacious sun-dappled woods, inhabited by towering trees. Above our heads was a mottled canvas of yellow and green, the tree branches still clinging tightly to their foliage. However, this forest had seen many an autumn past, evidenced by the deep leaf litter in which we sank. It was just six o'clock in the evening, still rather early, and we were in good spirits. We may not have made it up and over Peekamoose, but we estimated we'd made it roughly two-thirds of the way up, having not given into our fears of ascending an almighty Catskill High Peak. Scott offered to cook up dinner for the both of us and I happily accepted. It was nothing unusual for Scott to prepare me a five-star meal at home but, given that I wanted him to relax and recover when he got to camp, out here I'd largely taken on the chore of cooking. So, while he prepared our dinner of Kraft Mac and Cheese with greens, I got to hanging our bear hang.

"I didn't know if I'd make it," Scott said suddenly as we sat eagerly spooning bright orange noodles and deep-forest-green waterleaf leaves into our mouths.

"What do you mean you didn't know if you'd make it? What, up Peekamoose?" I asked, shoveling another spoonful into my mouth.

"Yeah. We've been doing some hard climbs and I knew, given the elevation change, that this could be the hardest one yet. I've been worrying about it for days. Every time I was hiking up some other less-than-remarkable mountain, I'd wonder how the hell I was going to do this one," he explained, stirring his noodles.

"But hon, you've been doing awesome! We've kept the same pace the whole time. These climbs haven't been easy for me either."

"I know. But I worried about the Catskill peaks before we even left home. I didn't know if I'd be conditioned enough . . . but this wasn't so bad," Scott said, now looking around at the forest surrounding us, as if marveling that we sat in this very spot.

"Oh hon, we didn't have to take this on today. I had no idea. You were the one that wanted to go farther today," I countered, surprised now that we'd even attempted Peekamoose today.

"I wanted to get it over with so I could stop thinking about it!" He chuckled.

I poked at my bowl of noodles, hesitant to speak my thoughts.

"There's going to be more, love," I said quietly.

"But now I know I can do it! I mean, sure, it was a hard climb, but we moved at a steady pace and it didn't feel all that much harder than any of the others we've done. In fact, it was easier than those climbs in the Palisades," he replied, relief washing over his face.

"That's because your body has adapted now. I told you it would," I replied, so very proud of how far he had come already. "Nothing prepares you for hiking a long trail than hiking a long trail."

"My body feels strong, like I can really do this now. I mean . . . we're doing it. We're *really* doing it." He put his empty pot down in the leaves.

"We're definitely *doing* it," I agreed. Now, more than ever, I wanted to see just what these mountains had yet to reveal.

That night we lay wrapped in each other, as a strong wind blew over the shoulder of the mountain, billowing the walls of the tent. And with each gust, it was as if another layer of worry fell away. He was right. We'd climbed this mountainside smooth and steady and *together*. And *together* we'd make it over all the mountains to come.

CHAPTER TWO

"My-my-my-my-my-my MY Sherona!" We sang in unison.

Despite the work ahead of us, we were psyched. And there was work. We still had 1,000 more feet to climb this morning to summit Peekamoose and doing so would only check one of the eleven High Peaks we'd have to climb in our roughly ninety miles through the Catskill Park. A Catskill High Peak is any summit that reaches over 3,500 feet. This elevation doesn't mean much when hiking mountains out West, but here in the Catskills, above 3,500 feet is virtually another world, altogether different from anything even 500 feet lower. But the morning air was chillier than any we'd yet experienced and kept us cool as we climbed. We were enlivened.

"My, my, my, my, WHOO!" Scott belted out.

Ironically, this melody was what played through both our heads. It seemed a strange choice until we then remembered that we'd heard it while shopping in Walmart a couple days ago. With so little sensory input as far as radio, movies, YouTube, Facebook, and all those impressions to which we're normally subjected daily, it's amazing how one played-out pop song can suddenly take on new life. *By God, I think it was the catchiest tune I'd ever heard!*

Gradually and then suddenly, the woods dramatically changed. Its eerie silence drowned out the melody playing in our heads, and its gnarled tree roots, sharply turning trail, and lichen-covered rocks demanded our attention. We'd entered the boreal forest—a forest that normally exists in more northern regions, like Canada and Alaska, however, it also exists here in the Catskills above 3,500 feet. This forest is nourished by the moist air from the southeast and southwest that rises over the Catskills, cools, and turns to rain or snow. Conditions are cold and moist on the High Peaks and support regionally rare plants, those one is unlikely to encounter in a lowland or deciduous forest. Just like that . . . we had climbed into a whole different biome.

The towering hardwood trees nearly disappeared, largely replaced with balsam fir, red spruce, and eastern hemlock—the forest was dominated by conifers and our senses by their overwhelming aroma. It is not always easy to distinguish these trees from one another; however, some key characteristics make identification easier. Balsam fir has needles that resemble eastern hemlock—flat with two white stripes on the underside—but fir needles are longer and spirally arranged on twigs rather than laying in a horizontal plane. Spruce needles are altogether different from the latter, being four-sided and spirally arranged. When cones are present, these too provide distinctions. Balsam fir cones look as if they have been dunked in sap and perch erect on branches, whereas spruce cones are usually smaller and dangle. The cones of eastern hemlock are tiny, no bigger than a thimble.

Over boulders and underfoot snaked the roots of yellow birch, a tree that likes to perch atop large slabs of stone and decaying logs. Yellow birch seeds germinate readily in the thin soil and sediment found on boulders and stumps rather than in the thick leaf duff of the forest floor, and saplings will grow into mature trees despite their precarious perch. In fact, often a yellow birch will persist beyond the decay of its nurse log—that log or stump atop which it germinated—and it will stand with roots exposed like long straggly legs. Yellow birch is also one of the best medicines a backpacker can stumble upon. Its inner bark contains methyl salicylate, the same stuff found in the black birch we'd shared trail with throughout our hike and the prolific wintergreen we'd encountered in the Shawangunks. Yellow birch is easy to recognize by its peeling golden bark and, when a twig is snapped, its strong minty smell. Simply break off some low-hanging twigs, break these into even-smaller pieces and simmer a small palmful for a muscular pain-relieving tea. What backpacker couldn't use an aspirin-like medicine from time to time? Though, given their inherent vulnerability at this elevation, we would not harvest from these trees today.

Our ankles brushed rare edible plants that were once common vegetables to the Native Americans. Clintonia, a plant with fleshy basal leaves, each one shiny and elongated, sported its perfectly round blue berries on long slender stems. Had we been here in spring, we would've seen its bell-shaped flowers with flared yellow petals instead. But it's not the berries or flowers of clintonia that are edible, but rather their substantial leaves. Four-leaved bunchberry, the smallest member of the dogwood family, sat square and stout, each plant so close to the next that they formed a carpet. This plant also bears berries, red in color, and if the animals don't lay claim to them first, you can nibble them for an astringent Vitamin C morsel. Centuries ago, Natives Americans and settlers alike would gather baskets of these berries to make a jam. Interspersed were the heart-shaped leaflets of wood sorrel, often mistakenly called clover because they are shaped like a shamrock. Flip one of these green leaflets over to spy its deep plum-colored underside or place one on your tongue for a lemony zing. Here, the wood sorrel seemed to prefer the mossy tops of rocks to the forest floor, evidence that in these hard-to-survive woods, adaptability was key. I hoped that we, too, could muster adaption.

Suddenly, we walked the level trail toward a gigantic boulder that sat at a sharp turn. Apparently, we'd lost ourselves in the mystery of the boreal woods, for without our hardly knowing it, we'd reached the summit of Peekamoose. We laid our hands atop its cool surface. There's something to be said for hiking a trail that is constantly twisting and turning, weaving its way up the mountainside, rather than gazing straight ahead at an immense climb up a steep incline. It's easier to take one step at a time than to know the challenge that lies ahead. The darkness of these woods, too, seemed to transport us; had we not had a watch, we wouldn't have known if it was morning, high noon, or evening. This quality coupled with plants that harkened of generations past rendered this place timeless. After a pregnant pause, we shattered our moving meditation with hoots and hollers, exuberant in our reaching the top.

"You did it love," I whispered to Scott once we'd quieted down.

He beamed. Although we'd been pushing ourselves harder than ever while on this hike, looking at him now, I couldn't help but notice how young he looked. Even with his normally smooth-shaven face now bearing a full beard, his smile was boyish, the lines in his brow softened, and his eyes bright. His hair was a wild spray of blond curls rather than well groomed—just how I knew he liked it—and contrasted with his gray beard. It was as if in just a couple of weeks, he'd hiked off years of stress and worry, returning to himself.

Hiking has a way of doing that—peeling back the layers that we accumulate over time. With nothing to do but walk, there's a whole lot of time to think and ultimately to ruminate. One might suppose that all this time to dwell on the state of things past and present could be detrimental, hard to shake without distractions, but rather I've found it quite the opposite. It's true, my worries, anger, regrets float up to the surface and I have no choice but to think long and hard about them. But, being so attuned with my own body, I cannot help but notice how these various feelings create tension throughout my body, each constricting or expanding a different area. I find at some point it reaches a climax, a point at which I must let it go because I know that if I don't it'll consume me . . . and so that's what I do. I hike it out. I cannot tell you how many times on my long treks I've found myself suddenly sobbing or screaming in the woods at the dialogue in my own head . . . and then all in the same instant I hike on, breathing and repeating aloud, *Let it go.* The difference was this time, we weren't only releasing, creating space to breathe and move forward, but refilling those empty spaces with love.

We affectionately termed Peekamoose "Peekaboose," given that its summit had appeared virtually out of nowhere, and hiked on to Table Mountain, which although a High Peak, was nearly level with this summit. Once at the shoulder of this ridge, we descended steeply, gradually leaving the shadows of the boreal forest behind and walking beneath the ever-growing tops of oaks and maples. Reaching a sunny meadow, we walked a wooden bridge across the East Branch of the Neversink River. This wasn't the first encounter I'd had with this waterway.

I could walk this river south and eventually end up in Port Jervis, a little town that I'd once called home during a tumultuous time in my life. I'd lived there during the time between my two Mountains to Sea Trail hikes and I'd served as a rock to childhood friends and a drug-addled boyfriend who, like waves, relentlessly crashed against me in their turmoil. I'd regularly visited this river seeking solace. After two years of this storm, I knew it was time to either hike it off or drown. I finished my first book, which I had long set aside, and hit the trail. And afterwards, I did not return to this riverside town. Instead, I headed back to Asheville, with its calm waters and friends who didn't summon storms but supported me. I then journeyed to western New York for a long hike on the Finger Lakes Trail. I would redefine my experience of the Northeast, my first home and one that I refused to give up on. After two months on that trail, finally having let go of so very much, I walked along the shores of the Neversink River to its eastern terminus. I had cried on the cliffs of this river in despair, walked its stony shores in my power, and the message it'd spoken to me subtly, but repeatedly, was just that . . . *Never sink.* Three days later, I'd walk into the restaurant where Scott worked, and he'd ask me if I'd like to join him for a hike.

We followed the river until we reached a humble wooden sign nailed to a tree.

Finger Lakes Trail, Eastern Terminus.

We dropped our packs with a thud. Then with one hand I grabbed his and placed my other against the rough bark of the tree. Being here now with him by my side was evidence of just how far I'd come. I had walked not only thousands of miles to create the life I wanted but in doing so had found the man I love. He was the greatest reward I could receive for all my efforts. Now I stood at this Finger Lakes Trail terminus, my love's hand in mine.

"I hiked the Finger Lakes Trail and found you," I said to him, peering into the eyes that I now knew so well. I remembered how the very first time I met him, his eyes had intrigued me and how I'd longed to know them better.

He brought his lips to mine and as he did it was as if I could see and feel all the poignant moments that had led to this one. I didn't believe I'd ever find a man to share my love of the trail. Not one that I'd care for at least. I'd long relinquished that dream. And if I couldn't find a partner who'd hike with me or at least stay out of my way so that I could, I'd do without one. But he had proven me wrong. We pulled out our food bags to revel in a long-anticipated lunch of the usual—English muffins and hard cheddar.

"You know, hon, back when I hiked the Finger Lakes Trail, I'd considered linking it with the Long Path. I thought maybe I'd hike to where the Shawangunk Ridge Trail joined with the Appalachian Trail and then follow the AT to Culver's Gap and walk home to my parent's house. But that would've meant another two weeks on the trail and I was tired. *So tired.*" I spoke while gazing back at the sign that pointed south on the Long Path.

"What, and make me wait another two weeks to fall in love with you?" he replied, rolling his eyes at me and shoving half of his sandwich in his mouth all at once.

"Yes, that would've been silly," I agreed, chuckling at his cheeks so swollen with food he resembled a chipmunk with a cache of nuts. "All this time I guess I've been saving this trail for the right person, for us."

After lunch, we would've been happy to kick up our feet on our packs, bask in the dappled light, and call it a day, but Slide Mountain, the tallest mountain in the Catskills, awaited us.

"You got this, babe," I said to Scott once we'd shouldered our packs and again faced the trail ahead.

"*We* got this," he replied, giving me a quick peck.

As we ascended, the trail was so wide and well graded that it felt like we were riding an escalator to the top. This gentle ascent continued until the spruces and yellow birches greeted us in the boreal forest. We maneuvered a narrow trail for a short spell over boulders and under low hanging evergreen boughs, and then again the trail widened and became nearly level. The temperature dropped as a breeze blew strong, carrying the sweet aroma of the dwarfed balsam firs to either side of us. Although intoxicatingly fragrant, they offered little protection from the elements. We followed a tiny side trail between their scratchy boughs to the edge of the ridge and here, for the first time, we grasped just how high we'd climbed. We teetered hand in hand and gazed across the expanse of jagged peaks, green with dense conifers, highlighted sporadically with yellowing birch leaves. We peered into the deep cuts, the narrow cols within these peaks where perhaps a slender stream trickled. The black outline of a distant bird soared on the wind's currents. The grey, cloud-filled sky provided a dramatic backdrop to nature's show. There was no denying the enormity of Slide Mountain. I felt a wave of fear and when Scott took a small step back, I knew that he had too. Remembering our offering to Peekamoose—I hoped that it extended to this mountain as well.

We stepped back onto the main trail and walked the spacious path between the trees to Slide's true summit of 4,180 feet, and then just a tad farther, where we found a flat-topped boulder to rest. It was here that we found a plaque memorializing John Burroughs. Reportedly, he slept several nights beneath the ledge of this very boulder, with nothing more than balsam boughs for a bed. Burroughs, who was born in 1837, spent his childhood at the foot of the Catskills in a town near Roxbury. Later, as an adult, he returned to New York State, taking up permanent residence in what is now called Esopus and at the turn of the century took to summering in a farmhouse he called Woodchuck Lodge near his birthplace in the Catskills. Throughout his life, he was continually inspired by and called to the mountains, which became the subject of many of his nature essays. He kept the company of historical figures such as Walt Whitman, Theodore Roosevelt, and John Muir. Through his explorations and writings, he introduced the public to the Catskills' majesty. And now, over a century later, as we began our traverse of what is now called the Burroughs Range—Slide, Cornell, and Wittenberg mountains— the line from his essay *In the Heart of the Catskills* encapsulated our feelings perfectly: "Here the works of man dwindle."

His beloved boulder provided us with respite as we cracked pistachio shells and swilled water and spied, through windows between the evergreens, the foggy blue Ashokan Reservoir in the distance. The wind blew ever stronger, forcing us to put on long sleeves and hats. "That ascent was nothing!" Scott said proudly.

"I know. You would think for the highest mountain in the Catskills it would've been an ass-whooper," I echoed, skimming the details of our upcoming miles. Suddenly I picked up on a description I hadn't seen before. "For our descent, the guide says something about ladders and rock ledges." I said, reading these directions over for what must have been the tenth time that day. Somehow, I hadn't caught those details. It's amazing how many times one must read them before they stick.

"Hmm. Well we've got some time, right?" Scott asked, not seeming too shaken.

"Yeah. It's four-thirty, so we've got about two and a half hours to go our last four miles. We should be fine," I answered with ease, although inside I felt a pang of nervousness.

"Oh yeah. We'll be good. At least it's not uphill!" Scott said with a wave of his hand. I didn't have the heart to tell him that in my experience, downhill did not necessarily equal easier.

Our descent began steeply by way of three tall wooden ladders that had been built into the side of the rock face, each step a solid foot away from the next. As I watched Scott descend first, his back to the sweeping view of the mountains to come, I reminisced on the many ladders I'd had to climb along the AT. It was hard to believe we were in New York. This felt more like the rugged terrain of New Hampshire or Maine.

At the ladders' base we found a trail that led off to the left. Following a narrow ledge between scrubby pines, we reached a small metal pipe that jutted from between the sharp rocks in the mountainside. Water poured from its opening into a small gravelly pool at its base.

"I'm thinking we should fill up, hon, just in case we don't make it to our expected camp for the night," I suggested. The wind blew harder here, pummeling us with mist and enshrouding us in fog. I was becoming increasingly aware of the toughness of Slide.

"Yeah, you're right. We should probably give the Phoenicia Lodge a call too for tomorrow night, just in case we don't have service farther down," Scott added.

"From *here*?" I could hardly think straight here, let alone dial a phone number.

"Yeah. If we don't get a room, what will we do?" he replied tensely.

Given Slide's conditions, he was more concerned with the luxuries of town than tonight's camp. But he had a point. If we simply hiked into town tomorrow and they were full up, there'd be no way to clean up and resupply on our food stores . . . and these were *necessities*.

"Okay, well give me your water bladder. I'll fill up on water while you give them a call." I said, taking off my pack and carefully leaning it against the cliff-side. And there, while trembling in the cold biting wind, Scott pulled out his phone and, with just one bar of service, dialed the lodge, paid for it in credit, and secured us a room. This procedure, so common in civilization, seemed rather absurd from our wilderness perch. But hey, God bless modern conveniences. Now chilled from our exposure on the cliff's edge, we pulled on our wool vests and gloves, loaded up our water bottles, and continued our descent.

"At least they gave us ladders!" Scott proclaimed, followed by a nervous chuckle.

"Yeah, they weren't kidding when they said a *steep* descent!" I replied, raising my voice over the wind that still blew between the trees. We hiked for a short while down the nearly vertical winding trail, both of us quiet, keenly focused on each step and too cold to care for conversation.

"Where's the trail?" Scott suddenly asked.

I stared at the sheer drop-off before us, looking left and then right for the next blaze. There were none. I looked straight ahead and that's when I saw it, the metal disc on a yellow birch tree roughly thirty feet away at the bottom of the drop-off. Suddenly I felt colder than ever.

"It's here," I answered numbly. I realized then that I could no longer feel my fingertips.

"What do you mean it's here?" Scott said looking to the ground far below.

"Look," I said, motioning toward the tree. "We're going to have to throw our packs down." The last time I had had to maneuver such a task, my pack had nearly tumbled off the side of Mount Katahdin.

"There's got to be another way down. I mean this is crazy," Scott said, pacing the top of the rock ledge.

He was right. They couldn't expect us to scale this sheer rock face without ropes. There had to be another way down. I investigated the webs of leafy tree branches and brush to either side of us but found only more perilous drops. Scott had doubled back on the trail some yards to see if he could find a way to bushwhack to the bottom. But inevitably we both returned to the edge of the cliff that dropped twenty vertical feet to the ground below.

"We'll have to wedge our feet into the rock," I said, pointing to the shallow chinks in the rock.

"You can grab hold of these roots." Scott followed, nodding his head toward a yellow birch root that snaked downward, smooth and scraggly from many a hiker's tight grasp.

Whether we liked it or not, this was indeed the intended route. We took off our packs, stepped close to the edge and let 'em drop. They landed with a loud thud and after a couple of rolls came to rest beside some large rocks. Our hiking sticks followed suit, landing in a clatter.

"I can go first," I offered, thinking of Scott's fear of heights.

"No, no, no. I will go first," he said with a wave of his hand. Even when boldly confronted with his phobia, he still insisted upon being the *man*.

Turning to face me, he knelt and then slowly began descending, pressing his whole body against the smooth rock face until his feet reached a small ledge. Releasing his grip on the rock's upper lip, he wedged his hands into a small crevice about a foot from the top.

"Be careful, honey," I urged him. I was powerless to help him.

"I am. I know. I got it." He sounded angry, but I knew he was just scared out of his wits and sharply focused.

He shimmied across the rock face to grab hold of the birch root. Grabbing hold, he then scaled down like a spider, lowering one leg and then the other to another ledge that only he could see. I held my breath and hoped that he would not lose his balance and fall backward onto the rock-strewn ground beneath him. Then he surrendered. Letting go of the birch root, he leaned into the rock, pressed his hands into a depression, lowered a little farther, and dropped to the ground, landing on his feet. I exhaled.

"Good job, love!"

"Yeah. Thanks," he muttered, dusting off his hands. "Okay, your turn. It's not as bad as it looks from up there. You'll be fine. Just take your time."

Apparently, he'd found his courage, but in watching him descend, I had lost mine.

Whatever. None of that matters now. You can do this shit, I told myself. I followed the same route that he had chosen and was thankful for the agility my trail runners afforded as I lowered my feet to the first small ledge. I pressed my body hard against the cold rock and wished that I could at least regain feeling in my fingers. I reached over and grabbed hold of the birch root, more thankful than ever for this tree. Suddenly I realized I could feel its smooth wood against my skin. I tightened my grip. Here, I was strong. Apparently, its medicine goes above and beyond its medicinal constituents.

"Now lower yourself. I'm here below you, I got you," I heard Scott say from behind.

I took a deep breath and trusted, searching for the next rock lip with my toe. Found it.

"That's it," Scott said, assuring me.

"Okay. I'm coming down."

"I got you," he said again.

I lowered my other leg, let go of the birch root, and, all in the same instant, felt Scott's hands around my hips.

"I got you," he said again, this time as if reassuring himself.

"Jesus," I gasped, turning 'round to look at him and then back up at the ledge from where we had come.

"Yeah. That was bullshit," Scott replied and went to gather up our packs.

He was fumbling through the hip pockets on his pack when I suddenly remembered we hadn't even thought to secure our more fragile items: phones, camera, and his glasses.

"Are they okay?" I dared to ask as he pulled his glasses from the pocket.

"Whew! Yeah, they're fine. So is the phone," he answered, now pulling the phone from the other pocket.

All the fragile items in my pack had also survived the fall. Funny, how when standing on the edge of a cliff, these items don't even warrant a thought. Even if some, like those glasses, are integral to the journey.

"I guess that's what they meant by *steep*," I said, hoisting my pack.

"Huh. Yeah," Scott said with a grumble, buckling his hip belt.

"That's got to be the worst of it," I added, feigning confidence in my statement. I hoped I was right.

"Can't be worse than that!" Scott replied, passing me my trekking poles and then collecting his own, which had landed at the base of a nearby tree.

Turns out we were wrong. Well, none as bad as the first, but we scaled several more sheer rock faces along our path, each one requiring a strategic maneuver to descend. Later I would read in full, in Burroughs's *In the Heart of the Catskills*, his description of his ascent of Slide:

"The mountain rose like a huge, rock-bound fortress from this plain-like expanse. It was ledge upon ledge, precipice upon precipice, up which and over which we made our way slowly and with great labor, now pulling ourselves up by our hands, then cautiously finding niches for our feet and zigzagging right and left from shelf to shelf."

Clearly our ascent had not been his route. He had chosen a path that provided terrain better likened to our descent. Humans were surely made of different stuff back then, bodies as rugged as the mountains they scaled. I could not imagine climbing without a trail what we had just navigated.

"That better be the last one," Scott said, giving me a sideways glance at the bottom of yet another cliff. "How much farther do we have?"

I unfolded our weathered directions.

"Over three more miles?"

I looked at my watch to see that already one hour had passed. We were moving at half our usual speed.

"How the hell is that possible? *That* felt like three miles!" Scott returned.

"I know. It's the rock scrambling," I said, hanging my head. "It's slowing us down."

Already our foggy daylight was turning to dusk. This was no place to venture a night hike— that much I knew. Thankfully, we had filled up our water reserves so we could camp sooner than we'd planned if needed. We hiked, now gradually descending on the winding trail, still in the thick of the boreal forest. The wind had stopped. And in its absence, we were immersed in silence, a forest silent, all except for the call of a single bird, the hermit thrush. Its song resonated like that of fingers drawn along the rim of a wine glass. Warmth flooded through me all the way to my toes. I'd heard this very same birdsong frequently in the northern evergreen woods along the Appalachian Trail. Now here I was sharing space in these dark woods, the man I loved hiking beside me. This bird of the hinterlands carried a message: *I am just where I am supposed to be.* Somewhere around 1,000 feet below the summit, in the col between Slide and its neighboring giant, Cornell, we found an open patch of flat ground at the base of a small embankment and decided to call it home for the night. Later that evening, as we nestled into our sleeping bag atop the soft bed of dry pine needles beneath us, we felt like victors. We may not have made it the fourteen miles we'd wished to, but we'd made it down one of the most challenging climbs I'd encountered since Mount Katahdin. If we could tackle that, we could tackle anything. Somewhere, from off in the darkness, an owl hoo-hooted.

CHAPTER THREE

We awoke at first light, when the sun's rays had finally penetrated the thick evergreen boughs in our little nest. It would be a full thirteen-mile day summiting two more high peaks—Cornell and Wittenberg—then three more modest mountains—Cross, Pleasant, and Romer—but, by God, we'd make it to that little motel room in Phoenicia. The morning remained cool, making for perfect hiking weather. We hiked between moss-covered rocks and beside rocky cliffs and spied the first threads of *Usnea*, a fruticose lichen, hanging hair-like from the decaying fallen trees that crisscrossed the path overhead.

Like all lichens, *Usnea* is the resultant organism of a symbiotic relationship between two distinct organisms—algae and fungus. The algae photosynthesizes, providing food, and the fungus provides a larger surface to catch rain and absorb water from the humid woods, retaining moisture. Lichens use trees or rocks as their substrate, creating a home on the fine sediment or dust that collects on the surface of these solid unmoving beings. Slow-growing and sensitive to air pollution, it takes a lot for a lichen to persist. And these *Usnea* were *thriving*. Here in these woods, apparently the evergreen-infused air was as clean as it smelled, enabling lichen growth. Discs dotting their thin gray threads evidenced that this *Usnea* was reproducing. But *Usnea* is more than just an indicator of air quality. Much more. It's also a valuable medicinal offering antibiotic-like qualities.

For centuries, it has been packed into wounds to reduce bleeding and prevent infection. Today, modern herbalists use it most often in an alcohol extract taken internally to heal bacterial and viral infections of the lungs and urinary tract.

Our ascent from the col was so gradual, dream-like, that before we knew it, we were up and over the tree-covered summit of Cornell. We began our descent and were soon torn from our dreams and smack! Back into the reality of the Catskills. "You're kidding me?!" Scott exclaimed.

"Shit," I echoed.

We stood at the edge of yet another precipice. This time with a sheer drop between the bosom of two large boulders that sat atop an even larger boulder. We'd later learn that apparently, this is what hikers call the Cornell Crack.

We slouched off our packs—we knew the drill. This time we removed our valuables, slipping them inside our pockets, and literally threw our packs off the top of the boulders. They landed with a kaboom, bouncing several times down the trail before tumbling to a halt. Our hiking sticks we dropped down the crevice. "I can go first, babe," I offered, although I knew by now he'd only turn me down.

"No, I got it, just give me a hand," he replied sharply.

I laid on my belly atop the flat rock and wished that this time a birch tree or two had chosen this place for a perch. Now my arm would serve as a root. Scott turned around and grabbed hold of my forearm, shakily lowering himself down into the crevice. I prayed that this would not end like some bad adventure movie where I lost my grounding and went down with him or he lost his hold on me. If one of us slipped there was no chance of a soft landing on the forest floor below—only bone against rock.

He slid his grip down my forearm to my hand and lowered himself down to the boulder below. There, he came to a squatting position and cupped his hands to provide a foothold for me.

"I got you," he said again, a calm confidence that hadn't been there on the first descent now strong in his voice. His certainty gave me certainty.

That and the fact that I hadn't severely injured myself yet on a trail. Surely it wouldn't be here and now. Hiking requires a good deal of that . . . a faith . . . not so different from that of a strong relationship, I'd also learned. I turned around and, grabbing hold of the top of the rock with my open hands for traction, lowered myself down, soon feeling his hands beneath my feet and then his body wrapped around mine.

"Whew!" I hollered. "Holy shit, babe."

We gave each other a kiss and then took to maneuvering our way down the large boulder, hugging it with our whole bodies.

"That better be the last one!" Scott exclaimed, picking his pack up off the trail. "I fucking mean it."

From here, we hiked what's known as the Bruin's Causeway, a narrow path along the ridge leading to Wittenberg. At 3,500 feet, this col has one of the highest elevations in the Catskills. Reportedly, many an animal track can be found here in the mud, such as bobcat and bear—hence this portion's name—which enjoy meals of the smaller critters that can easily get stuck in this steep-sided col. I just hoped we hadn't been so foolish ourselves to suffer such a fate. But before we knew it, we were climbing the winding trail up short switchbacks through dense woods to the grassy summit of Wittenberg.

The Ashokan Reservoir laid before us like a foggy blue inkblot amidst the green mountains. We climbed atop a flat white boulder and gazed out over the erect sap-seeping cones of the balsam fir that grew below. In this moment, all alone on top of this giant, we were the only people in the world with this view. We hooted and hollered in celebration. Yet we were not conquerors of this mountain, rather grateful recipients of its beauty. Like excited children, we explored Wittenberg's summit, darting from one end of the boulder to the other, and finally collapsed on our backs, letting the sun warm our bones.

But there wasn't much time for basking in this bright light with three more mountains to go. The trail led us steeply down the side of Wittenberg on a loose rock trail, our feet and hiking sticks skidding with each step. We slithered and slid our bodies over boulders of every shape, but not once did we have to launch packs off cliffs, and the descent ultimately proved easier than those of Slide and Cornell. Our morning bled into afternoon while we maintained a slow steady focus. When finally, the fir and birch morphed into oak and maple, beech and witch hazel, the trail snaking long before us through forest bright with yellow midday sun. It felt strange. We'd spent two days in not only the darkness of the boreal forest but also its quiet, sometimes the only sounds the dripping of moisture from the trees' boughs and our own padding feet. Now the forest was illuminated and alive with birdsong and buzzing insects. We were thrust from a dream, from one trail onto what felt like an entirely different one.

Over the next nine miles we rolled up and over Cross, Pleasant, and Romer mountains, essentially three peaks along the same ridge, each close in elevation. However, the trail still paraded us up and down stone steps, between boulders, and over loose, carefully laid flat rock. This new portion of trail, which had recently replaced a lengthy road walk, was meticulously well maintained, evidence that the folks who curated this section clearly loved it. They wanted only to share that love with fellow hikers. We passed a father and his two daughters going the opposite direction, planning a night out in the woods. They were chipper, clearly enjoying the scenic stretch, but we could think only of getting to Phoenicia, each mile seeming longer than the next.

The trail finally spit us out on Lane Street—one mile outside of downtown Phoenicia. We walked the residential roads holding hands swinging, so grateful to be on easy terrain and headed for our hotel. On the sidewalk along Main Street, we found downtown quiet in the late afternoon. Silently we looked to each other and rejoiced for the quaintness of this little town. Although town days are much anticipated, once actually in town, it can quickly become daunting. Not only do you encounter more people in a few short hours than you've encountered for an entire week, but the onslaught of stimulation from speedy cars to blinking streetlights to the buzzing of electricity all around you is in stark contrast to the peaceful forest. And that's just outside. Inside stores you're confronted with a myriad of choices, all while music plays overhead, and florescent lights flicker. The everyday stimulus that we're typically accustomed to suddenly seems assaulting. After six months on the Appalachian Trail it was *another* six months before I could run errands without anxiety. But from the looks of it, Phoenicia might just prove to be our pace while still offering everything we needed.

We found the business district, if one could call it that, which consisted of just two blocks with a campground and post office on one end and a library on the other. In between were a handful of artsy shops, an outfitters/hardware store, a country grocery, a liquor store, a gas station, and a Mexican restaurant and Italian restaurant side by side, seemingly under the same ownership. We hit a couple shops for supplies and then headed straight for our hotel a little over a mile outside of town.

We fell in love with the Phoenicia Lodge upon first sight. It consisted of a stand-alone office—also home to owners Brian and Sara, who had renovated the motel and grounds—a simple strip of rooms, each with its own screen-door entrance and a little bench. Cabins with fire rings and picnic tables dotted the lawn out back. We asked Sara about laundry facilities and although they were out of order, she happily offered to do our laundry for us. This is no small gift to a hiker. She also informed us that they had bicycles that we could take at our leisure into town to save us having to walk any more miles. *Had we fallen to our deaths from one of those boulder climbs and gone to heaven?*

Once inside our room we found it incredibly small but oh, so adorable. This hotel had surely been here a long time, harkening back to when people were content with less. The double bed sat in the center of the room and absorbed most of the space. However, the owners had still managed to squeeze in a tiny table complete with two retro-style vinyl-upholstered chairs. On the table was a rotary phone and on the bedside table was an alarm clock that had two hands and a knob to wind it. In the bathroom was a stand-up shower, toilet, and the tiniest sink I have ever seen. Yet, with everything crisp and clean, and a screen door and windows that we could actually open, we didn't feel like we were in a sterile stuffy box. We each cracked a can of soda that we'd acquired from the general store in town, poured them into our camp mugs, and wandered over to the ice chest—a real one—at the end of the patio to procure some ice.

That evening, with headlamps beaming, we rode into town on a dark street. I hadn't ridden a bike since I was twelve years old. Scott on the other hand was an old pro, having whizzed around Manhattan on two wheels during the many years he'd lived there. Pedaling behind him and clinging tight to my handlebars, I felt alive, awakened by the magic of this moment in which I never could've expected to find myself. Seated at a sidewalk table, we devoured plates of food and pints of beer at Brio's Italian Restaurant and marveled at the patrons around us. Scott remarked on how they appeared like automatons in the video game Sims. People moved around each other without any real acknowledgement and void of wonder for this starry night. This dinner so very different from our pots of noodles and dirt speckled water in our tiny tent in the woods, we took nothing for granted.

Afterwards we rode back to our room in the quaint motel by the light of the moon, the dimly lit street periodically illuminated by the garish lights of a passing car. And later that night we made the most of our real true bed, careful not to disturb our neighbors with the squeaking of springs.

CHAPTER FOUR

Scott had the honors of balancing the box on his hip as he rode, one-handed, back to the lodge where we could sort out its contents. We had ridden our bikes into town to pick up our mail-drop from the post office. I watched him weave and wobble in front of me and I hoped he didn't swerve into traffic. That'd be a crappy way to end a thru-hike.

He deftly maneuvered his way into the gravel parking lot with a snazzy skid and we slipped back into our room. In the process of unpacking HEET, pistachios, organic Pop-Tarts, Aquamira, and, most importantly, another small bottle of whiskey, I planned our miles for the upcoming week. A stay in a motel never means complete rest and relaxation when hiking a long-distance trail, what with all the resupply and planning that must be done before checkout. Somehow, we still managed to be out by noon and then made our way the mile into town, by foot, and with *nearly* full packs. There was still more shopping to do.

With just four miles planned for the day, we would peruse Phoenicia. I've learned that it often makes more sense to hike a short day into town or a short day out rather than take a full "zero" mileage day for a number of reasons. Firstly, one can easily tack many more days onto a hike with days off. Secondly, it's far more costly to secure two nights in a motel room as well as meals and luxury items such as cold beers, purchased in town. Thirdly, one's body will actually ache more after a day of not hiking than if you hike at least a few miles to keep your body in a rhythm.

As we made our way around town, we noticed something about the people we encountered. They seemed content. Rough-around-the edges local folks, blue-collar workers, business owners, and many an artsy Manhattan-type transplant—each one more friendly than the last. Several asked us, "Where you headed?" Others simply stated, "Nice day for a hike!" Perhaps it was our backpacks that welcomed an interaction. In turn we explained that every day was a *good* day for a hike for us and that we were heading to the Adirondacks. This in turn earned us wide-eyed expressions and words of excitement or support.

Despite having enjoyed the substantial continental breakfast earlier that morning at the Phoenicia Lodge, our bellies soon lured us back to Brio's, where we dropped our packs by an outside table. While we waited for our second breakfast to arrive, I pulled out our maps and the guidebook pages for the next couple of days. That's when it dawned on me . . . tomorrow we'd hike the infamous Devil's Path.

The Devil's Path stretches twenty-four miles in length and is considered the most rugged trail in all of New York State due to its rocky terrain, steep ascents and descents, and boulder piles that must be traversed. Doing the math, I figured out that the Long Path only followed it for an eight-mile portion, but still, Scott had put down his egg and cheese sandwich and was rubbing his brow.

"They call it the most rugged trail?" he asked, looking me square in the eye. What he really wanted to say was, *Why didn't you tell me about this earlier?*

Perhaps this was a bad time to tell him that it also looked like Phoenicia could be our last stop in a town and that springy bed could have been the last time we laid our heads atop pillows until we completed our hike.

"Yes. But we're only hiking eight miles of it. There are a few peaks in there, but we've already climbed so many. How bad can it be?" I said, trying my best to act aloof, although I too was wary.

Scott rolled his eyes at me and reached for his sandwich.

"Well. Eight miles. That's not so bad," he said after swallowing. "Where's our next stop?" He was picking up the little bits of egg that fell to the plate.

"Umm," I stalled, folding up the maps in haste. "I think this might be our last." Perhaps he wouldn't hear me over the crinkling.

"What do you mean? Aren't we resupplying somewhere?"

"Well, yeah. But at the post office. I don't see any more hotels within a reasonable walking distance ahead."

"Oh wow," Scott said, forcing his food down in a big gulp.

"Yeah. I know," I said sympathetically. Suddenly it felt as if we were hiking into the wilderness for the first time all over again. How would we fare without a breather in civilization?

After a long pause, Scott said, "Well Phoenicia has been awesome. Here's to hiking on!" He shoved the last of his sandwich into his mouth.

And just like that the prospect of sleeping in our tent for the next so many nights seemed alright. If Scott was okay with it then I was too. Although we did laze about on that patio for an especially long time.

Late in the afternoon, with four liters of water each and three days of food to carry us to Palenville, we began our *easy* four miles up the side of Mount Tremper. But with the humidity high and our bellies so full I was pretty sure they were creating drag, we had no choice but to take our time. And finally, at the 1,500-summit, we set up camp just past the lean-to at a flat spot in the woods.

My eardrums vibrated with a low hum, a buzz. Still half-asleep, I laid beside Scott utterly confused.

"Do you hear that?" I asked him, disregarding whether he was still asleep. I had to know—was I really hearing this buzzing or was it just in my head? It was so constant, I couldn't tell.

"Yeah. That buzzing?" he answered and sat up swiftly, looking around the tent that shone bright with early morning light.

"What is it?"

"Shit," Scott answered. And suddenly it dawned on me too . . . *bees.*

Scott was once attacked by a swarm years ago and his hands swelled up like balloons. Ever since then he's had a good, healthy fear of buzzing things with stingers.

"You think so?" I asked, now scanning the walls of our tent. If so, we were surrounded.

"What else would it be? Maybe we disturbed a hive in the night." Scott said, his tone growing more tense.

"But we were sleeping," I answered, still staring hard at the tent walls. I imagined a big fat black bear sitting outside our tent with a paw full of honey having just knocked down a sugar-laden hive.

"Well I don't know!" Scott said, now frustrated that I was debating with him how or from where these bees had appeared.

We sat a few minutes longer in silence, listening to the buzz that, like a whirring engine gaining speed, grew louder. The sun was rising above the ridge, creating shadows that played on walls of the tent.

"Should I look?" I asked.

"I don't know." He said tersely and without moving a muscle.

"Well we have to get out of here somehow!" I said. "I feel like an idiot just sitting in here scared."

Carefully I reached over and unzipped the tent inch by inch, in case the bees were waiting just outside to swarm. Peering out, I saw the trail of a flying insect zip by in the misty morning light and then another. Out I crawled and zipped up the tent as fast as I could, so to not let any inside.

I was surrounded by hum. As my eyes adjusted, I could see dozens of flying black specks zipping past my face. I managed to follow one with my gaze and saw it land on a broad witch hazel leaf. *Oh my God. This was a story to tell no one.*

"It's flies!" I shouted giddily.

"Flies?" Scott asked, still confused and not sounding all that relieved.

I looked around at the moisture-laden leaves on young saplings and at the forest floor bespeckled with black, fuzzy-bodied flies. They might have been nothing but horse flies, but they were in numbers. I poked at one and it didn't even flinch. And they were stupefied. I poked at another and it moved a couple slow steps to the leaf's edge before taking off in a buzz. The sound we'd been hearing were simply the flies awakening. A memory resurfaced of getting up in the night while camped on the Mountains to Sea Trail and when I'd shone my headlamp on a garbage bag left out to dry, I'd found an army of flies simply snoozing in the night air. In the morning, when I'd awoken at dawn, they'd stirred, but slow as molasses in December. Then as the sun had risen higher, one by one they took to flight. I guess everything must sleep sometime, even flies.

"They're waking up!" I said to him, unzipping the tent's door in a flurry.

Scott clambered out and peered around at the black glistening beads, some sleeping, some zipping, but all buzzing.

"Eww," he said with a sneer. "This is going to make the morning poop fun."

"Oh god, you're right," I said with a grimace. Ain't nothin' like flies on shit.

Once on the trail, the day was cool and crisp with clear blue skies. We hadn't had a morning this cool since the beginning of the trip. The first few miles were easy and level with a long descent to Warner Creek, and we found ourselves singing and goofing our way down the trail. We stopped and snacked, taking in the hammering of a knock-knocking woodpecker overhead that we never did see despite our peering through the dead snags. Later, when snacking by the creek we had two orange-and-black butterflies with elegantly curved wings flitting ceaselessly around us, showing off their colors. When one alighted on the handle of my trekking pole, I glimpsed on the underside of its wings the characteristic white crescent and dot that earns them their name, the question-mark butterfly. But upon crossing that creek, our morning stroll changed shape.

We began our ascent of Edgewood Mountain, which would require climbing 1,500 feet over less than two miles, stumbling over loose slate stone and clawing through blackberry brambles and wood nettles. Wood nettle, a relative of the European stinging nettle, is one of the most loathsome plants a hiker can encounter, even if tasty and nutritious. Every part of the plant is covered in tiny translucent hairs, each which contains a bulb of fluid at its base. When an unassuming hiker brushes by, the hairs effortlessly pierce the flesh and inject that fluid, much like a hypodermic needle, sending a cocktail of chemicals into the bloodstream which causes an allergic reaction. If one is lucky, a burning, tingling sensation will ensue for about five minutes; if one is less lucky, up to an hour. But heat destroys those stinging hairs and the leaves of wood nettle are a delicious edible green when steamed and tossed with some pasta or eggs. Even the question-mark butterfly agrees, as it is one of the host plants they enjoy as caterpillars. The ol'-timers in the Appalachian hills claimed that rubbing wood nettle leaves on achy joints had an analgesic effect, but from our inadvertent stings we felt no relief. Using my bandana as a glove, I plucked a handful of leaves to add to dinner later that night. They were past their prime—the plants having already flowered—but they would still add some vitamins and minerals to our sorry pots of noodles.

Mingled amidst the nettles were the delicate seed heads of ramps—that's what we call them down south at least—better known in these northern parts as wild leeks. Each head sported an umbel of slender stems, each bearing a small, shiny, ebony seed. Ramps, a wild member of the onion family, are comprised of an underground bulb, from which two to three broad green leaves unfurl to the abundant sun of an early spring forest. Ramps' leaves wither away once trees leaf out, by which the plant sends up a flowering stalk in summer, producing seed come late summer and early fall. Ramps are considered a delicacy, every forager's delight, and sought by upscale restaurants. However, because ramps are so desirable, they have suffered the abuse of overharvest. The most sustainable way to harvest ramps is to simply pluck a leaf from each plant, therefore allowing the plant to continue to photosynthesize and go onto reproduce by bulb and by seed. It takes five to seven years for ramps to reach maturity from seed, so consider the impact of digging up the plant to acquire bulbs. Additionally, given the protected nature of the Catskill Park, this was no place to harvest a plant that in some places hangs in the balance.

Climbing up over several boulder jumbles, we finally reached Edgewood Mountain's long flat summit, still thick with deciduous trees. It was hard to believe we were still 500 feet below where the boreal forest begins. We found a grassy picnic-like spot to lunch in the shade and reveled in our hard rolls and cheese from town, reluctant to reach the meal's end. But end it did.

We descended steeply, reached Silver Hollow Notch, and then ascended again, about 800 feet to Daley Mountain. We zigzagged through boulders encased in yellow birch roots thicker than my thigh, and it felt as if these trees literally called to me to stop for a spell. They had wisdom to share, if only a patient hiker would take the time to listen. Just then, Scott stopped in his tracks and gazed upon the curling golden bark of a tall fissured tree.

"You have a nice life. You don't have to work or worry. You have just to be. That's all," he stated plainly, as if his insight came direct from the tree itself.

We spend so much time running circles in our daily lives, circles that we've created, convinced that work and the minutia of daily interactions are of the greatest importance. More so, we believe that that which we produce is a testament of our self-worth or value to society. Are we not valuable simply because we are living, breathing beings? And who's to say our purpose is any more than that? It seems in our nature to desire a purpose, but we often forget that we can create what that purpose is and allow it to enliven rather than enslave us. A long hike helps one to remember that. It strips off the layers of identity that arise from working a particular job or earning a certain income, driving a Mercedes or a rattling tin can, living in a luxurious home or a trailer home, those things that we allow to measure lesser or greater, and one is reminded that they are simply a human being, a living creature on this planet like everything else. Let the trees be our examples.

CHAPTER FIVE

I could hear nothing but the sound of my own gasping breath as we pushed our feet into root and rock, leaf and dirt, climbing the last half mile to the summit of Plateau Mountain. When I lifted my gaze, I was face to face with a wooden sign that read: The Devil's Path. We'd been working so hard all morning I'd nearly forgotten that "the most rugged trail in New York" awaited us at the day's end. I looked to Scott, whose face had changed abruptly from red to white. We considered a break but decided against it. Keeping our momentum going was the only way we'd make it down this trail today.

This fierce path of fire and brimstone began with a ridge walk across the aptly named Plateau Mountain amidst old-growth spruce and fir forest. The sweet aroma of evergreen boughs was intoxicating. It's easy to understand how humans intuited that these trees held medicinal properties. The growing spring tips, when steeped in hot water, may be ingested or inhaled as a steam to clear bronchial passageways and open lungs. From between the trees we glimpsed a sweeping view of the deep valley and the mountains yet to come. Our descent was rugged with many a large flat-faced boulder to navigate and loose scree rolling beneath our feet. Likely this was the start of this path's devilish antics. We continued this tricky bouldering for what seemed a very long time, so long that our day, which had begun at nearly first light, was now reaching its close at nearly dark. Still, we delighted that we had not encountered any sheer rock faces requiring us to throw down our packs and leap. Guess it's all relative.

Before us on the darkening path we spied a lithe figure approaching, a four-legged animal trotting in front of him. Suddenly we had a blond labradoodle sniffing our dirty sneakers and a barefoot Ken Posner standing before us, one hand on a lightweight trekking pole. Ken is a board member of the New York–New Jersey Trail Conference, a volunteer crew leader for thirty miles of trail, and the organizer of the Long Path Race Series, which includes the infamous Shawangunk Ridge Trail Run. We had chatted with him via Facebook some days previous and had given him a rough idea of where we might be on the trail, but we certainly hadn't expected him to pinpoint us so perfectly along our route. This man could predict mileage! Although we hadn't yet met in person, who else would be hiking barefoot up the Devil's Path?

"Ken?" I asked.

"Heather and Scott?"

"Yes!" we answered, chuckling.

"Great. I hoped I'd find you guys here. You said you might be staying at the lean-to in Mink Hollow, so I figured I'd try and meet you. If it'd be alright, I'd love to hike with you two tomorrow, learn some more about the plants."

"Sure thing!" I answered and then followed with my burning question, "How far are we from the lean-to?"

"Oh, you're just about a half mile, all downhill," he answered with a wave of his hand.

"Awesome," I answered, smiling at Scott.

Ken Posner is no average hiker, in fact he's hardly a *hiker*, he is an elite athlete. But he'd never tell you this. In 2013, he started out from the West 175th Subway Station, in New York City, on August 25th and finished September 3rd in John Boyd Thacher State Park, running the Long Path in a mere nine days and three hours and breaking the previous fastest known time. Upon completion, he wrote a book about his experience, titled *Running the Long Path*. During his thru-run he'd wore sneakers. He now hiked barefoot because of an injury that he'd incurred while running. Hiking barefoot, he explained, helped to adjust his footing and slow him down. I was pretty certain that learning about the plants would slow him down too.

"Okay, well I'm just going to head up to the summit quick for a little night hike and I'll be right back down. I'll meet you guys at the lean-to," he said with a nod, pulling his headlamp out of his shoulder bag.

"Sure, have a good hike!" Scott said with a nod, then, turning to me, added, "Just gonna hit the summit real quick? Have fun with *that*, bud."

And so, while Ken continued up the long descent we had just traversed, his dog Odie at the helm, we continued creeping our way down the slippery rock. We stopped just before the lean-to at a piped spring that trickled water from between boulders, creating a small creek along the path. Filling up our bottles, we looked at each other and shook our heads.

"He was barefoot," Scott stated.

"I know. Barefoot on a night hike," I clarified.

Ken Posner gave new meaning to "hike your own hike," a figure of speech in the hiking world that essentially means there is no right or wrong way to hike a trail. We just hoped we could keep up.

Upon reaching the lean-to in the dim evening light, we were devastated to find it occupied by a dozen other hikers. Too tired to care about pleasantries, we made a beeline toward what looked like a camping area just beyond it. Besides, those at the lean-to seemed so busy chatting it up that I doubted they even saw us. For us our campsites were not "camp-outs." Our campsites were "home," and we just wanted to get our chores done and kick up our feet after a long day on the trail. Finding a wide patch of dry moss, we dropped our packs and set up our tent by headlamp. Once finally nestled into our sanctuary, we changed clothes and got to making dinner. Just as we were just beginning to wonder where Ken might be, we saw a bobbing headlamp.

We spent dinner talking trail. We learned that Ken was from Manhattan. He had discovered the Long Path while running carriage roads in Minnewaska State Park and, with further exploration, soon fell in love with it. After thru-running the Shawangunk Ridge Trail, he got the idea to set his sights on the Long Path. Mind you, he had completed seventy marathons prior to his success on the Long Path, and so he knew very well what it was to push one's body to the limits. Still, his thru-run of the Long Path, had been no easy feat for him. He told us of running on little sleep and through rainstorms, and of his injuries near the end of the trail during which he'd even considered throwing in the towel, but still, he'd endured to the end. Since that time, he has dedicated his energy to the trail so that others may discover its magic as he did and continues to today. He told us that he comes to the Catskills every weekend and although he has dreams of doing a long hike someday, work is still an obstacle. He suggested, "Perhaps many weekends spent in the woods can have the same effect on a person as one continuous hike." Scott told him of his time wandering in the Rockies with nothing more than a knapsack, while I shared bits and pieces of my experiences on other long-distance treks. But tomorrow would be a full day of getting to know each other and identifying the plants, so before too late we bid farewell and retreated to our tents.

We began our day with a steep ascent up Sugarloaf Mountain and we moved slowly. A plant walk is a very different thing from a hike. Rather than hiking, strong and steady like a machine on autopilot, one's pace is unpredictable and irregular, like that of a question-mark butterfly, flittering from this plant to that as one feels called. Today's route would also require our utmost attention as we climbed over boulders the size of cars along the Devil's Path. Ken was still barefoot but given the way he adeptly maneuvered atop the path's boulder-lain jagged terrain, there was no denying he was fully attuned to these mountains. He knew them, but more than that, trusted them in a way that we were still learning to do so. It was as if his body were a natural extension of the mountain itself.

Native plants abounded along our rugged path. We chatted about the scarlet, Vitamin C–rich berries of the leafy, cliff-dwelling mountain ash and the antimicrobial resin of spruce and balsam fir. We spotted the toxic but intriguing

American yew, which this time of year could easily be confused with a young eastern hemlock due to its similarly shaped flat needles, but come summer when it bears cup-shaped fleshy fruits, its identity is unmistakable. Indian cucumber also grabbed our attention, sporting its cluster of blue-black berries atop a slender stem skirted with a whorl of broad leaves. Tempting as its berries may be, they are toxic to ingest, but its pencil-thin lateral root is quite edible and provides a delicious crisp morsel.

We soon learned that Odie, with a periodic boost from the rear, was very adept at picking our best route through the boulders, finding a path where we wouldn't have seen one. However, even with Odie's help, when we reached the top of Sugarloaf Mountain, we'd hiked for over an hour and a half but traveled only one mile. The plant walking was slowing us down but not so much as the high heat of the day and the fact that we'd ascended 1,200 feet in that meager mile. And so, without time to waste, it was time to begin our descent.

We slithered and scrambled over sharply angled rocks that looked as if the gods had simply tossed them onto the trail from on high. We slid alongside the snaking roots of yellow birch and then stumbled over the knobby network of evergreen roots that hold the thin soil of the boreal forest in place. Mountain ash berries littered the trail, as did wild cherry, and so we couldn't help but nibble as went along, sampling these fruits with a sprig of lemony wood sorrel that grew in clumps at the base of trees.

Reaching the col, we ascended again, this time Twin Peak with its west and east summits. These climbs were not lengthy but challenging in their technicality. Along the way, the three of us chatted about Thoreau, Muir, Burroughs—the writers who brought the beauty of wilderness alive both on the page and in our minds. I had not discovered Burroughs until this hike, however, by my own choosing, I had read Thoreau's *Walden* in high school and fallen in love with the idea of living self-sustainably, especially in a humble cabin amidst the woods. Thoreau had also spurred in me a pride. "Why should we be in such desperate haste to succeed, and in such desperate enterprises? If a man does not keep pace with his companions, perhaps it is because he hears a different drummer.

Let him step to the music which he hears, however measured or far away," Thoreau wrote in *Walden*. I, too, preferred to spend my days quietly wandering the woods, observing and experiencing my natural landscape, and Thoreau's writings affirmed for me that this was indeed a worthwhile pursuit, a noble one in fact. I would continue for some years to read all I could of Thoreau. Later, after I had hiked the Appalachian Trail, I realized how utterly inseparable I was from nature, that I needed it to thrive. "I think I cannot preserve my health and spirits unless I spend four hours a day at least—and it is commonly more than that—sauntering through the woods and fields absolutely free from all worldly engagements," wrote Thoreau in his essay "Walking."

I found my way to Muir when I became curious about the great West, to which I had never traveled. His poetic descriptions of the Sierras made me swoon, and I read with pen in hand, marking up paragraphs about isolated peaks, sweeping flower-filled valleys, and fortifying atmospheres. I had found the writer who spoke to my soul. Muir could convey in words the beauty with which I felt imbued when outside in the natural world. He revered the mountains as I did and aspired only to experience them in all their grandeur. "And when they are fairly within the mighty walls of the temple and hear the psalms of the falls, they will forget themselves and become devout. Blessed, indeed, should be every pilgrim in these holy mountains!" exclaimed Muir in *My First Summer in the Sierra*. Nature was his cathedral, and it was mine too. Later, Muir would inspire me, with my father and a pickup truck, to explore those places he described out West and I would weep at their beauty.

I wanted badly to know more of Burroughs, for perhaps he too would kindle a spark. Ken, having spent so much time in Burroughs's home range, was just beginning to give us some background, when we rounded a bend where the trees were sparse. The three of us fell silent and peered out over the spikes of balsam firs into the layers of mountains draped across the landscape. Given the beauty before us, words would have only served to disfigure its majesty.

After a moment, Scott reached for his water bottle and Ken spoke. "To the north," he said, pointing towards the rippling humps of mountains in the distance, "those are your peaks to come, the Blackhead Range."

"From here, I feel like I could see all the world," Scott replied.

"You can," I answered with a wink.

We resumed hiking and were approaching the summit when the faint aroma of bug spray wafted by, then the sound of voices up ahead—we had company. We tread the green moss–lined corridor, the tan dirt here fine and sandy, evidence of the many feet that visit this peak, when suddenly we were awash in color. More people than I cared to count had crammed themselves onto this small rock overlook, among them at least two families with teenage children and a dog, and a slew of selfie-snappers. We politely said hello and squeezed in amidst the low boughs of a nearby spruce tree. Had it not been high time for lunch, we would've kept right on hiking. Apparently, everyone else deemed this a perfect lunch spot, too.

Ken sat down and quietly got to unpacking Odie's food, seemingly unaffected by the crowd, while Scott and I exchanged grumbles and fumbled with our large packs that were far too big for this little rock, at least today. Ken had brought no food for himself as he was on a thirty-hour fast. Last night, while we'd poured crushed crackers into our pots of instant rice, he'd sat peacefully empty-handed and explained that he periodically fasted while hiking to encourage his body to burn fat rather than rely on sugary snacks. Yet another astounding feat in my book considering we had to snack roughly every couple of hours to keep our energy up and our mood stable. All I could think about was food right now. Quickly as possible, I got to slicing cheese for our English muffins when suddenly one of the families' dogs came over and shoved his wet nose into my hands, eager for a taste. I gave him a shove and he backed off only to return a second time, and a third time, before its owner called him over. A lot of good that did, Bucko. On a small rock between us, I managed to spread out lunch when that thieving mutt darted back, shoving his snout right into my open-face cheese sandwich. I pushed him away hard, but he only lunged towards us again.

I persisted to protect our food by leaning over it with my body while beside us a teenage girl smeared lavish amounts of goat cheese on a long crusty baguette.

I leaned over to Scott and whispered in his ear, "I swear to God, if this dog steals our cheddar, I'm ripping that baguette right out of her hand. Eye for an eye."

Scott nodded, "Works for me."

Meanwhile Ken got to chatting with the father of the goat-cheese smearer and his buddy. They boasted about how many times they'd hiked this mountain and Ken listened intently, never mentioning his record-holding. Once we were fed, Scott made a point to educate the men on Ken's accomplishment and although Ken barely acknowledged his feat, the men stuck a sock in it.

I often feel guilty for resenting large groups of people on the trail, but that doesn't stop me. Rationally I know it's good that so many people *want* to visit the woods in their free time, but having grown up where I did, surrounded by thousands of acres of woods where the only trails were mostly those left by hunters, I rarely shared them. As I grew older, the woods became my refuge from the rest of the world, the place where I released my teenage angst and, as an adult, where I planned my dreams. Because of these experiences, I've always sought trails that were less traveled, and they're a large reason why Scott and I chose the Long Path. The wilderness is and has always been his place of solitude. It's true I've met some special people along a dirt path, but never have I found them, or rather, had a chance to get to know them, in a large group setting. Stimulus is smothering when one purposely seeks quietude.

As soon as we finished eating, we packed up and hit the trail. We hiked onto the east peak of Twin Mountain and we watched as Odie sure-footedly made his way over roots and rocks with grace. Perhaps Odie was more mountain goat that dog. This would later become Odie's trail name and Ken, well, we deemed him the Flash. Even if presently nursing an injury, only a superhuman could complete the Long Path in nine days. When he and Odie got low on water, Ken surrendered to his speedy inclinations and took off in the lead while we continued making our descent steadily. We found him waiting for us in Jimmy Dolan Notch at a cluster of trail crossings. It was time for Ken to try and hitch a ride along the nearby road back to his car. "Thank you both for further raising awareness about this trail. More people need to know about it," Ken said with solemnity.

"Our pleasure. If only folks knew this ran practically through their back-yards," I replied and Scott nodded in agreement. I only hoped that, in the future, those people wouldn't visit the trail the same days that I did.

Once Ken and Odie were out of sight, we collapsed atop a large rock mark-ing the intersection and pulled out a crumbled bag of cookies. It was three in the afternoon and we'd hiked a mere four miles, which had felt like forty. The Devil's Path had been arduous, some of the toughest miles we'd hiked. Yet Ken had been a welcome companion for the day—offering his knowledge of the region and a shared reverence for these mountains. Nonetheless, with just half the day's mileage completed, there was no time for resting.

Brushing the crumbs off our faces with dirty hands, we shouldered our packs and started up Indian Head Mountain. The ascent would be short, at only 0.6 miles, but by no means quick with a 400-foot elevation gain. We climbed hand over foot over flat-rock ledges and zig-zagged between tree roots and sharp rocks, swooshed through a dark damp spruce forest and suddenly emerged on a rock that jutted out from the side of the mountain like a jagged tooth.

We stood with our chests heaving, our bare skin beaded with sweat, and gazed out over green mountains in the foreground, the blue-grey spikes of yet more Catskill Mountains in the distance. Behind these were a shadowy line of mountains, the topography reminiscent of a steady heartbeat on a hospital monitor. Ken had told us that from this peak we would be able to see Vermont, Massachusetts, and Connecticut. I now stood gazing at some of the same peaks I'd hiked on the Appalachian Trail, and though I knew that they lay far away, I felt connected. We cognitively separate mountains by the valleys that divide them, and define them by their summits, but in truth, there was no separation between the mountain atop which I now stood and those in the distance. I had tread through their forests, drank from their springs, and gazed from their rocky outcrops, perhaps even looking back at where I now stood. I knew them well, not in their entirety, but I'd never want to. Their mystery was my heartbeat.

Just then I heard Scott flick his lighter, and the smell of tobacco smoke stirred me from my thoughts.

"Was that it?" Scott asked while exhaling. "This is the top of Indian Head?"

"Yeah, this is definitely it," I replied with a chuckle, but I knew what he meant. The intimidating ascent had gone by in a breeze.

"That wasn't so bad," he said, a smile stretching across his face.

"Thank God," I echoed, smiling in astonishment and motioning that I wanted a drag of his cigarette.

With this expansive vista and not a single soul around, we dropped our packs and treated ourselves to a lengthier break than before. Scott shot a text to Star Left with our location. We would meet her this evening and we looked forward to it.

When we loaded up our packs again, we knew there was no way to go but down. We were giddy. Like children, we teased each other while carefully maneuvering between yet more rocks and roots, shuffling and sliding down loose rock. Suddenly from around a car-sized rock, Star Left appeared, as soaked in sweat as we were.

"I can't believe you guys hiked the Devil's Path in this heat! You two are hardcore!" She announced upon seeing us, already winded. "And look at you, you're still smiling!" she said to Scott.

"I'm just happy to be done with the Devil's Path," he said, rolling his eyes.

"That makes two of us," I said.

"Well, it's all downhill from here!" replied Star Left, who had been hiking *up* to meet us from where she'd parked.

Our rambling tales then unfolded, as we told her all about the past week. She was serving as our in-person journal, an ear to our joys and hardships from the past so many days. And while Scott took the helm as narrator, it dawned on me that in the thirty minutes since we'd met up with her, I hadn't thought about my aching feet or heavy backpack. I could tell from Scott's demeanor that he too was simply reveling in the company of a friend, the day's wear falling away without notice. As we descended through lush, leafy woods we intersected, finally, with a wide path—the Overlook Trail—which we followed just a short distance to our much-anticipated lodging for the night, the Devil's Kitchen Lean-to.

Our hearts dropped. The lean-to's floorboards were crumbling and covered in black soot. An equally sooty fire ring sat directly in front of it—one too many fires had been built here on windy nights, capturing the smoke inside the shelter's three walls. Devil's Kitchen seemed a more appropriate name than ever. But there was nothing we could do—this was it. We pulled a couple of garbage bags from our packs and took a seat, and when Star Left then presented us with two homemade salads loaded with veggies, we could've been sitting in the fire ring for all we cared. We chatted between mouthfuls of crunching lettuce, carrots, and broccoli, and she shared with us that she wouldn't be spending the night because she had to work the next day. She had driven two hours just to feel the trail beneath her feet and to bring us this vegetable bounty.

"This is probably the last I'll see you until the end. I had to make it a good visit!" Star Left said with a big smile.

"Ah really? We will miss hiking with you, and you've been such an incredible trail angel too," I replied, motioning to the salad in my lap. "Do you have a big workload coming up?" I knew Star Left's job at the office could be demanding.

"Oh, just the usual, but I'm going down south this weekend, and then by next weekend you'll be done!"

My stomach dropped like a lead weight atop that sooty ground. I counted up the miles remaining in my head. Roughly 150 at the most. She was right. We hadn't even bothered to look at how many miles we had left in the journey. Each day I had simply focused on this or that ascent, one resupply or another.

"Is that right?" Scott asked, clearly as surprised as I was, although he didn't seem as somber.

"Sure is. One hundred and fifty miles. That's roughly two weeks," I answered plainly.

"Shit."

"Oh no, I'm sorry guys! I didn't mean to bum you out! You two aren't ready to be done yet, are you?"

"I'm not," I answered pitifully.

"Hmmm . . . well," Scott started with a sideways smile.

"You're ready?" I blurted at him.

"No, no, not really. I'm not ready to go back to the *real* world, but I mean, I'm ready for a shower, a cold soda, and to sit on a toilet instead of squat in the dirt."

Star Left gifted us two bottles of water, big hugs, and headed for her car. In her absence we started to hem and haw about going on farther for the night. Early this morning we'd planned to do twelve miles despite the dreaded Devil's Path, a notion we had well abandoned a couple of peaks ago, but it would be nice to at least hit double digits for the day. Not to mention, this lean-to in disrepair only dampened my spirits even more. Scott agreed and thanks to Star Left we were replenished. It was decided. We would push on another mile and a half, descending into Platte Clove. The trail was easy and graded, in fact, almost level, as we hiked on quietly. I couldn't shake the thought that within two weeks, I wouldn't be looking for a campsite or thinking about where we would get water. All that would be provided without effort, but our days would feel insignificant. We reached, in what seemed very little time, a country road flanked by a large barn, and after passing through a parking lot, shortly thereafter found a level leafy clearing just off an old woods road to set up our tent.

Scott had handled the hard day's hike on the Devil's Path in stride. I couldn't have been prouder of him. In turn, I made dinner for the both of us. It was a small token, but I had little else to offer as reward. After devouring our bowls of noodles, we hung our bear-hang in a nearby tree and in the darkness of the night laid down to sleep atop our pads. The air was warm and muggy, still I wrapped my body close around his. Soon his breath deepened and within minutes he snored lightly. While he lay fast asleep, I stayed awake, listening to the coyotes yip and howl somewhere off in the distance, imprinting the sounds, the smells, the feel of being alone in the woods with my love after a day of high mountaintops and sweeping vistas. In the treetops overhead, an owl hooted.

CHAPTER SIX

We were low on fuel and food, and totally out of whiskey. It was imperative we reach the small town of Palenville by five o'clock to pick up a maildrop of supplies from the local post office. So, although we would have preferred to spend the day in our satin sleep sack drinking crappy instant coffee, as soon as the day's heat began to soak the tent, we got a move on.

Our first climb was gradual, one in which we could just use our legs rather than our whole bodies, and after our traverse on the Devil's Path, we were relieved. However, as we continued on our way to the northern shoulder of Kaaterskill High Peak, the sun rose higher and the humidity grew heavier, making the ascent ever more challenging. When we reached our highest point at 3,000 feet, we were rewarded with a level walk through the Pine Plains, a picturesque forest dominated by spruce and eastern hemlock, reminiscent of those forests normally found at higher elevations. However, since we had reached Indian Head Mountain, we would walk the Catskill Escarpment to its end near Windham High Peak. The escarpment, which consists of the northeastern corner of the Catskill Mountains, broken only by Platte Clove, Kaaterskill Clove, and Dutcher Notch, is remarkable for its steep slopes, which with its heightened exposure and shallow soil promote lower elevation boreal forest species. Here the boughs shaded us from the sun, and we could feel cool moisture rising from beneath our feet. Walking on, the woods became dappled with hardwoods, then morphed dramatically as we strode beneath a leafy canopy, which then transformed again as we passed into a dark forest consisting mostly of eastern hemlock. Suddenly we emerged into bright open woods, mountain laurel growing along the edges of trail. This trail was truly ever changing.

Around noon, we followed a well-marked trail that wove us through a corridor of trees atop the ridge. We began to cross a shallow rocky stream that lightly flowed right off the side of the cliff. Without a word, we pivoted towards the cliff, stumbling over hundreds of round stream stones, before reaching the smooth rock face that topped the lip of the ridge. Surely this was Buttermilk Falls. From this ledge, where the stream narrowed to a thin ribbon of water, its route was obscured, although we could hear it trickling far below as it carried on its way. In the distance before us stood the mountains, undeniable and inevitable. We'd already climbed so many mountains, but still there were so many more before we'd reach the Catskills' end. Pulling out the map, I could see that we'd cross yet another waterfall not far from here. That seemed a perfect place to break for lunch.

Within short order we reached a similar stream crossing, although this one more broadly flowing. Wildcat Falls. Here the waters tumbled over a rock ledge with several other steps of ledges upon which we could sit. We took off our packs and pulled out our usual English muffins and cheese, but with town now surprisingly only about four miles ahead, we did our best not to eat too much. Surely a restaurant awaited us just in time for a mid-afternoon meal.

Our mileage rolled by easily, so much easier than the day before. We followed the ridgetop that ran parallel to Kaaterskill Clove, a deep gorge over 1,000 feet below, gazing in awe at the exposed layers of rock on the tall mountain across from us, before beginning to descend. Carefully we tread over sharply angled rocks and then slipped and slid our way through loose gravel and scree. Exposed tree roots acted as barricades, halting us periodically in what was less like hiking and more like a controlled slide.

As we rounded a bend, two large wings arose, without a sound, from the grassy woods. A large bird took its perch in a tree before us.

"Babe, babe!" I said in a loud whisper, stopping in my tracks.

Scott knew better than to speak at all and instead stood perfectly still, following my line of sight. Slowly we approached together a couple more steps, cautious to keep our footfalls quiet. Through the leafy boughs of a birch tree, we spied the bird's distinctive brown and white mottled feathers, bright yellow bill, and dark round eyes, black as night. A barred owl. He stared back at us, his ebony eyes unflinching. Owls are typically nocturnal, hunting with their keen night vision in the cool darkness of night. During the day, they will rest in the camouflage of a forested area, but to catch a glimpse of one in daylight hours is quite unusual.

Scott took a couple steps forward, confident in his approach, while I stayed back, unwavering in my stance. Clearly, he felt akin to this creature in a way that I did not. He came to stand beneath this regal bird of prey and spoke softly to it: "Thank you for your protection."

The owl turned his gaze to Scott below but remained sturdy atop its perch.

Seeing this barred owl, whose call we'd heard so many nights during our hike, seemed an affirmation of our journey. I held my breath and walked towards Scott. I stared into the owl's black eyes and motionless he returned my gaze. Warmth washed over me. If he could speak, surely, he'd say, "Fear not, for I've been watching over you and I will continue to keep you in my care. You've come this far, now just a little farther." Standing there below him, I was vulnerable but secure. The owl settled his talons on his branch and lifted his gaze, looking out over the forest. And there he sat and there we stood, sharing this cove of birch, grateful to be in his company.

I lost all sense of time—it could have been fifteen minutes or fifty—when Scott and I finally looked to one another and nodded. It seemed this owl would've been content to spend the rest of the afternoon on his perch overhead, but for us, it was time to go. As we turned to walk away, he took to flight, swooping down and nearly touching our heads before again rising. He came to perch on a high branch, his back to us, facing northward down the trail. And so, under his watch, we too hiked northward, every step bringing us closer to our goal.

The trail led us down, down, down one of the steepest gravel roads I've ever walked in my life and in about a mile we emerged from the woods onto a paved road where we were met with one of the most glorious sights a thru-hiker could ever see.

Ice Cold Drinks. Ice Cream. Snacks. $1 each.

A chorus of angels sang on high as we read the chalk-scrawled message on a blackboard that leaned against a little red garden shed. The shed's large wooden doors were thrust open and surrounding it were vibrantly colored potted plants. Although our trail went left, we made a sharp right directly into this heavenly abundance of refreshment. Inside we found a full-size refrigerator/freezer beside a simple countertop lined with small baskets filled with little bags of chips, granola bars, packets of crackers, and my favorite processed delicacy—Cheese Doodles. Opening the fridge revealed three shelves stocked with flavored sparkling water, a plethora of fruit juices, and Scott's preferred trail beverage—Gatorade. In the freezer were boxes of every kind of ice cream cone and ice cream sandwich one could dream of, so jam-packed that a box tumbled out at our feet. Never had I seen so many frosty options. We stood in awe and for a moment I couldn't decide just what to grab first, but our indecision was fleeting; I grabbed a chocolate chip ice cream cone and an orange seltzer, Scott an ice cream sandwich and Gatorade, and took a seat at the provided wooden bench complete with an umbrella overtop. It wasn't until we'd crumpled our wrappers and were slurping our last sips that we remembered town still awaited. This could have been it and, I swear, it would have been enough.

Afterwards we cleaned up, courtesy of complimentary wet-wipes—also a hiker favorite—and grabbed a couple small bags of chips and Cheese Doodles for our packs. In doing so, we also found a notepad for comments and requests. We scribbled down a message expressing the deepest of gratitude, signing it Bot (short for the Botanical Hiker) and Wise Man, which Star Left had dubbed Scott. We looked to the farmhouse that sat back from the road, knowing that surely it must be home to the kind souls who provided this oasis, and smiled. On the trail, you never know just where generosity might appear. Likely this roadside stop offered reprieve to not only hikers but the other residents of this quiet street. Before shouldering our packs, we pulled out our Ziploc bags that served as wallets and were thankful to find some singles—we hadn't even bothered to look, but my God, we would have given any size bill for these amenities—and shoved them happily into the skinny slot of a tin money box. Although we had just one short mile left to go until downtown, Scott grabbed another cold Gatorade for the road.

We continued to walk the residential road a little way and then after straddling a guardrail, popped out on a main road. A roadside sign read: *Welcome to Palenville: Home of Rip Van Winkle.* "We've been here before!" I suddenly exclaimed. How could I possibly forget a town with a claim to fame such as Rip Van Winkle. In Washington Irving's *Rip Van Winkle*, he'd stated that Van Winkle had lived in a village at the base of the Catskill Mountains, mountains through which he'd regularly saunter. In the nineteenth century, Palenville, as well as numerous other small Catskill towns, laid claim to his place of residence, but given Palenville's popularity, it stuck. I felt a bit like Van Winkle myself, having wandered out of the mountains to find myself in a familiar place, and like him, I was changed, although not only outwardly but inwardly, from that person I'd been when we'd last visited. "You're right!" answered Scott. "This is the way that we drove to Acra Point."

There is a certain reward in arriving in a known place by foot rather than by car, that knowledge that your *two feet* carried you here of their own volition. This very road we had driven numerous times, two hours from home, to one of our favorite spots for a two-day hike and overnight camp—a portion of the Long Path that led from Black Dome Valley up and over Acra Point to Windham High Peak. On this stretch of trail was where we had first fallen in love with the Catskills. It had ignited our interest in discovering more of this region and I had realized then that, even while hiking the Finger Lakes Trail, I'd never truly experienced the breadth of its majesty. Now we had returned to this town and would revisit this portion of trail as thru-hikers, but not without some serious sweat. Palenville does indeed lay at the very base of the rocky Catskill giants, and typically, when we reached here by vehicle, we still had thirty minutes maneuvering a winding road through a narrow pass, traveling up, up, up, before we'd even reach the trailhead. On one occasion, my truck had overheated in its strain. If that had seemed an arduous journey by automobile, it would surely prove an even greater one by foot. I could hardly wait.

We walked the narrow shoulder of a road, bustling with tourists seeking their own experience in the Catskills, and soon reached a little market that had been listed in the guidebook as a good place to stop for resupply: The Circle W. Just outside the front door, an old-fashioned thermometer read: ninety degrees. Ungodly hot for late September. But once inside, we were blasted by cold air conditioning that chilled the sweat pouring down our temples. On their modest shelving, we found an array of gourmet items with equally gourmet prices, but much to our delight, also a gourmet lunch menu that was, in contrast, very affordable. The bounty of Palenville just kept on coming as we ordered two paninis complete with horseradish cheddar, caramelized onions, fresh wilted spinach, and sliced tomato, and a large Greek salad on the side. We sat down at a small table nearest the outlets and pulled out our devices to charge up: two phones, one camera, and a tablet. When these were finished, we would switch them out for our two backup battery packs. When not in use we kept our electronics off, but who knew when we might see an outlet again.

While waiting for our food, we saw a letter framed on the wall thanking the business owner for opening this little shop again. Apparently, the Circle W had been in operation since 1908 but had closed its doors in the mid-1990s. This shop had been a local fixture: the go-to diner, grocery, bait and tackle, and hardware and even a place where you could pick up a pair of dungarees. Roughly a decade ago, the business was purchased by Gary and Patti Harvey, a family whose ancestors had long inhabited Palenville. The Harveys renovated while still keeping in line with the shop's quaint charm, and breathed into it new life, as evidenced by the patrons entering and exiting in a stream. When our food arrived—crispy bread with oily melted cheese and our salad complete with feta cheese piled high and flanked by dolmas—it was even more delicious than we'd anticipated. After devouring as much as we could stomach, we wrapped half of our sandwiches in foil for dinner later that night and got to chatting with the employees. They were funky fresh in attire and attitude—think twenty- and thirty-something hippy meets hipster—and gracious enough to fill our water bottles for us with ice cold water and let us hang out as we waited for our electronics to finish recharging.

We were beginning to realize that these little Catskill towns had an earth-loving, artistic vibe that we hadn't anticipated, and it thrilled us to no end. Surely it was partly due to the influx of folks from New York City but rather than use their wealth to reshape these towns into mini city strips lined with stores out of touch with the needs of the locals, these new residents had seemingly used their affluence to enhance these towns, keeping within the down-to-earth feel of small town America.

After a good long while, we thanked our newfound friends and reluctantly exited the swinging front door into the hot sun. The heat hung so heavy around us it nearly took our breath away as we now walked with full bellies to the post office where we picked up our box of supplies and then onto the Dollar General to further resupply. There, we dropped our packs in a shopping cart and once again happily walked up and down the air-conditioned aisles selecting a box of this and a box of that. The amount of packaged food a hiker must eat is why I learned how to forage in the first place. But a hiker cannot survive on wild greens alone. When the tiny woman at the register overheard me telling Scott just how we would repack our snacks into Ziplocs, she offered us a handful of extra grocery bags. Such kind gestures take on so much more significance than in our everyday life simply because they *are* so much more significant. Plastic bags can mean the difference between wet or dry clothes after a heavy storm, or moldy or fresh bread because of the Northeast's humid climate. And the fact is, in our ordinary existence, many of us, *especially* those of us who have the luxury to take a long hike, take for granted such things as dry clothes and fresh food. Hiking makes you grateful not only for these simple needs being met but for those who help you along the way. Thank you, Dollar General cashier.

Outside the store we took a seat on the curb and emptied every single item from the body of our packs, then ripped into cardboard packaging, sorted food into dry bags, and with all of our might, squished our now very full food bags back into our packs amidst the rest of our gear. We aimed to pack the greatest weight in the center and against our backs: sleeping bag and tent stuff on bottom, food bags in the middle because they are the heaviest, and clothes on top.

We made our last stop at the Mobile gas station to load up on smokes. We had to drop our backpacks to dig out our money and also to search out a snug place to shove said cigarettes, and in our spectacle, got to chatting with the man behind the counter who had skin the color of dark sand.

"Are you two walking a long way?" he asked.

"Yes, all the way to the Adirondacks," Scott answered.

"How far is that?"

"About another 140 miles," Scott replied.

The man's eyes went large and a big smile formed on his face.

"Where are you coming from?" he asked.

"New York City," Scott answered.

"New York City?!" the man said with a gasp.

"Yep. It sure is hot out today though," I chimed in.

"Oh yes, it is. But I think that's great. Where I am from in India, people walk everywhere. I used to walk ten miles in heat just like this to and from work and to the market. No one walks here. Everyone drives," he explained, motioning to the many motorists zipping by on the road outside. "It's true. Too much traffic too," I said, rolling my eyes.

"Yes. I have a car, but I still like to walk. Keeps me in good shape," the man said with a smile.

"Helps to counter these!" Scott said with a chuckle holding up a pack of cigarettes.

"Oh yes, those are very bad for you. You should stop," the man said, shaking his head.

"I know," Scott said, shoving the pack in the top zipper of his backpack.

"Do you need some water?" the man asked as we hoisted our heavy packs once again.

"Oh no thank you, we filled up at the market a ways back," I answered.

And just like that, Palenville presented us with more kindness. Walking slows one down enough to not only appreciate it but to receive it.

Finally, it was time to head for those bare rocks we'd seen from the escarpment earlier in the day. They now rose roughly 2,000 feet above us to South Mountain on the escarpment. With our packs laden with four liters of water each—there was no guaranteed water source in our near future—and four days' worth of food, we took many a break along the endless zig-zagging switchbacks. We watched as the valley dipped farther and farther below us, and although it was a torturous climb, thanks to our visit in town, we still walked with smiles.

About one-third of the way from the top, we found a grassy spot at a bend in the trail beside a slender, dried-up streambed. A sweeping view of the mountains through which we'd traveled spread before us. An owl hooted, *hoo, hoo, too-HOO, hoo hoo, too-HOO-aw,* overhead . . . and just like that, we'd found our place of rest for the night. We pulled out the tent, put it up in a jiffy, and then wondered what to do next. Without water to fetch nor dinner to cook, making camp had been a breeze. So, we unscrewed the plastic cap from our bottle of whiskey, unwrapped our paninis and took a seat on a ledge just outside our tent. Darkness fell before we even finished eating and as we sat by the light of a slivered moon, a barred owl hooted faintly in the direction of the mountain from whence we'd come earlier in the day. From nearby treetops, we heard a bold, *hoo, hoo, too-HOO, hoo hoo, too-HOO-aw,* in response. Perhaps that owl we'd shared space with earlier in the day was passing along the word to keep an eye on us. It sure seemed something, be it the owl of the forest itself, had us in its care.

CHAPTER SEVEN

Teeny yellow worms hung wriggling on single strands of wispy silk from limbs and leaves. Repeatedly we had to stop to wipe clean our arms and legs and patiently pick them off each other's heads. The trail was a webby gauntlet. On Scott they particularly liked to dangle from the ends of his curls, swinging back and forth in his line of sight. For me, they preferred my eyelashes. These critters were harmless but gross, and we wondered what had deemed today Day of the Worm.

We reached the top of South Mountain and then stumbled upon two exposed rock ledges. Atop one sat a behemoth of a boulder, and the other was severed with crevices that ran deep and narrow down to the earth below, aptly named Boulder Rock and Split Rock respectively. These smooth rock ledges were formed by the scraping of a glacier. The boulder, too, sat here because a glacier had carried it, the same glacier that also had filled the wide valley we now saw below us. Boulder Rock and Split Rock quite literally have remained since the end of the Ice Age. From here we surveyed a tremendous view of the Hudson Valley. It was impossible to imagine before us a swollen landscape of ice considering the bowl of green, patched here and there in autumn colors, that now laid below.

It wasn't long before we reached the former site of the Catskill Mountain House, a once prestigious inn for the likes of politicians, renowned artists, and the wealthy. President Theodore Roosevelt and Thomas Cole were just a couple of its illustrious visitors. The Catskill Mountain House operated from 1824 to 1941 and was, for much of its life, considered a jewel set in the heart of the Catskills. For over sixty years guests endured a five-hour ride by stagecoach that carried them twelve miles, climbing 1,600 feet, to its doors. Later, when a railway was constructed, guests enjoyed the relative comforts of train service. The inn could accommodate two to three hundred people at a time. In its prime, four stories tall and built in neo-classical form, it resembled Greek architecture, a row of noble pillars holding it strong. But all that remained now were just a few flat slate rocks pressed into the ground and a couple of lonely-looking stone posts that had served as gates. A single stalk of yarrow, a resilient wildflower scientifically named *Achillea millefolium* after the Greek hero, Achilles, stood amidst the remains bearing a late-season cluster of ivory flowers.

When it was revealed in the 1880s that Slide Mountain, which lay far to the southwest of this site, was in fact the tallest mountain in the Catskills and not Kaaterskill High Peak, which can be viewed from the inn, the establishment weathered a hard blow. The inn was also discovered to sit on a precipice at 2,250 feet, rather than the 3,000 feet that owner Charles Beach had claimed. But eventually even these details mattered not, as its elite visitors' interest in the Catskills waned and they turned their attention and affection toward the Adirondacks. In 1962, the state of New York acquired the land and, in 1963, burned the inn to the ground. It seemed tragic that the structure had not been preserved, but we were grateful that at least the view remained.

The Catskill Mountain House, set before the flat rock ledge of a grassy plateau, had held vigil over a sweeping view into the valley and the mountains beyond. Servants would come knocking on doors to announce the sunrise— that's right, the sunrise itself—so that one could better appreciate the view from their balcony. Standing here, even in midday, I could understand why. From here we could see all the way to the Berkshires. With my imagination I drew a dotted line, like that which one would find on a map, up and over the mountains to each of those faraway peaks I knew from the Appalachian Trail. I envisioned a new line tracing my route to come on the Long Path. On numerous paths, my feet had crisscrossed these mountains, but this present experience was wholly new and different from those that I had experienced before. Even after so many miles I still didn't know what might happen next, what I might see or smell, or feel, or even fear . . . but for me, that is truly living. The mountains have the unintentional power to make me surrender to the unknown, and in that I find sanctuary. Perhaps this view had provided a similar experience, for its long-ago visitors—an all-at-once embrace of the future, a revelation of the possibilities, the giant scope that can be one's life.

When we reached the picnic area at North Lake campground, we found it, much to our delight, without another soul. Dropping our packs at a nearby picnic table, we pulled out a little vial of Dr. Bronner's liquid soap, razors, and combs. We'd learned from a couple of day hikers in passing that this campground, now abandoned for the season, had hot showers. Who knew when we'd get a shower again—and I swear I could still feel those teeny tiny worms wriggling in all the places I couldn't see. Stepping into the ladies' bathhouse I found a clean white shower stall with a wooden bench for my few belongings. I hung my bandana that normally served as a sweat rag on the nearby hook so that I could reach it easily upon exiting—today it would serve as a towel. But when I went to turn on the water all I spied was a tiny metal showerhead and a single large metal knob. *Just how did one use this thing?* I tried turning—nothing. I tried pushing it up and down—nothing. Finally, in frustration I punched it and oh, sweet Jesus! Hot water sprayed out of that little spigot like a firehose. For a whole thirty seconds. *What the hell?* I punched it again and sure enough, more water! So be it. I must have punched that knob twenty times by the time I was finished.

"Man, I don't feel like going anywhere now," I proclaimed, plopping down beside him and lay my bandana out to dry in the hot sun.

"I'm relieved you're saying that. It's like all the energy has drained right out of me, I'm so relaxed," he said, wriggling out his arms.

"I know I feel like I'm wrapped in a silky robe reclining in a lounge chair not sitting in my sweaty hiking clothes on this hard-ass wooden bench."

"We could just stay here the rest of the day, go for a swim in the lake, and take another shower. Hell, we could take showers all day!" Scott exclaimed.

This indeed sounded like a perfect plan—a level tent site in a completely empty campground with running water. But we had a schedule to keep up. It was already midway through the last week in September and Scott had to be back to work by the start of the second week in October. We were cutting it close. "I wish we could just keep hiking," Scott said, as if reading my very thoughts. "What if we didn't have to get back to work?"

"One day babe. One day," I replied and gave him a kiss on his forehead. We had worked hard all summer at building up our company, Hike Local, offering guided hikes and plant walks in our region, and had done well, but not well enough to quit our day jobs just yet, which was our ultimate goal. With a successful hiking company, we could offer hikes wherever we wished on our own schedule, but for now we swung both the dream and the demands.

"How about a snack for now," I said.

"Deal," Scott replied.

While eating, I pulled out the guidebook and found that it would be seven miles until we hit another water source, at a place called Dutcher Notch. Once at the notch we'd then have to climb 500 vertical feet over a mere three-tenths of a mile to reach an allegedly dependable spring. We'd already learned the hard way that in autumn, our *dependable* water sources were not always so dependable. We questioned if we should simply fill up our reserves for camp that night, but that would mean carrying a whopping four liters each, which translates to eight pounds each. Screw it, we'd take half that and trust the spring would be running.

Reluctantly we packed up our gear and, at nearly noon, set out for ten more miles of hiking, our sights set on the Batavia Kill Lean-to, the very place we'd camped during our first excursion into the Catskills together. When we were last there, the Batavia Kill which ran beside the lean-to was fast-flowing, so perhaps we could avoid that awful descent in the notch altogether and just push on to camp.

Leaving the picnic area, we walked a sandy trail littered with pine needles between enormous boulders, each boulder comprised of thousands of small multicolored round stones, each a different expression of earth's hues. We surveyed our picturesque surroundings from one lookout after the next: Artist Rock, Newman's Ledge, and North Point. At North Point we twirled around, appreciating a 360-degree view. Heat radiated from the rocks beneath our feet, which had been baking all day in the sun, and a heavy haze of humidity shrouded the mountains farthest away. Just beyond the flat-faced boulder, we lucked out on a grassy patch beneath the cover of a birch tree and broke for lunch. On this ninety-degree day in September here in upstate New York, shade was a real commodity. We chuckled again at our having ever set out with a fifteen-degree sleeping bag for this journey.

After lunch we carried on to the summit of North Mountain, whisking through a spruce-fir forest thriving below 3,500 feet, and then Stoppel Point. It was here, while descending its northern side, that we spied the ghastly wreckage of a small plane. In May of 1983, twenty-six-year-old Rex Miller ignored warnings from a flight school manager that weather was bad and visibility poor, and took flight from Poughkeepsie, heading for Watertown. Within thirty minutes, he tore through the treetops at roughly 3,400 feet, crashing to his death on the rocky peak. We looked up at the bright sunlight shining through the open canopy and wondered if this window to the sky had always been so. The heaps of wreckage were the only memorial to this man who had flown solo. Had he had left family behind? Friends? What a terrifying end he must have faced in his last seconds.

After lingering long enough to conjure too many dreadful images, we made a steep descent towards Dutcher Notch. I tuned into the swishing of our feet through the leaves underfoot and imagined the sound sweeping away all that darkness. Suddenly the sound of voices trickled through the trees below and I lifted my gaze to see four hikers approaching. They hiked slowly but steadily ascending the steep mountainside, each with packs as large as our own. As they grew close, we could see three men and a woman huffing and puffing, looking just as weary as we likely did.

"Hi there!" the broad-shouldered man in the lead announced himself. "Hey!" said the strong-bodied woman beside him with a smile. She had a long braid just like my own and I had the feeling that she was as pleasantly surprised as we were to see fellow backpackers. This was Duke and his wife Lilah, out for a hike with their friends Damon and John—and John's teenage nephew who had breezed far ahead—on the twenty-four-mile Escarpment Trail, which for most of its length runs concurrently with the Long Path.

"How y'all doing?" I returned. Perhaps we could also get some reliable information from these folks about the trail ahead.

"Where are you coming from?" Scott asked them, as if reading my mind.

"Batavia Kill Lean-to," John answered.

"Oh wow. Awesome. Is the stream there running?" Scott asked in return.

"Yes!" John answered, as if relieved by this fact. "But not at the lean-to. You'll have to hike about three-tenths of a mile beyond it to find water."

"Are you two planning to fill up at Dutcher?" Duke then asked.

"Yes. Is it running?" I asked again.

"Barely. We climbed down, I mean *straight* down, to get water from the spring but it was basically a leafy puddle. We pumped everything we could out of it. Do you have a pump? If you don't you won't get anything out of it, and there's probably hardly anything left," Damon explained.

"Nope, no pump," Scott said.

"Well, we did run into a ranger that claimed three-quarters of a mile to the east is a stream that's lightly running, but there's no sign of that on the map and who knows when he was actually last down that way," Lilah added.

"Damn," I replied, dumbfounded with just how we were going to get more water. I was already beating myself up for only taking two liters each. Who knew how much we had left in our bladders but with the afternoon as hot as it'd been, likely we were near the end of our stores and we still had two more summits to reach before our descent to the Batavia Kill.

"Okay, well thanks so much for saving us the haul. We'll just hike onto Batavia then," I said with more confidence than I felt. It was already nearly five o'clock in the evening.

"Yeah, the lean-to is really nice. It's brand new and you can't miss it. Don't stay at the one that has been eaten by the porcupines for the last quarter century. The new one still smells like fresh lumber. Even left you guys a bundle of wood! We were in no hurry, so we chopped up some downed trees for the next hikers," John said, giving us something to look forward to.

"Wow. Thanks guys," Scott said, then added, "Hey, we're thru-hiking the trail, check out our journey online at the blog if you want, we'll definitely give you a shout-out. You guys were a big help!" He motioned to me to give them a business card.

"That's so cool. We're just out for a couple nights but maybe we'll see you on down the trail one day," said Lilah.

And with that we wished each other luck and headed our opposite directions. Little did I know then that Duke and Lilah—two months later while out for a motorcycle ride—would, by chance, stop into the little café where I worked a couple days a week. Every once in a while, the serendipity of the trail does sometimes bleed into everyday life. The key is that all persons remain attuned to that trail state of mind.

"Shit, we were counting on that water," I mumbled to Scott under my breath as we hiked on.

"Yep," Scott replied.

CHAPTER EIGHT

"How much do you have, babe?" I asked, as I struggled to wrench my water bladder from my backpack.

It was five-fifteen and we'd just reached Dutcher Notch. Even now as sat atop a downed tree, our legs quivered from the long descent. The air felt heavy and wet, far too hot and humid for autumn.

Scott slid his Gatorade bottle out of his stretchy side pocket and held it up. "About half a liter."

Maybe that was the trick—good ol' fashioned water bottles. A water bladder fits inside a sleeve on the inner backside of the pack, therefore, to reach it requires removing half of the backpack's contents. You'd think by now a backpacking company would come up with a better system.

"Okay, let me see what I've got here. Maybe I have enough for both of us."

With a tug I ripped the bladder from my pack and held it in the air. My already dry mouth suddenly felt like sandpaper. The bladder was nearly sucked dry. Maybe a half liter at best.

"Shit," I said with a sigh. "The one time we choose to trust the water source and it's dry." I internally chastised myself for not taking just one more liter each.

"That's all you've got?" Scott said, his eyes wide.

"Yes. That's it," I said, pulling out my water bottles to double check. Both were empty.

"How far are we from the lean-to?" Scott asked.

I was already pulling the map from the top of my pack. Unfolding it hastily, I read the mileage between the tiny red triangles that served as waypoints. "Looks like three-and-a-half miles."

"Well that's not so bad. I mean I'm tired but that shouldn't take so long," Scott said with a shrug.

But he couldn't see the story the map was showing. Two summits stood in our path—the Arizona Plateau and Blackhead Mountain. To better understand our route, I unfolded our crinkled trail guide pages. It looked like we could summit the plateau within just eight-tenths of a mile, but it would require an 800-foot ascent. From there we would climb another 600 feet to the top of Blackhead Mountain. But there then was more:

Reach the summit of Blackhead Mountain, the second highest point on the Long Path and the fourth highest mountain in the Catskills. The Long Path drops precipitously down the north face of Blackhead, plunging over ledges in one of the steepest descents in the Catskills.

Visions of Slide Mountain flashed before my eyes. *Plunging over ledges in one of the steepest descents in the Catskills?* My heart fluttered and I felt my breath catch in my chest. I passed the pages to Scott, my whole body filled with dread.

"What?" Scott asked innocently.

"Read it," I said, dropping my gaze to the dirt at my feet.

"Fuck," Scott said, letting the pages fall to the ground. "How is that possible? Steeper than Slide?"

"*One* of the steepest," I clarified. But I knew I was full of shit and I folded. "You're right. They didn't give us that kind of warning for Slide. I don't know that it will be worse, couldn't be really, but it might be just as bad. The climb alone will take us longer and then we have to go down *that*? Shit, if we only had water we could camp here for the night and tackle that in the morning."

"We could try the stream to the east. Where the ranger said there was water," Scott suggested.

"Yeah, we could. But what if there's no water there or we can't find it? If we hike down that trail and find water then yeah, we can just set up camp here and hit it in the morning. But if not, we will have wasted valuable time and then still have to make the climb." I could hear my speech getting harried.

We gazed to the east in bewilderment. Then I saw Scott shift his gaze to our feet, following the Long Path northward as it snaked across the ground, disappearing into the wall of trees covering the mountainside. My heart still fluttered. Literally. I didn't know if it was the heat of the day or the stress of the circumstances, but with every other breath I took it felt as if my heart had tiny wings that pitter-pattered. To be honest, this had been happening for the last couple of days and I knew climbing another mountain, exhausted and dehydrated, was the last thing I should do but the thought of a dry camp and a dry climb in the morning depleted me even more.

"I don't know, hon. What do *you* think we should do?"

I was tempted to hike on, but I knew he was exhausted too, and the last thing I wanted to do was push us *both* up these mountains in compromised states.

He looked at me long and hard.

"We should do it," he said, his voice now calm.

I looked at my watch. In all our indecision we had already wasted thirty minutes. It was now five forty-five. "It's possible we won't be to the top until dark."

In the beginning of our hike, the sun didn't set until eight-thirty, and we'd reveled in our long days. However, we'd been growing increasingly aware, especially over the last week, how we repeatedly erred in our estimations. We had after all been hiking for nearly a month, and the sun now set roughly an hour earlier.

"Not if we hike fast," he said, continuing to eye the trail that disappeared into the darkness of pines.

"Hon, we can't hike that fast, especially with the little bit of water that we have."

If we hiked on, I needed him to have a realistic handle on the commitment we were making. My heart still fluttered. Likely this was my body telling me to *slow down*.

"What do you want to do?" he asked me then.

"I want to hike on," I answered fast and without thought. "I mean at least we know there's water at Batavia."

"Exactly. We can do it," he said, taking a meager sip off his water bottle and shoving it back in his pack.

"Okay. But we have got to pace ourselves a little. Promise me you won't barrel up the mountain."

I knew he could push himself too hard and quite frankly so could I, and this wasn't the place nor time to do it. I was keenly aware of our isolation. In this moment, I was acutely aware that we were small and the mountains so very big, and all the rest of the world seemed well beyond walking distance. I checked my phone just for the hell of it. No bars—there would be no calling for help. Reaching the Batavia Kill depended solely on us.

"Yeah, sure," he said, already picking up his pack. He was used to my being concerned about him, but what he didn't know was that this time, I was also concerned about me. I didn't feel right. But I wasn't about to tell him that now.

"Alright, that's it then. Let's hit it," I said, taking the smallest sip from my water bladder's hose and stuffing it back inside my pack along with my clothes bag and food sack.

I took a deep breath and let him lead the way. The sweat that had covered my body finally felt cool against my skin and the black dirt beneath my feet was cold and damp through the soles of my shoes. We disappeared into the trees at the base of the Arizona Plateau and Scott started up with a steadiness. I lagged and paused, turning my gaze to the treetops. Our first climb up Peekamoose had been humbling. I knew better than to approach this mountain with the mentality of a conqueror. It was formidable and we would only make it over its summit safely with the mountain's acceptance. I silently asked the mountain for grace.

But rather than form actual words in my mind, I requested with my whole self: *Please be good to us.*

We slipped on loose scree as we climbed rocky trail that shot, nearly vertical, up the side of the mountain. Scott gained speed, moving faster than I'd ever seen him go, like someone had lit a tiny flame beneath each foot. I ascended steadily behind, pacing my breath and breathing deeply through my nose as slowly as I could. I urged him to slow and he paused to take a drink from his water bottle, shoved it hard back into its sleeve, and carried on with the same momentum as before. I drew my attention to my heartbeat, which in this moment felt solid. Perhaps I could will it to remain so—grounded and steady. I connected each fleeting footstep with the damp ground beneath my feet. When we could see the edge of the plateau, we collapsed, still strapped into our packs, against the sloping mountainside. We were just fifteen feet from the top. We took luxuriously long gulps from our ever-depleting water caches and hastily ripped open granola bars, shoving the dry bars into our mouths.

"Shit," Scott said, still regaining his breath and rolling his eyes. Sweat poured from his temples.

"I know." This was all I could muster.

"How much farther now?" Scott asked.

"Three more miles," I answered. If he'd take that as good or bad news, I didn't know.

"Fine," he simply replied.

After a few minutes of break, we helped each other up to standing and pushed on. Once atop the Arizona Plateau, we persisted on thankfully level trail. We would walk this flat ledge for about a mile before beginning the final climb to the top of Blackhead Mountain. Perhaps it was the way the day's yellow light was turning golden or maybe just endorphins, but I felt my concerns burn off, dissipate into the ethers, as we hiked over the now-grassy trail lined with paper birch, mountain ash, maple, and beech. Their leaves were yellow and scarlet and every shade of brown. Thorny blackberry brambles and drying blueberry bushes lined the trail and boulders sat in this mountaintop garden like elders keeping vigil. Now and again when the trail would widen, we could glimpse Blackhead's rounded summit looming before us. When we passed grassy clearings, I envisioned us stopping and standing still with arms spread wide in reverence for this place. Despite our pointed focus on reaching camp and finding water, this shoulder of the mountain had such power of presence it demanded our attention.

"How many feet is the ascent?" Scott stopped suddenly just as we started to ascend, and asked without turning around to face me.

"Six hundred feet." Again, was my answer good or bad?

"Okay. Two hundred less than the last one."

He was behaving so stoically—too stoically—it made me nervous. Surely he wanted to throw down his sticks and scream. I knew because that's what I usually do. I have noticed that sometimes the calmer I am, the greater the storm inside me, a sort of overcompensation.

I took a deep breath and a small sip from my water bladder, which gurgled, a sure sign that it was nearly empty. Yet still my heart did not flutter. Maybe I was wrong about Scott's stoicism. Maybe the plateau had taken effect on him, too.

The ascent was relatively gradual to start, along a grassy trail, but it soon grew steep and we forced our feet against loose rock, climbing with our whole bodies over sharply angled stones and boulders of every shape. The sun was blindingly orange-red as it started to set behind the dark outline of Blackhead Mountain. From this height, I swear I could reach out and touch it. This place was strange—beautiful and rugged—and so was the collection of plants at my feet. Dandelion, blackberries, Virginia waterleaf, and violets—plants normally found at lower elevations in the Catskill region—mingling with the typical evergreens and birches of the High Peaks, provided evidence of the many intrepid hikers that had sought this summit. These plants had likely been carried on the soles of their shoes, worked into the loose soil with each footfall. We may have been alone on this mountain, but we were not alone in our desire to be close to it, to touch it, to feel it, to know it. Just then, when nearly to the top, I heard Scott gasp. I looked up to see him gazing out over breathtaking view of the valley below and the many smaller mountains encircling us like islands in the sky. We both halted and I nearly went weak at the knees.

"Woohoo!!!" Scott let out a battle cry that ripped the silence and raised his trekking pole high to the sky.

"Oww oww!!" I hollered back, standing on my tiptoes, overlooking the land we now knew well below.

We turned and shouted big open mouth cries at each other. Wide grins stretched across our faces. We were so close now.

Grabbing thick roots for handles and pushing against sharp rocks for steps, we finally climbed our way to the summit. Suddenly we were swallowed by the boreal forest. The air was cool as we tread swiftly between the stout balsam firs, their needles scratching our arms and imprinting their sweet scent upon our skin. Finally, we reached the large boulder that marks its summit . . . and collapsed. Relief swept over us as we rolled off our packs and laid on our backs flat atop its cold solid surface in a nest of dark fragrant evergreens.

"It's getting dark fast," I said to Scott while peering up at the sky that was quickly deepening into blues and grays. I thought I could even see a couple of stars peeking out.

"Sure is!" he replied, his tone oddly giddy. "You feeling okay?"

"Yeah, I'm alright, kinda heady," he said, pushing himself up to a sitting position. "Whoo!" he blurted stumbling back onto his elbows.

"How much water do you have left?" I demanded, pulling his water bottle out of its sleeve.

I held it up only to see it held nearly the same amount it had down at Dutcher Notch.

"You hardly drank a thing!"

"I'm fine. Had to save it," he said with a slur.

"Drink, now," I ordered, shoving it at him.

"We have to save it!" He said, with a wide-eyed crazy look.

"Not that bad. You have to stay hydrated!" I ordered back. "I still have some. We'll be fine," I added, although I didn't really know how much I had left in my bladder.

He needed food. Hastily I rummaged through the top of my pack and pulled out a granola bar.

"Eat this," I said, sliding it across the rock.

"I'm not hungry," he said, after a big gulp of water.

"Hon, we just ascended 1,400 feet. We have a mile and a half to go. We need to eat."

I pulled out another bar for myself. I too felt heady even if my fluttering heart had finally grounded itself.

"Okay," he whined, like a little boy being told to eat his greens.

We unwrapped our bars sloppily and shoved dry-as-sand granola into our mouths. By the time we'd finished, it was nearly dark.

"I needed that," Scott said, already sounding more normal. "Where does the trail go from here?"

I looked around and saw the faint shimmer of a blue metal disk on a nearby evergreen tree. Walking across the boulder, I could faintly see the outline of trail leading into blackness, complete and utter blackness.

"Over here. We're going to need our headlamps," I said, my thoughts shifting into gear to figure out just how we were going to descend this mountain that we'd worked so hard to climb.

"Shit. I can hardly see the trail," Scott said, now standing beside me. "We sure will."

I squinted to see the time on my digital watch, seven-fifteen. It shouldn't be this dark yet, but time was different here in the boreal forest. That, we'd already learned. It may as well have been midnight.

"Are you ready to descend the steepest mountain in the Catskills?" I asked, peering hard into Scott's eyes, searching for a confirmation that he felt more centered.

"What choice do we have?" he replied, his gaze steady.

"Not much."

"Let's get started then. We'll take it slow," he said calmly.

"Yes, we'll have to. Let's just hope it's not like Slide."

"It better not be."

We strapped on our headlamps and slipped off the boulder into the darkness, hoping against hope we wouldn't have to shimmy our entire bodies down smooth rock faces for the next two long miles. In short order we were navigating makeshift stone steps three feet tall, turning around to hug each boulder as we descended what felt like a tremendous spiraling staircase. This was probably one of the dumbest decisions we had made yet . . . but these are the terms of the trail . . . once you've set your course, there's no turning back.

By the light of headlamps that illuminated no more than fifteen feet ahead of us, we shuffled our feet over loose rock and eased our way down steeply sloping smooth rock. We scrambled down more boulders, using birch roots, when available, like ropes, and skated over scree. The trail at times looked like a black shoot that, should we lose our footing, could send us sailing right off the side of the mountain and into the starry sky. Lights from homes and roadways speckled the surrounding mountains and valley below, and as the night grew darker and our eyes adjusted, the sky was ever punctuated with twinkling pinholes of starlight. For a time, my fear vanished, replaced by sheer exaltation. This was just us—two bobbing headlamps in the darkness—and Blackhead Mountain. It was an honor that we experience her in the quiet black night. She was a slumbering giant granting us safe passage. No longer could I focus on reaching the lean-to and finding water, but rather I was wholly present in this dream, her dream, where anything could happen and all that mattered was our next footfall.

Roughly two-thirds of a mile down Blackhead, the trail shifted from a rocky slalom to something that resembled a true trail. Rather than sharing space with the stars, we resumed our place amidst the trees, deep in the forest. The descent was still steep but at least we could *hike* rather than climb. Now moving swiftly as we could, we were alert to periodically lift our gaze from the trail so to see the next reflective metal disk that marked our route. Thank God trail maintainers had thought to use these, for we never would have found our way otherwise. Moths circled the bright lights from our headlamps incessantly and our ankles rolled on the rocky terrain. We hollered curses in frustration while the coyotes yipped in chorus somewhere in the distance. My fears threatened to overwhelm me . . . *What if one of us twisted an ankle or fell and broke a leg . . . there's no way we'd be able to hike out of here.* An owl hooted from the canopy above, a reminder to keep faith and surrender to the moment.

"How much farther do you think we have?" Scott asked, his tone anxious.

"I don't know. It seems we must have gone a mile, but we've been moving so slow."

We kept our eyes sharp on the trail markers, hoping that the next one would be yellow, blazing the way to the lean-to and even more importantly, the Batavia Kill.

"There!" Scott shouted, stopping dead in his tracks.

I shone my headlamp in the direction of his and spied a yellow disc.

"Oh, thank God, hon, I don't think I would've seen that," I said.

"We're not missing this camp!"

That last quarter mile to the lean-to felt like the longest we'd ever tread. We hiked on, shining our poor headlights through the darkness in search of the new lean-to that the other hikers had told us about back at Dutcher Notch. *You can't miss it!* one of them had said.

Finally, we arrived before the familiar Batavia Kill Lean-to that was just as we remembered . . . porcupine-chewed and mouse-ridden. It was nearly nine o'clock.

We dropped our packs and headed farther down the trail to where we knew we'd intersect with the stream. *It's running three-tenths of a mile farther down the trail,* one of the hikers had told us. When we found the stream filled with only dry smooth stones, I hoped to God they were right. We left the trail and walked the edge of the dry streambed until suddenly I saw the shimmer of wet rocks.

"Look, babe! Water!" I said with a gasp. Scott seemed to still hold his breath.

We kept walking until those wet rocks, became a trickle, and then pools of water. The water was so clean and pure that it reflected the round beams from our headlamps brightly, like two round moons.

"Shit yeah!" Scott declared.

I got to filling our bottles and bladders while precariously balanced on a couple large stones in the streambed. I then passed the full bladders to Scott and tossed the full bottles up on the stream's embankment. We hustled back to where we had dropped our packs, water sloshing at our sides, to start purifying and try to find that damn lean-to.

For thirty minutes we looked through the darkness, climbing farther up into the forest, doubling back on the trail from where we had come, and searching in the woods to either side of the old lean-to. Nothing. If those hikers hadn't told us they had stayed there I wouldn't have believed it was even there. How does one lose a lean-to?

"That's it. I give up," Scott said, throwing up his hands, his headlamp blinding me in the darkness.

"Screw it. We're here. We have water. We descended the steepest mountain in the Catskills in the fucking dark—," but before I could say any more Scott finished my statement.

"Let's set up camp."

"Doing it," I copied, starting to pull the tent from my pack.

By ten-fifteen, we'd finally finished dinner. Laying atop nothing more than our lightweight silk liner, we laughed lazily, resting against each other's sweaty bodies. The night was still sweltering, and we couldn't seem to drink enough of that precious water from the Batavia Kill. We were all at once triumphant and exhausted. Who needed a lean-to? We'd made it.

CHAPTER NINE

Our bodies felt as if they'd been run over by a steam roller. But that didn't change the fact that we had a full day ahead. Ignorance is bliss and we were all too wise when it came to these mountains. Today we would summit Acra Point, Burnt Knob, and Windham High Peak—the very places that we'd visited on our short overnight hikes last summer and had so looked forward to seeing again on our thru-hike. Ah well. We'd dig down deep and summon the energy to greet these peaks with the same enthusiasm we always had. Oh, and that lean-to? We found it. On an unmarked side trail, it sat clean and welcoming, a neatly stacked pile of firewood in the corner. Go figure.

As we proceeded onward and upward to Acra Point we went through bright woods already growing hot. Along the way I snapped a couple twig tips from yellow birch, passing one to Scott and sticking the other between my teeth like a toothpick. Scott did the same. Some minty refreshment would do us good, as would its pain-relieving properties. As we crested the mountain, the trail plateaued, following the ridge through the start of the boreal forest. Sneaking through a narrow pathway between the evergreens we emerged onto the sun-drenched slab of rock called Acra. Across from us we could see the three peaks of the Black Dome range, which we'd also hiked last summer. As we took a break and ate some cashews, I sat and dreamed.

The last time we were in this very same spot we had entertained the idea of a thru-hike on the Long Path. This little section of the Catskills had become our solace from everyday life. It wasn't every weekend we could get away but as soon as we'd lined up two consecutive days off with nothing else planned, we'd usually visit this spot on the map. We noticed even in the mere twenty-four hours away from home how much our general mood changed. It was as if for that short time we viewed the world with new eyes, with not only wonderment for the beauty around us but also patience. We rolled with the punches that the trail dealt us and handled them in stride as a couple. We would return home renewed. We got at least a few days or so out of that renewal before it would fade. If surface change could occur that quickly, how would hiking a month together transform us?

"Isn't this amazing, honey?" I asked, breaking my gaze finally with the mountains to look at Scott.

All I got was a snore. He laid resting against his backpack, his head thrown back, mouth agape. I gave him a little nudge.

"Oh, oh, sorry," he apologized groggily.

"You still tired?" I asked.

"Yeah, I just feel like crap. I don't know, I must still be recovering from last night. Sucks. I really want to be enjoying this, but I can't help it," he explained.

"This is our place baby!" I said, going to him and giving him a big hug.

"I know. It's awesome," he said, and gave me a kiss. But I could see in his eyes that seemed to sink ever deeper into his face, that he wasn't himself.

"You should drink some more water, hon. You're probably still dehydrated from last night. I know I am. When I peed it looked like Gatorade."

"Oh! A Gatorade. How good would that be?" Scott said wistfully.

"I would slam anything on ice right now," I seconded as the sun poured down upon us on the exposed slab of rock. Instead I plucked a couple ripe mountain ash berries that hung heavy on a low branch and offered them to Scott, hoping their vitamin C could provide him a boost, but he only sneered.

After resting here for about a half hour while Scott dozed in and out of sleep, we hiked on over rolling rocky trail to the jagged outcrop of Burnt Knob. Scott had livened up along the way and once here he rallied, taking a series of photos of us on its edge. But the temps were rising and here we could not only feel but see them. Our view was hazier than usual, the day's humidity shrouding peaks we'd normally still see in the distance. Scott pulled out his phone and checked the weather . . . it was already ninety degrees . . . we both wilted a little more. The day was forecast to only get hotter, reaching ninety-five at its zenith. Depleted, we hiked on.

We were just a couple miles from Windham High Peak and now traversing trail that was a fraction as difficult as that which we'd been hiking the last few days. However, Scott's pace continued to slow, so much that we were completing only a mile an hour, which was at least half our normal speed. We continued to take breaks and snack and drink water, but I could see that he was beginning to walk like a drunken sailor. Something was *definitely* not right. Still, slowly but surely, we crisscrossed up switchbacks that grew gradually shorter approaching Windham's peak. After what seemed a tremendously long time, we reached its grassy level top. Scott had been tripping over his own feet the entire way up and my calves ached. Both of us poured sweat. A day that I had envisioned being magical had magically morphed into sheer work.

We dropped limply atop the large flat rock that marked its summit. Embedded in the stone was a steel National Forest Service emblem displaying the mountain's elevation and location by longitude and latitude. We'd reached it. But not a single leaf rustled overhead for the air was suffocatingly still and thick. Unlike our experience amongst the other high peaks, which provided the cool damp climate of the boreal forest, here we felt exposed, baking in the midday sun. Windham High Peak, although towering at 3,524 feet, is one of the few High Peaks that remains blanketed in grass and dotted with deciduous hardwoods. I could hear Scott wheezing and my lungs also felt tight. We chugged from our water bottles and then peeled ourselves off the hot rock to descend into a hopefully cooler valley. I had to start thinking about our options.

With the humidity and heat, it was insane to hike on, but once again we were low on water. Despite our having filled up several liters at camp before leaving, we didn't possibly have enough to carry us through the night. The next stream was at the lean-to about two miles ahead. We'd have to at least make it there.

We hadn't even made it a mile before Scott pleaded to take a rest again. Without hesitation, I obliged. I was fading fast, too. I slapped peanut butter on English muffins and then pulled out our guidebook pages.

"There is a motel about three miles down this road." I pointed out the listing in the guidebook to Scott.

"A motel? I thought there were no more motels?" he asked, suddenly perking up.

"Well it is *three* miles off trail and there's few services surrounding it, so I never marked it in our itinerary. But it's here, plain as day."

"How much farther to that road crossing?"

"It's just past the lean-to, so about another mile."

"I think we should go."

"I want to too, but those are miles on open road, likely without shade. What if we get there and there are no rooms?" I countered. A motel sounded grand, but we could get there only to turn around. That would be a total of six miles out of our way. In our current state, that would be six miles too many.

"I don't know, but I can't do the miles today," Scott said, his eyes heavier than before. "I'm sorry but I just can't."

"I can't either, hon. It's just too hot," I said, taking off my bandana and wiping my forehead again. "We'll aim for the lean-to and take it from there. How about that?" I offered.

"Sounds like a plan," Scott said.

The next mile was comparatively easy, but it still took us nearly an hour to reach the lean-to. When finally we spied it down in a clearing, we scampered downhill only to reach its wooden plank floor and collapse again. I pulled out our guidebook again, surveyed the map, and then on my phone, got to Googling. From what I could tell online, there were at least some services in Windham. It was, after all, a ski town. It was hard to imagine snow on these mountains. I mean, how the hell could it be *this* hot in late September? I called the several motels shown online but still only got through to the one listed in the guide. They had one room available, but at a hefty price. This late in our hike we had to be careful of what we spent or else we'd return home broke.

"What do you want to do?" Scott asked, leaning against his pack.

"What do *you* want to do? There's supposed to be water here . . . somewhere," I said, looking around at what looked to me like a dry camp, although a water source was listed.

He didn't answer and neither did I. Instead we both simply sat, staring out at the woods that now felt painfully indifferent to our struggle. Mother Nature offered no reprieve, no gifts, no magic. All I could think about was the long hot night ahead of us if we stayed here.

"Fuck it. Let's go into Windham. We'll hitch it. And surely there have got to be other motels with rooms available." Dismissively, I tossed down the guidebook pages on the wooden floor.

"Yeah, I don't think we have any other option. If we camp here for the night, we're just going to keep on sweating. It's too hot. We're both exhausted and dehydrated," Scott said, then added, "and I want a Gatorade."

By the look of his cracked, pale lips, I knew he needed one. I had a feeling, motel or not, both of us were delirious enough that we might walk six miles just for a cold drink.

"Alright. Let's get the hell out of here."

We soon hit pavement . . . white-hot pavement without a smudge of tree cover. Cars zipped by at regular intervals, and with each one, I stuck out my thumb. Not one even hit the brakes. In the opposite direction, a jeep drove by and gave a friendly honk. *Screw you buddy.* One woman drove by and mouthed "sorry." *Yeah, not as sorry as me.* I was beginning to think the town of Windham could suck it. We walked the entire three miles, every single step, and then spied a sign: The Copper Kettle Inn and Restaurant. This wasn't the one in the guidebook, nor one we'd seen listed, but it was worth a shot.

"Look, look! Come on!" I said, literally pulling Scott by the hand towards the humble establishment, which sat beside a steel bridge. "Maybe they have a room . . . and a Gatorade!"

We walked up to a door with an office sign above it and turned the knob . . . that didn't budge. Locked. A piece of paper was taped to its glass window that read: *Closed.*

"You have got to be kidding me!" I exclaimed, just about ready to kick down the door.

"Wait, maybe that's just for the restaurant." Scott pointed to a menu on the door that listed the hours for the grill. *Open Friday through Sunday.* It was Thursday. We stood there on the stoop, peering about dumbly, a tiny seed of hope still in our hearts that we could at least get a room. Then, just as we were about to turn 'round and submit again to the sizzling pavement, a woman's face appeared behind the glass, then a man's. By the expression on our faces we must have looked like two kids on Christmas, or deranged serial killers, I don't know, but they looked startled. Frightened or not, they fiddled with the knob and opened the door.

"Hi guys, can we help you?" the young woman asked.

"Do y'all have a room?" I blurted out. "We're thru-hiking the Long Path and we just walked here from the trail three miles away." I shared details hoping to better convey our misery.

"Well, we have a group here this week doing dog training. We're pretty full. But you guys are hikers?" She asked.

"Yeah, we hiked from New York City," Scott added.

"Wow. Yeah, well come on in. Let me see," she said

We walked into dining area of the restaurant and followed her towards a tall counter. I scanned the establishment. Surely there had to be some kind of ice-cold refreshment to be had here.

"Do you guys want something cold to drink? Maybe a soda or something?" the man spoke then, as if reading our minds or perhaps our weary faces.

"Yes, how about a Gatorade?" Scott answered before I'd even opened my mouth to speak.

"Well, we don't have any Gatorade," the man replied.

Scott's bright eyes went dull and then he just stood there, clearly having not thought of anything else but that Gatorade for the last three miles.

"Do you have a Sprite, or, err, a Coke. It doesn't really matter." I spoke for him now.

"Yes, we do have Sprite. Do you want ice?" the man replied, and I swear a halo appeared over his head. He was a true trail angel and he didn't even know it.

"Yes please!" Scott answered, his eyes again bright.

"Sure thing!" the man said kindly and then added, "I'm Dave and this is my wife, Lisa," motioning to the young woman now behind the counter at a computer.

"Hi, I'm Heather, and this is Scott," I told him.

"Okay, Heather and Scott, I'll hook you guys up," he said, turning for the back room.

Boy, that was awkward. I was glad he had taken our over-eagerness in stride.

"Let me see here," Lisa said, now punching some keys on the keyboard and squinting at the screen.

We waited with bated breath. *Please, oh please, we'll sleep on the front porch if we have to!*

"Looks like we do have a room open still. What kind of bed were you guys looking for?" she asked.

"Doesn't matter," I answered frankly.

"Okay, I have one with two double beds. Our queen and kings are all taken."

"That's perfect. How much is it?"

"I can do $80," she answered hesitantly. I had the sense she thought this might be too steep for us. However, it was still half the price of the other motel that we had called in advance.

"Great," I replied and shoved off my pack to look for my credit card.

Before we knew it, we had a real, true hotel key in hand.

"Do you guys have a laundry room?" I asked, now that our other needs were filtering through my heat-induced haze. I hoped we could luck out with some clean underwear.

"Hmm no, sorry, our laundry is out of order. But I could probably do a load for you. Do you have much?" she asked sweetly.

"Oh, just a small bag," I said, motioning to our packs."

"Duh. Of course. Guess you two can't carry much in there! I know how it is. We do a lot of mountain biking and when we stay at a motel, laundry is essential," she said with a smile.

"You have no idea!" Scott chuckled, pulling on his collar as if to air out the stink.

"No problem. Just bring over your bag once you guys get showered and such," she said with a wave of her hand.

Just then, Dave appeared then with two large to-go cups.

"What do we owe you?" Scott asked as Dave placed them in our hands. The cups were wet with condensation and cold, so cold.

"Don't worry about it," Dave said and added, "Glad we had a room here for you."

"Oh my God, thank you both so much," I proclaimed, and Scott echoed the same.

Hoisting our packs from the floor and, with a clatter, gathering up our hiking sticks from where they leaned against the counter, we headed out the front door and into the bright afternoon sun. We crossed the parking lot and climbed the few steps to the front door of our room. It was bordered by two Adirondack-style chairs. Beside one was a small table and ashtray. This place was getting better by the minute. Pushing open the door, we found a room that was country and quaint. Most importantly, we had fresh running water from the tap, an air conditioner, and a shower. Perfection. Scott dropped his pack and fell atop the nearest bed with a thud, cold Sprite still in hand.

"This is amazing," he said, taking a long slurp.

"Doesn't get any better," I replied, already peeling off my clothing to take a shower. We drained our sodas, showered, and drank another liter of water each, but still we hadn't peed. It dawned on us then just how severely dehydrated we'd become.

"We needed this room," I declared while lying beside Scott.

"Of course, we did!" Scott said emphatically. "Well I knew you were hurting, hon, but I didn't realize how overheated I had gotten too. I feel so heady."

"Babe we've been hiking for days in ninety-degree weather over the highest peaks in the Catskills. Yesterday we hiked until ten o'clock at night. Today we summited two more peaks and walked for three miles down a wide open road. Yeah. I think we're a little worn out," he said, while stroking my hair.

"Well when you put it that way!" I laughed at him.

Even after all these years of hiking, I still have a need to justify taking a break. Back when I hiked the Appalachian Trail, I was so hell-bent on proving myself, not so much to other people, but to myself, that my drive usually resulted in a minor injury that would take me off the trail for a couple days. Ironically, when I would tally up my mileage, I would realize that I had gained nothing. I might have pushed myself to go those extra miles, but I'd only lost them in the end. Now with the wisdom of experience, I usually know when to slow down, but still, a tiny part of me feels like I'm making excuses.

We went outside and took a seat in our real true chairs with backs.

"Hi there!" an older man called out to us from where he sat enjoying his identical chair one room down. "Couldn't help but notice your big backpacks. Where are you coming from?"

"The Big Apple," Scott answered back with a broad smile across his face.

"Get out!" the man guffawed, leaning forward in his chair.

"But we just got *here!*" Scott shot back, and the man chuckled at his bad joke.

And with that, we were no longer strangers. We learned that Dave, along with his wife Cindy, were traveling from their home in rural Pennsylvania. I mentioned we were from a town near Milford—no one ever knows where Lackawaxen is—and in turn he named a nearby business that he frequented,

Alice's Wonderland. Alice's was the small family-owned outfitters I'd worked at off and on for some years, and it, too, is in the middle of nowhere. Typically, only locals knew of it. He offered us a ride into town so that we could pick up any needed supplies when he and his wife went to dinner. They would be leaving shortly, but he assured us they would happily wait for us if we needed time to get ready. Without hesitation, we disappeared into our room and grabbed our wallets. There wasn't much we needed considering we had not planned to make this stop, but we could grab a real dinner somewhere . . . and another bottle of whiskey.

When we emerged, Cindy was by his side on the front porch.

"Well hello there! Are you two ready for dinner?" she asked as if we were longtime friends.

"Well, uh," I stuttered. *Were they inviting us to dinner with them?* "We really appreciate you giving us a ride into town. That's so nice of you," I finished, still uncertain as to how to reply as we walked with them towards their car.

"It's our pleasure. But to be clear, we'd like you to *join* us for dinner. We're going to the Chicken Run. From what we hear it has the best food in town!" Dave explained.

The Chicken Run. This didn't sound like a very vegetarian-friendly establishment. Scott looked as speechless as I did. But it was so very sweet of them to offer and they seemed so nice, we couldn't possibly turn down their offer. Besides . . . we could probably put a hurting on some mashed potatoes and slaw.

"Wow. That's so kind of you. We wouldn't want to impose," I answered, truly hoping that they weren't feeling obligated to invite us.

"Not at all. We love meeting people when we travel. It's half the reason we do it!" Cindy assured us.

"Okay then, the Chicken Run it is!" Scott declared.

When we drove a few miles before seeing any businesses, we were even more grateful to be in Dave and Cindy's car rather than on foot or, worse yet, back at the hotel room eating boiled noodles again. We reached the heart of town, which was surprisingly well developed with a number of restaurants and a variety of small businesses, but Dave just kept on driving. As we approached a large gravel parking lot that wrapped around a sprawling shack on the edge of town, Cindy exclaimed, "Oh! Here it is!"

Dave parked the car and the four of us stepped from the sedan. The establishment looked well-kept but comprised of a patchwork of additions, each a little different in style. To one side of the building a tall wooden fence ran its length. "I wonder if that's where they keep the chickens," Scott said to me under his breath.

"I wonder if that's where they kill 'em," I replied.

Scott ran up and opened the door, holding it for us as we walked inside.

"Welcome!" announced a cheeky waitress with bright red lipstick, a voluminous bouffant hairdo, and a well-endowed bosom who stood proudly in the entrance.

"How maaany?" she asked with a southern drawl that seemed out of place for New York State.

"Four," answered Dave.

"Great!" she said, flashing us a smile the size of Texas. She led us through the many rooms of the restaurant, and as she did, I couldn't help but notice her equally well-endowed rear end—yet she navigated the tables effortlessly. Red and white checkered tablecloths were spread atop each picnic-style table, and in the corner of one room was a jukebox, in another a pinball machine. Adorning every available surface and space were tiny figurines, statues, and paintings—all chickens. She sat us at a long table against a wall in the back of the restaurant and presented us with our menus.

"I'll be back in a jiffy!" she said. No way this woman could be this chipper about serving us dinner.

We opened our menus. *Fried Chicken. Roast Chicken. Half a chicken. Whole Chicken. Chicken fingers. Chicken breast. Chicken Soup.* I could see Scott flipping through the pages quickly, scouring the menu as well. I took a look at the sides. *Mashed Potatoes. Cole Slaw. Green Beans. Cornbread. Grits.*

Okay, doable. Then I saw it, on a tiny corner on the backside of the menu. *Vegetarian fare: Veggie Burgers. Veggie Lasagna. Tossed Salad.* Score!

I flipped over Scott's menu for him and pointed it out.

"Yes!" Scott blurted.

"See something you like?" Cindy asked.

"Oh um, yes the veggie burger. Perfect," Scott said sheepishly.

Dave and Cindy looked at each other. "O-oh," Cindy stuttered.

"We're vegetarian," I said.

"Oh, okay," Dave replied, seeming a little concerned but, all in all, still hopeful in his new friends.

The waitress returned, placing a salad bowl full of popcorn on the table between us as a starter and took our orders. Needless to say, Dave and Cindy got chicken and by the time our meals arrived, the four of us were already in full conversation. We talked about Scott's music career and the names with whom he'd played. Cindy shared with us their daughters' mission work abroad. Dave told us about his work doing antique restoration and I told him about my grandmother's china closet we'd lovingly had restored. He told us, too, about his younger days when he shot speed and drank all night. Cindy, who seemed wholesome as apple pie, more than once commented on how she and her husband were complete opposites, yet for them it worked. This woman knew well the man that she'd married. She handled him with care, kept him in line, and loved him dearly. Turns out they had met at the disco thirty years previous and the rest was history.

We finished dinner with ice cream sundaes and when the waitress brought us the bill, she got to talking about the ample entertainment they had there on the weekends.

"You should come see our stage outside! And you have to see our chicken!" she said with genuine enthusiasm.

"Well sure," Dave said, winking now at Scott. It seemed even Dave had to wonder what chicken we had not yet possibly seen. Maybe they indeed had a coop in the backyard.

She led us out two glass doors and that's when we saw it.

"That's where we have the musicians come and play," she said, motioning to a stage beyond the more obvious focal point: a six-foot statue of a rooster with a yellow beak, red comb, and wattle. She followed our gaze. "Oh yes, and that's our chicken!" she added, placing her hands on her hips proudly.

"Holy shit," I heard Dave say under his breath.

"Dave," Cindy shushed him.

"Haha! Now that's a cock!" Scott exclaimed while I stood speechless.

"Hey, how about a picture?" Cindy suggested.

"Yes, yes, here you four get together," The waitress offered, corralling us together in its shadow.

We laughed the whole way back about that cock. Dave and Cindy were also so kind as to make a stop at the liquor store so we could procure a small bottle of whiskey. Once at the motel, we said our goodbyes, exchanged phone numbers with plans to keep in touch, and then disappeared into the sanctuary of our room. Although we hadn't had a drop to drink, we already felt drunk from dinner and laughter and likely dehydration. We laid about on our bed, alternating with drinking cold clean water from the faucet to our hearts content and whiskey on the rocks until we simply dozed off.

In the morning, we were startled awake by the foreign sound of an alarm clock. Despite the rude awakening, we both remarked on how much more human we felt. My head no longer felt like I was under water, and Scott stood up straight, walking easily rather than shuffling to the bathroom. We had at least eleven miles planned for the day and possibly an additional three miles back to the trailhead—a long day in the mountains and one that we could have only been attempted in good health. We threw on our clothes from the night before, and while Scott went outside for his early morning smoke, I brushed my teeth, stuffed toiletries back into stuff sacks, and wondered at how we'd spread out so much of our gear in such a short period of time. Perhaps I needed to greet the day, too, before getting into all this.

"Holy shit! It's cold out here!" I exclaimed as I was slapped in the face with a frigid gust of wind. Scott wrapped his arms tight across his chest. I squinted at the thermometer that hung on the post just outside our room. Forty-eight degrees. In the night it had dropped over forty degrees. I dashed back inside and grabbed a blanket, wrapping myself up in it before sitting down beside Scott, who was already somehow sipping on a tall cup of steaming hot coffee.

"Hey! Where did you get that?" It appeared I had been slighted by the coffee fairy.

"Dave! Don't worry he got you one too!" he said, presenting me with an equally tall cup of coffee.

"Really?"

"Yeah, he said he went out this morning and thought of us, so he brought these back. He just dropped them off while you were inside."

"That's amazing!" It truly is the little things that count on the trail.

"What's amazing is how cold it is out here!" Scott returned.

"I know. What the hell? Yesterday we were suffering heat exhaustion. Today we'll be trying to keep warm." I could see Scott was already Googling the weather on his phone.

"Says the high is going to be 56, and tonight—" he paused. "A low of thirty-six." His rosy, coffee-warmed cheeks turning pale.

"Thirty-six degrees tonight? Are you kidding me?"

"No joke."

I thought of our sleeping bag that my father had retrieved from us in Nyack, New York. It a had luxuriously warm rating, good down to fifteen degrees. The warmest one that we had now was rated at thirty-two degrees and our other lighter weight bag was rated to fifty degrees. Now let it be known that these ratings in no way guarantee to keep a hiker toasty at said temperatures, rather they ensure one doesn't freeze to death. I was less than confident that even our heavier weight bag, would keep us warm. Add to our situation that we hadn't actually been using these bags as intended—one to a person, zipped all the way up and cinched—but rather as quilts, unzipped with one laid beneath us and the other atop. Oh yeah, and did I mention that these bags were ten years old, which meant compressed loft and therefore less insulating ability. Our stated temperature ratings were far from true. The only thing that might save us was our silk sleep sack, made for two, that supposedly added ten degrees of warmth.

"Are we going to be warm enough?" he asked, clearly seeing that I was lost in thought.

"I hope so. We'll boil some water and fill a Nalgene if we need to, stick it in the sleep sack like a hot water bottle. Old-fashioned style." I hoped he couldn't sense my worry.

"Ah, we'll be fine," Scott replied, and with a toss of his hand seemed to dismiss any concern.

Just then I saw Lisa, from across the parking lot, push open the office door, our tiny bag of clothing in hand.

"This hardly qualified as a load!" she said with a chuckle, standing before us.

We got to chatting and she offered us not only a ride to the trailhead this morning but even a lift across the bridge to a little café for breakfast first. Despite the cold temps, it was becoming apparent, the Trail Gods had stockpiled some trail magic for us here in this little town of Windham. So, we packed up our things quick as we could, said goodbye to Dave and Cindy on the front porch and hopped in Lisa's car.

Once at the coffeeshop we sipped more coffee and ordered egg and cheese sandwiches. As the cold wind howled against the large window beside us, I felt the day's promise deteriorating. Multicolored leaves whisked across the parking lot. Overnight, autumn had arrived. While lingering longer than we should, I took out our guidebook pages and studied the upcoming miles on the map. That's when it dawned on me. Yesterday, when we had hit pavement, we had not only exited the woods, but the Catskill Park.

"Honey, we did it!" I suddenly exclaimed. Scott peered out the window looking forlorn.

"What do you mean? We still have over 100 miles to go!"

"Yeah, I know. But we finished the Catskills! Well the worst of it, there's still a few Catskill humps, but we're headed into the Schoharie Valley."

"Well, ho-ly shit. I didn't think I could do it. Wasn't that ninety-some miles through those mountains?"

"Ninety-four, to be exact." I leaned across the table and gave him a smooch. "Babe, you did it. *We* did it."

A sweeping view of the valley

PART SEVEN:

THE SCHOHARIE

VALLEY

In Mine Kill State Park - getting closer!

CHAPTER ONE

The sound of Lisa's motor trailed off into the distance and suddenly there we were on the roadside, hoisting our packs for the miles ahead. "We got this shit," Scott declared. He studied my face, then added, "God, I love you."

"I love you, baby. We're amazing," I replied to this man across from me, a very different man from the one I'd started this trail with.

Scott's beard was thick, all salt and pepper—I could barely remember what he looked like clean shaven—and despite the gray, he looked younger than ever and so strong. We were changed people, but not just on the surface. I could feel pride welling up in my chest like a balloon filling with helium. I felt light, almost heady. Together we'd taken on this journey, each of us weighted with concerns about what might transpire, uncertain of its outcome. Our apprehension had been much like that which we'd felt in beginning a relationship together over two years ago. But just the same, we'd leaped. Then and there we had embarked on a journey and our journey had led us here . . . prepared to venture further into the unknown on a blustery day in a tiny town in upstate New York.

Our first steps were easy as we traced a plank walkway that wound us through level woods. Inevitably, we would eventually climb steeply, but our trail was leafy, void of enormous boulders and rock scrambles. The woods were open and bright, filled with mostly young deciduous trees. The Catskill Park had been magical and rugged and raw—beautiful and hard—but these mountains, they were gentle, welcoming.

We summitted Mount Pisgah, Richtmeyer Peak, and finally Richmond Mountain, adding layers when the wind blew strong at elevation and shedding layers when tucked in the gaps. From the top of Richmond Mountain, when we spied a view of jagged teeth–like mountains, nearly black against the blue sky in the distance, we were paused amidst the frigid, gusting wind. As we huddled side by side for warmth, I pulled out our map. Lo and behold, we were gazing at the Blackhead Range and the Devil's Path, which now looked so very far away. Victorious, we took pictures from our relatively modest perch, which had required a fraction of the effort to climb in comparison to those high peaks.

We descended through majestic plantations of towering Norway spruce, labyrinth-like, with only aqua blazes leading the way through the darkness. Gradually we drew ever closer to a stream that trickled in a ravine. The sides of the ravine were gutted and rocky, evidence of this water's force in a wet season. Thankfully, we found a deep pool of water captured in a cluster of boulders where we could fill up our water bladders and bottles, and shortly thereafter, found a level spot in the woods just before dark.

Dropping our packs, we hastily began setting up our tent in the dying light. I laid out the nylon shell atop the leafy ground and was just beginning to lock together our poles when Scott nudged me. Thinking it was an accident, I ignored him, but then he nudged me even harder.

"What?"

"Look!" he whispered loudly through clenched teeth.

I followed his sideways stare about twenty feet away to the biggest porcupine I'd ever seen, standing upright. Unflinching, its eyes were locked on me.

"Whoa," I said louder than I'd intended. "Look at that guy, he's two feet tall!"

The porcupine settled back on his haunches, his coat of sharp spines radiating like an aura. Just then, he started in, chirping and clicking at us, maintaining his stare with beady black, marble-like eyes. I didn't know porcupine-speak, but something told me he was not pleased.

"What should we do?" I asked Scott. I was completely and utterly intimidated.

"How should I know? I thought you said you'd dealt with these things all the time?"

"Well yeah, I mean, I did. I've never faced off with one! Shit. This is like Grandpa Porcupine—big and old and cranky—you don't mess with Grandpa Porcupine," I said to Scott without breaking my gaze with the porcupine. I couldn't let Grandpa know I felt threatened.

He remained completely still, all except for his little mouth, which persisted in chirping and clicking.

"Maybe we should get out of here. I don't want to mess with Grandpa," Scott said sheepishly. I could tell he felt as silly as I did, being bullied by a porcupine, but there was no denying this guy was pissed. We were on his turf.

I scanned the darkening woods around us and peered up at the grey sky through the treetops. The shadow of night was quickly descending upon us and from the chill on my skin I could tell the temperatures, too, were dropping. My anxiety rose.

"But what if we can't find another campsite?" I posited.

"Okay, then we'll stay," Scott said, trying to sound tough. He resumed snapping together the tent poles, while keeping a close eye on Grandpa.

I started to fasten the plastic hooks around the poles, but when I looked up again, still Grandpa hadn't budged.

"Babe, he keeps staring at us!" I said again, feeling paralyzed now by those black eyes.

Scott dropped the poles. "I thought you said you wanted to stay!" he said in a huff. I knew he was growing angry with my indecision, but I couldn't help it.

"I never said that! I just said it was getting dark. I don't know. Maybe we should go."

The porcupine clicked and clacked and dropped his stubby front legs, coming to squat on all fours.

"Let's go," I suddenly declared, and hastily gathered up the nylon shell of the tent in my arms.

"Wait. Hold on," Scott put his hand on my shoulder.

"What?!" I replied shrilly.

Grandpa was waddling slowly toward us. That's it. We're toast. I could beat him off with a tent pole if I had to, but would it reach far enough? I'm not one to resort to violence but my animal instincts were kicking in. I envisioned us as pin cushions, dozens of spines poking from our arms and legs, when, all of a sudden, Grandpa took a sharp turn, waddling swiftly down the hillside below our campsite, and disappeared into the thick of the foliage. When I heard Scott exhale loudly, so did I.

"He's gone," Scott said, squinting through the darkness at the wall of vines and trees at the base of the hill that had absorbed him.

"I guess we're staying." I let the tent fall back to the ground in a heap and as I did, I felt my face flush with embarrassment; I had to fight a sneaking smile. To think a porcupine had almost gotten the better of us.

"That guy was scary!" Scott said with a grin, snickering nervously.

"I know! I was ready to throw the tent at him and run! Let's hope that's the last of him."

By the time we got our tent erected, the sun had set. We strapped on head-lamps to prepare a couple of the remaining meals in our food sacks—yet more Knorr Pasta Sides. But with the steam roiling up to our faces and the heat of our aluminum bowls radiating through our fingers, neither of us cared that we'd eaten some variation of this meal nearly every night we'd been out here. In fact, all I felt was gratitude. We had already put on our long underwear, wool vests, and knit hats, and had wrapped our lower bodies in our sleeping bag. Later that night, as the temps dropped swiftly, this meal would keep our bellies warm as we drifted off to sleep.

My eyelids thrust open and I laid stone still, listening to loud rustling uphill from our tent. Instinctively my body tensed as twigs snapped and the rustling came closer, closer, *closer* to our tent. That was no squirrel . . . and it was picking up speed, running straight for our tent!

"Do you—" I mustered but before I could finish, Scott bolted upright, pulling the sleeping bag from my body.

There was no more time for fear. I scrambled to my knees.

"Hey! Hey you!" I yelled at the top of my lungs.

Scott too came to kneel, and we stared hard at the nylon door of the tent, illuminated by the moonlight. Whatever it was had stopped in its tracks.

"What the fuck is that?" Scott asked.

"I don't know. But it's close," I replied. My body trembled, whether from the cold or from fear I couldn't tell.

Just then it started coming forward toward us again. I clapped my hands so hard that it stung—then again and again, hoping the loud noise would scare it off. Whatever it was stopped once more, sounding now as close as a few yards from our tent.

"Maybe it's Grandpa?" I suggested, breaking my gaze with the tent door to see Scott with eyes as wide as pie tins. The creature rustled through the leaves, back and forth, as if it were pacing outside the tent.

"That's too loud to be a porcupine," Scott said then, saying aloud the very thing that I was already thinking. "Besides, it came from uphill. We saw Grandpa go downhill."

"Shit," I said with an exasperated sigh. "You're right. That's got to be a bear." I knew this routine all too well. We could likely scare if off but then we would sleep with one eye open the rest of the night.

"Oh shit!" I then blurted out.

"What?" Scott asked in a panic, then seeing what I saw, added, "Oh, fuck."

We peered down at the food bag at our feet. It had been so depleted, and we had been so warm snuggled in our sleeping bag, that we hadn't bothered to do a bear-hang. Of course, on this night, of all nights, we'd given into our comforts. We *always* hung a bear-hang.

The nearby rustling continued, sounding as if it might be coming closer. Just enough, I unzipped the tent to reach the rock that I'd used as a level surface to cook on earlier in the night. Although tempted to throw it into the darkness at this elusive creature, instead I started pounding it against the ground. I'd use recommended protocol—make as much noise as possible to scare it away—even if I had, by now, encountered enough bears to know that this rarely worked. But hey, it was worth a shot.

"Light a cigarette," I ordered Scott as I rustled through my backpack for my own smokes.

"You got it." Scott quickly grabbed his pack from his bedside. He knew *my* protocol from my own stories of bear encounters in camp.

While thru-hiking the Appalachian Trail, in Massachusetts, I'd set up my tent next to a meandering stream at a campsite called Limestone Springs, leaving the lean-to to an older couple, Moxie and Tecumseh, with whom I'd been hiking. I'd no sooner turned off my headlamp when I heard a loud scuffling in the nearby leaves downstream. I yearned to holler for help, but I was ashamed of my bear phobia, which my nearby hiking pals knew all too well, so instead I resigned to suffer in silence. *I will be fearless, dammit. Besides it's probably just a squirrel*, I told myself. The rustling grew closer, until I heard definite footfalls and there was no denying that whatever was out there was much larger than a rodent. I laid on my back motionless, knife clenched to my chest, scared for my life and certain that this bear would eat me. *Surely it could smell the very blood coursing through my veins.* The footfalls shuffled around me and just then, a large snout pushed against the side of my tent, swishing back and forth across the nylon. That snout gave three large sniffs. *If this bear doesn't eat me, I'll die of a heart attack anyway.* He took another sniff, this time next to the tent pocket at my head where I'd stashed a cigarette butt, and let out an exasperated huff. He'd caught one whiff of that stale tobacco and retreated. The next day I learned from a ridge runner that I'd met "Ol' Limey"—a harmless but very curious 500-pound male black bear that liked to frequent Limestone Springs. I'm afraid that sealed the deal for me and cigarettes.

So, there we sat puffing hard and fast, blowing big billowing clouds out into the cold night air to either side of the tent. The movement through the leaves continued.

"Yeeeowwww!" Like a banshee I hollered into the night in between drags. "Oww oww owwww!" I screamed again. Then there was that other time on the Appalachian Trail when my father and I were camped somewhere in Virginia. I'd awoken in the night to a similar scuffling of leaves and called to my father in his tent beside mine. When we'd shone our headlamps out into the woods, we'd seen two eyes twinkling back at us. After much clapping in vain and the bear still lurking at the edge of camp, we got to hollering and shouting, screaming, and screeching, so much that campers downstream from us called out to ask if we were okay. Although I think they were more annoyed than concerned, nonetheless we'd scared him off. Strong vocal cords run in the family.

I continued to shriek my most fearsome woodland wild woman shriek while Scott bellowed in a deep voice, "NO! NO! NO!" like a monstrous commanding giant of the forest. Just when we thought we could hear nothing more than our own voices resounding through the trees, we heard scuffling in the leaves near the foot of the tent and then a hasty swooshing whisking swiftly downhill and into the bushes at the far edge of our camp.

My heart beat so hard I thought it might jump from my chest; Scott held his cigarette mid-drag. Farther off now, we heard twigs breaking, and then silence.

"I think we scared him off," I whispered.

"I'm not surprised," Scott said, and then after a moment's silence, broke into laughter.

My body erupted with laughter and suddenly I could feel the tension in my upper body evaporate. Warm air billowed from our mouths in the cold night air. "Well it worked didn't it?" I said, collecting myself.

"I think we just scared off every living thing for a square mile radius," Scott said, lighting another cigarette.

"Yep, probably. But that's alright. No way that was a porcupine."

"Oh hell no. That was a bear," Scott replied, taking a long drag. "What are we going to do about this food?" he added, gesturing to the sack that we'd cinched tight, as if that would have made any difference to the bear.

"I'll never sleep tonight if we leave it in here. We'll have to hang it." I reached for my watch and pushed on its light. "Oh my God, it's three in the morning!" I said with a groan.

"Well, let's do it then. Better bundle up. It's cold out there."

Outside we found a smooth stone, tied our cord around it and tossed it up over a long limb a good hundred paces from our tent. Thankfully Scott got the pitch on the first try. We replaced the stone with our saggy, nearly empty sack, and Scott hoisted it into the air, while I took the remaining cord and nearly hugging the tree's trunk, wrapped it three times around. Maybe now we'd have a *chance* of sleeping sound the remainder of the night.

My hands had grown cold from fussing with the bear-hang, but once back in the tent and wrapped up with Scott in our sleeping bag, I could feel the heat returning. Within minutes his breath began to deepen. Bear or no bear, apparently this man was going to get his due hours of rest. I laid there for a long while feeling his chest rise and fall beneath me, grateful for the warmth of his body pressed against mine. Countless times I'd been roused in the night by woods sounds and laid there *alone* in the dark straining my ears, wondering if I should be worried. There were other nights where I'd wonder if I might develop hypothermia, become delusional, and wander out in the snowy night. Sometimes I was simply so very aware of my aloneness it was overwhelming, my complete and total isolation in the dark. When I'd first started backpacking, camping was the very worst part of the trip. I was always scared at night. On the Appalachian Trail, I would set up camp near other hikers simply for the psychological security. Then, somewhere along the way, after many nights wrought with worry and many mornings of awakening safe and sound, my fear dissolved. I began to revel in the stillness of sleeping in a forest alone. Yet even now there are certain moments—a bear wandering into camp is one of them—that I want nothing else than to not be alone. Although I've worked through many fears through hiking solo, I don't think that I shall ever be fearless. To know now that every night when I laid down to sleep, I would not be alone, but comforted by the person who comforts me most: this was truly a gift.

· We awoke in the chilly morning groggy and reluctant to leave the warmth of our tent. We'd slept through the rest of the night without another visitor but stirred each time one of us accidentally rolled away, losing the other's body warmth. The temps had remained in the high thirties, luckily making the chilly night bearable, but not comfortable. At least the sun now poured through the treetops; this gave me some hope for the day. The morning began with a steep climb through a cobwebbed forest and then a long descent into the valley where we walked for three miles on a mostly level road. We reveled in the sun that warmed our bones. Along the way we passed humble homes and dilapidated trailers tucked into the hillside, many with livestock just outside their doors. Goats and horses peeked their heads from their paddocks as we hiked swiftly past. Around noon, we took cover behind a crumbling, junk-filled garage to strip off our long underwear. This was the first day we'd hiked for hours in long sleeves and pants, and although it was still brisk, it was important to get these clothes off before they became wet with sweat.

As we hiked into the town of Conesville, we passed older one- and two-story homes, some in sorry shape, others prim and proper, with small lawns that abutted a narrow sidewalk. We stopped to ask a woman walking her dog if there might be anywhere to get lunch and she informed us that there were no such conveniences in Conesville; but her voice grew bright when she added, "But we're getting a gas station soon!"

We started up a steep hill, leaving behind the main street and when we reached its top, turned sharply into the woods. Here we followed a trail on private property through which the landowner had given permission for the trail to pass. The tall trees here had already begun to shed their leaves and so the woods felt open and bright. We swooshed through leaves up to our ankles, which, although picturesque, proved quite the challenge, as they hid rocks of every shape and size beneath them. The leaf litter eventually thinned, and we followed aqua blazes that zig-zagged us, without explanation, through the forest. We took lots of breaks simply because we felt like it and lingered at the edge of a high precipice overlooking the Manor Kill, which ran swiftly at the bottom of a deep gorge. At two-thirty, well past the lunch hour, we gave in and pulled out our food bags. These, we knew, would be only a disappointment. We were due for a maildrop in Gilboa, but the post office closed at three o'clock. There was no way we would reach it in time.

The contents of our sacks laid on the ground before us: two packets of ramen noodles, two crumbling bagels, a packet of peanut butter crackers, and a granola bar. This is the problem with planning your food down to the day. Our planning had not yet caught up with our stomachs. And sadly, you see, the longer you hike, the more your appetite grows, along with your desperation. I sliced down the center of our bagels and placed them face open on a rock. Scott ripped open the packet of peanut butter crackers and carefully topped each bagel with three. We squished our sandwiches snuggly shut and chowed down, taking giant bites of our carbohydrate-rich delicacy that left our mouths dry but our bellies full. Well, full enough.

Descending through the woods, we hit a road again. The movie reel of trees to either side of us continued until suddenly we spied a rectangular sign with block lettering, illuminated with yellow globe-shaped lights around its border.

Lunch. Dinner. Cold Beer. Welcome to Clark's Tavern.

We'd stumbled upon an oasis. This humble country tavern, which looked like it had sat here for decades, may as well have had a red carpet stretched out before it. I suddenly regretted eating that awful peanut butter cracker bagel sandwich; but it mattered not, for those calories were long burned.

We entered through a side door onto hardwood floors that had been well worn by many a patron before us. Adorning the walls were beer signs of every brand, each neatly hung on its hook. Across from us sat a pool table, and on a corner wall was a dart board speckled with holes. Evidence suggested this was likely the local hangout, but there wasn't a soul to be seen. Could they be closed for the afternoon? We held our breath and approached the tall wooden bar lined with taps. I eyed a basket of little bags of chips that sat atop the counter and, behind that, a cooler filled with cold beverages. There was still reason to hope. If nothing else, we could at least score a cold soda and a snack. We stood about waiting, waiting, and waiting some more, when finally we heard the clanking of pots and pans from behind a swinging door. Just then, a middle-aged man with a slight build pushed through the door and gave a jump, clearly surprised to see us.

"Oh, hi! I didn't know you were here. What can I get for you?" he asked kindly.

"Could we get something to eat?" I asked in turn. I couldn't help but wonder if it sounded a little like I was begging. After all, I was inside.

"Sure, here ya go," he said, reaching beneath the counter and pulling out a vinyl covered menu.

"Oh, thank God," Scott said then, causing the man to study us.

We skimmed the pages of burgers, steaks, chicken wings, and the like, and finally laid eyes on a veggie burger. Scott promptly ordered one up and I went for a basket of cheese fries—something I hadn't ordered since I was a teenager—and a salad with chunky blue cheese dressing. We topped off our order with two frosty sodas. Our bill was just over ten dollars. This place really was like stepping back in time.

"So where are you guys coming from?" he asked cautiously while giving us our change.

"New York City. We're hiking the Long Path," Scott answered.

"Oh yeah, the Long Path. We've had a lot of hikers in here from that trail. Nice people," he replied.

Scott and I looked at each other in astonishment.

"You have?" I asked.

"Oh yeah. A lot of hikers stop in here. I mean there's not really anything else around for miles."

"Yeah, our food bags are about empty, and you just get so damn hungry out here. Are you owner?"

"This is my dad's place . . . but will probably be my place one day," he said with a roll of the eyes. I had the feeling he would prefer to be on the trail rather than behind this bar. Likely he'd been standing there since he was tall enough to see over it.

"We're so thankful you're here," I replied, wanting him to know that even if he wished to be anywhere else but here, that what he did mattered.

"Pays the bills! Well mostly!" he said with a chuckle. "Go ahead and have a seat guys, I'll have this out to you in a bit," he said.

"Sure thing. Hey, thanks bud," Scott said, reaching out his hand to the man; he accepted the shake with a small smile.

We passed into a side room and found a selection of wooden tables, each with a checkered red and white plastic tablecloth—clearly the favored motif around these parts—complete with silverware and a mug at each setting. Against the wall was an ebony upright piano with an open music book perched above its yellowed keys. We chose a table nearest to the outlets and got to charging. When our food arrived in short order, we didn't speak another word until we were finished. The cheese dripped with oil and stretched like elastic from the plate to my mouth and the iceberg lettuce crunched with each bite, cool and refreshing. This meal was more than just nourishment, it was a sensual experience.

"Dear God, that was heaven," I said, slumping against the back of my chair.

Scott leaned back, rubbing his belly in contentment.

"You ain't kidding!" he replied. "But I don't think I can move."

"I know, me either. Hey, is your vision a little blurry?" I asked, blinking my eyes. I may have only eaten a plate of fries and a salad, but to my weary body, it resembled Thanksgiving dinner.

"Yep," he said with a burp.

"And my face," I said putting my hands to my cheeks, "it feels like a furnace."

"That's called calories. Energy to burn," he said, shifting in his chair as if to make room for his food. I noticed then, too, that his cheeks were rosy as well.

We had been depleted. Eating dried foods for days on end simply doesn't nourish the body in the same way that a cooked meal does, especially one heavy in fats and an array of nutrients. Sure, we'd foraged some along the way, but harvesting calorie-dense foods in autumn is labor-intensive—roots take tools to dig and nuts take time to shell—and we hadn't the tools nor the time to dedicate to it that we would have liked. Our bodies were speedily digesting and assimilating all the nutrients from this meal at a rate we never experienced in our everyday life.

For over two hours, we enjoyed this little corner of Clark's, and we would have idled even longer had the seats around us not begun to fill. Patrons filed in, taking their seats in groups of two and four and six. An older white-haired man stood at the door greeting people who responded with big smiles and hearty handshakes. We imagined this was Pa Clark himself, and his face beamed at each and every person that entered. Having finally sobered up from our indulgence in real food, it was time to mosey down the trail. Clark Junior was kind enough to fill our water bottles for us, and we purchased another can of Sprite for the road. Without far to go, it seemed permissible to make this twelve-ounce weight exception.

"Thank you for coming to Clark's," Pa Clark said to us as we headed for the door.

"It was the best food we've had in miles!" Scott replied, holding his stomach again.

"Good, good!" he replied, giving Scott a pat on the shoulder.

We stepped outside into early evening air heavy with humidity. I could hardly believe that we had been so chilly the night before; it felt more like a midsummer's night than an autumn evening. The Gilboa post office sat just one short mile down the road. Had it not closed so early we would've been able to make it. Alas, such are the complications of mail-drops. But with no grocery store in sight for the next five days, the post office had been our only choice. We'd have to stealth camp nearby and reach it first thing in the morning. Neither of us felt much like walking any farther now, anyway.

While at Clark's, we'd studied our location on Google Maps and seen that our road walk ran along the enormous Schoharie Reservoir, which was buffered by a wide tract of woods. Those woods could serve as a fine stealth campsite. We walked the narrow shoulder past a forest thick with trees, the reservoir's waters only a momentary shimmer through a tangle of branches and vines. But when we spied a wire metal fence, chest high, that trailed the embankment below us, we realized it wouldn't be as easy as we'd thought to dip into the forest's shelter. We took turns scuffling down the loose rock and leaf litter where we thought the fence might be low enough to straddle, but each time found it just as high as before. About a half mile later, we reached an informal pull-off and spied a narrow foot path that led to mangled fencing—clearly, we weren't the only ones who wished to make use of this land. We waited until the passing motorists were well out of sight and vanished, sliding in leaf litter and gravel down the embankment.

Carefully we straddled the flimsy fence and continued to scuffle and slip down rough trail, steeper than before, to the water's edge. We stood before a vast expanse of water protected by towering trees, our feet deep in driftwood and trash on its rocky shore. We tip-toed through the heaps of rubbish—golf clubs, a Hershey's syrup bottle, a smashed microwave, a dog crate, a baseball mitt, beer bottles, soda cans, milk cartons, a single black and white Converse sneaker—hoping we didn't wound ourselves on a piece of rusted metal or broken glass. Sadly, this reservoir was also a dumping ground. *We* would be the least of its concerns. Where the ground leveled out, eagerly, we dipped back into the woods. Once amongst the trees, we wandered, far enough to lose sight of the trash but not so far that we lost sight of the shimmering water. As we did the landscape changed dramatically; we stepped over the gnarled trunks of fallen trees, startling chipmunks from their homes, and through knee-high asters gone to cottony seed, which brushed against our bare legs. Proof that one may stumble upon beauty in the most unlikely of places.

We followed the contour of the forest until we reached a clearing where a strip of land jutted into the lake, forming a sort of peninsula. The sun was starting to set and, in the distance, we could see orange lights near the shoreline. We might have been very much amidst civilization, but here we were in our own private wilderness. Our tent was up in short order and with full bellies, there was no need to cook dinner. It would be an easy evening. Scott cracked open our cherished can of Sprite, and with our little plastic bottle of whisky, mixed us cocktails in our camp cups. We stripped off our sweaty clothes and laid about in our underwear, now reveling in the warm night air. Outside a light rain began to fall and the dusky sky darkened to black; we laughed like children about nothing much at all and soon we were kissing, tangled in each other's bodies. For nothing more in the world could we want.

CHAPTER TWO

We awoke chilled in the damp morning air, our bodies and sleeping bag veiled in moisture. The light drizzle we'd fallen asleep to had apparently continued through the night, and still the rain pitter-pattered atop our nylon ceiling. I pulled out my phone and checked the temperatures for the day. The prediction was dreadful. It would only reach a high of forty-five degrees with the nighttime temps at thirty-two degrees. It would be our coldest night yet and rain was predicted throughout the day. Hiking all day in the pouring rain and then climbing into our tent in near freezing temperatures—a combination perfect for hypothermia.

I thought back to the day my father and I had hiked out of camp in a down-pour in the mountains of North Carolina on the Appalachian Trail. Relentlessly, the skies soaked us and for five miles we wound through trees and hopped rushing streams as fast as we could simply to stay warm. When we reached the bald summit of Walnut Mountain, we hiked through fog so thick we could barely see and struggled against strong winds and sideways-blowing rain that pelted our exposed faces and hands. Finally, we reached a lean-to but found it full with a group of teenagers from nearby Asheville who had set up home there, squatting, not camping. Stretched across the floor of the lean-to was a rat snake that they informed us they'd beaten to death. "We thought it was a rattler," a boy with stringy black hair had said. Although we'd hoped to stay there, this would not be our fortune. Desperate to get warm, we layered our fleece jackets beneath our raincoats, but our fingers were so numb neither of us work the zippers to zip them shut again. I could no longer feel my lips or my toes. Our hoods cinched around our faces and our arms wrapped tight around our torsos, we put our heads down and hiked on. Thankfully, we descended from there, and by the end of the day, reached Hot Springs, where we took shelter inside for the night. Had we had to hike on and sleep another night in the wet and cold, I don't know that we would have made it.

"Today is going to suck," Scott said, pulling his coffee from his food bag. I had our stove going, heating up some water.

"Yes, it is. But there are a couple of places we can take cover along our route if need be." I already had the guidebook laid out in my lap.

"Any hotels?"

He knew as well as I did that our options were slim that way. I looked through the guidebook anyway, which listed none, but then took a look online. Lo and behold, there was another after all.

"Well there *is* one a couple miles away, but there's no services near it and then we won't get any miles in," I told him, denying the tug I felt just to call it then and there.

"Shit," he said, fumbling with his coffee packet. "I don't want to not hike today."

Damn. Miles more important than comfort. No denying now, he was a *true* thru-hiker.

"Me either. But good to know if we needed to double back," I answered, praying that it wouldn't come to that. Our water came to a boil and we poured in our instant coffee powder. Warming our hands on our hot coffee mugs, we gazed out at the rain dripping from the autumn-colored leaves around us, saturating the forest floor. We stalled . . . but there was no denying the inevitable.

Once started, we packed up camp speedily and retraced our steps through the forest to the trash-strewn shore of the reservoir, where the raindrops formed expanding rings atop the water's surface. Then clawing our way up the steep embankment, we returned to the road where we walked for only a short while before following the trail into the woods. The trail provided a short though steep and rocky shortcut past a public school to the Gilboa post office. Not only would we pick up more food, but I was due some new trail runners.

For the last week, I'd watched my trail runners slowly decay and tear. But today, they finally gave way, the ball of my foot literally sliding out the side of my shoe on the downhills. I have found myself in a number of precarious situations with worn-out shoes on previous long hikes— I've duct-taped them, sewed them back together with dental floss, hacked off the heels when they started giving me blisters, and simply gave up and hiked on in Crocs. On the Finger Lakes Trail, two sweet trail angels, Terry and Kim, delivered me a new pair on the trail, and another remarkable trail angel, Roger, gave me a ride into a tiny town for a new pair roughly two weeks later. I've since learned to purchase more pairs than I think I'll need and simply leave them with a family member to mail out at the ready. My mother had been sweet enough to drop a pair in the mail, scheduling them to arrive the same day as our food.

Dripping wet, we dashed in the door of the post office and requested our mail-drop from the mailperson behind the counter. For a moment, she simply stood and gave us a puppy dog sort of face. Her empathy told me *she* was likely someone's mom, too. She then disappeared and returned, proudly bearing two packages.

My gaze locked on my handwriting scrawled atop our food box and I felt my eyes start to start to well up. I remembered addressing all these boxes back in our house in Lackawaxen nearly a month ago. Although in the grand scheme of things, that wasn't all that long, it felt like another lifetime. I remembered what my jeans felt like against my legs as I sat atop our carpeted floor and the smell of the pine wood that lined our walls. I felt a tightness in my chest, a sadness . . . but I wasn't sad because I wished I were home . . . I was sad because this was our final maildrop, which meant that we were almost to the end. I wasn't ready for this to end. As much as I loved our home and all that we had created there, this trail was now home and I had equal love for this routine—wake, hike, eat, hike, eat, hike, sleep—our new normal.

"This is it, babe," I said, as we headed for an awning beside the post office to unwrap our goodies. The sign on the door behind us read: Town Court Justice.

"Ha! Look at that," Scott said. "This might be it! That is, if being a stinky hiker is a crime!"

"No *this* is it," I said, dropping the box on the concrete.

"What do you mean?"

"This is our last maildrop," I said, looking at box that now seemed even weightier than before.

"For real? This is it?" he replied, and I wondered if he too felt sorrow or just relief.

"*This* is it," I said, looking him in the eyes now.

"Wow. Well we better make the most of this then. We are damn well going to enjoy these last miles," he said, looking at me with those warm eyes with which I first fell in love. "Hey, do you think there's Pop-Tarts in there?"

There was no time for reminiscing. It was urgent we be here now; that was all that mattered. It was clear to me. This is was our adventure and right now Pop-Tarts were our only agenda.

He ran his knife down the packing tape and tore back the cardboard flaps. A silver package sat on top. Really, how bad could today get? For God's sake, we had Pop-Tarts.

Our spirits lifted with each item we pulled from the box: prehydrated Indian dinners, a tin of pistachios, packets of Starbucks iced coffee. Things we could not procure from a rinky-dink gas station. We promptly ripped the food stuff from their bulky packages and dropped them in Ziploc bags. Next, from a paper bag we pulled a small bottle of whiskey and a several packs of cigarettes. If you're going to mail yourself treats, one may as well mail all the treats—just be certain that they're well camouflaged during shipping, as the post office would not approve. I tore open our second box and pulled out my sneakers, which were so clean and new they still smelled of fresh rubber. Untying the sopping wet laces of the disintegrating shoes on my feet, I tugged them off, and placed them in the crisp box. Scott shot me a look of envy.

"That's not fair," he said, pouting. "I want dry feet, too."

"Oh honey, my feet won't be dry for long," I assured him.

We snickered at how we spread our things out as if we owned the place, never minding that we also were directly across from the police department. Just then a white sedan pulled out of the parking lot into the street and cruised over, parking directly in front of us. A man in plain clothes stepped out.

"I couldn't help but notice you two over here. Looks like you're on a journey. Where are you coming from?" he said with what sounded like genuine interest, although we remained leery, uncertain if he was an officer.

"We're hiking the Long Path. It starts in New York City. We're headed towards the Adirondacks," Scott answered politely.

"Wow. Are you serious? You two walked from New York City?" the man asked, his eyes shining.

"Yep. It's been a long journey but we're almost there now," I seconded.

"Well, you still have a way to go to the Adirondacks. Wow," he said, rubbing his head. "That's so cool. I mean, what a worthwhile thing to do! People don't live anymore, you know, leave their homes, their comfort zones. Good for you. Hats off," he said with a smile and a tip of his baseball cap.

"Thank you," we said with a stutter, both of us relieved and, honestly, happy to have been proven wrong in our preconceived notions.

"No, thank you. Really. That's so cool. Do you guys need anything?" he asked.

I thought for a moment. But with all this food and gear laying before us, I couldn't think of a thing.

"Nope, I think we have all we need," I said, motioning to our things and looking to Scott who nodded his head in agreement.

The man paused and then said with a smirk, "Ha! Well I guess you do." He paused again as if thinking of what to say next, then added, "Well, good luck, you two."

"Thank you, we'll need it!" Scott replied with a chuckle and a roll of his eyes. The man nodded with a smile and walked inside the post office.

Once we had repacked our food and gear, we were left with a heaping pile of cardboard packaging, two empty boxes, and one pair of disgusting shoes.

"Where are we going to get rid of this stuff?" Scott asked.

"I'll see if there's a trashcan inside," I said, and grabbed up what I could in my arms.

No sooner had I walked in the door than the woman behind the counter said, "I can take that for you if you'd like."

"Are you sure? It's a lot, plus there's some really nasty shoes in here," I said, wincing.

"Yeah, yeah. It's no problem. Here, give that stuff to me. I'll put it in the dumpster out back," she replied, barely flinching. She was *definitely* someone's mom.

"I'm so sorry," I said, grimacing as she took my half-open box of shoes that I could smell from where I stood.

"It's fine. Safe journeys!" she said without delay and headed for the back.

This little town seemed alright. In fact, it seemed the farther north we traveled, the friendlier people became. I hoped the trend would continue.

Cheered up by our goodies and shameless public display of "hikerness," we hit the road walking in a light drizzle. But that drizzle soon intensified, strengthening to blowing, cold, biting rain. Growing more frigid by the minute, we stopped on the side of the road and pulled on our vests underneath our rain jackets, then hats and gloves. That blowing rain soon heightened into an all-out downpour, the wind constant. By the time we reached Nickerson's Campground, our good spirits had washed away.

Suddenly we spied shelter, a humble building with a sign above the door that read: Camp Store. We jogged up to its doorstep, peeled off our heavy backpacks and stepped inside its heated sanctuary, where we dripped our way up and down its brightly lit aisles in search of a hot beverage. We found a coffee maker with a full pot of coffee and steam roiled up to our faces as we filled our tiny

Styrofoam cups. We would've holed up in this simple little camp store a good while if the urgency to pee hadn't hit within our first few sips. The lady working the register directed us to the camping area where we could find a restroom. "It's just down the hill," she told us.

With our hands wrapped around our warm cups, we walked what turned out to be half a mile through the campground to a picnic table beside a bathhouse. We took a seat on its wet wooden benches. The pouring rain had thankfully reduced to a mere mist, but we couldn't shake our chill. Children ran around gleefully in sweatshirts and jeans and rode their bicycles over the gravel. Under the shelter of a pavilion across from us, a group of children did arts and crafts under the supervision of two women in hoodies, their sleeves rolled up. We sat bedraggled, wondering how on earth these people weren't in distress in these temps. It's a strange thing that happens gradually on the trail: when calorie deficient for days on end while physically exerting oneself to the utmost limit, cold penetrates to the bone. Our fat reserves had all burned up. We weighed our options. I considered simply camping here for the night. After all, the bathhouse was heated and if it came down to it, we could always dip inside in the night to get warm. But it was only noon and after camping for free over the last month, it seemed outrageous to pay for a soggy site surrounded by people. Plus, if we sat still all day we'd only grow colder and probably eat more of our food than we could afford. I suggested to Scott we hitch back to the hotel, which was not far from where we'd been camped this morning. "Hell yeah," Scott declared. But when I called them, all rooms were full. We had our answer, the only one. Hike on.

Leaving Nickerson's, we were graced by Mine Kill State Park. For four miles we cruised, warming up and nearly gliding along the rolling edges of ravines which cradled wide shallow creeks, first the Schoharie Creek and then the Mine Kill, and in this place, we too were cradled. Tall trees stood all around, their boughs shielding us from the rain that we heard hitting the leaves overhead. Winding our way down to the water's edge we stopped and gasped at a small waterfall that sprung forth from a skinny crevice in the bosom of the cliffside.

And in the way that only the trail can, our spirits were lifted yet again, made bright by the beauty before us.

Climbing a sloping hillside, we were reluctantly thrust from our wooded shelter into an open field of calf-high, wet grass. The water seeped through our shoes, and with each step we heard a woeful wet sucking sound. The wind picked up again and spat rain against our faces, and I struggled to keep my hood around my hat so that it wouldn't be wet come nightfall. Mother Nature is not cruel in such moments, but she is indifferent. It was up to us to adapt. That's when I noticed the lacy leaves of yarrow growing amidst the grass. Yarrow, the same resilient plant that we'd spotted back at the Catskill Mountain House, is a native plant that grows not only in grassy woods and meadows but amidst areas disturbed by humans, which is quite fitting given the spectrum of medicinal properties it confers. Its leaves and flowers are antibacterial and anti-inflammatory, but most importantly in our circumstances, diaphoretic, especially good at bringing warmth into extremities. Chewing these leaves might just keep our body temperature up and keep our fingers working in this cold, wet weather. I knelt and pinched their stems, gathering a half dozen to carry on with us.

In short order we reached a large park administration building. We stood in the sodden fields surrounding it and scanned the landscape for an awning. But there was none. Neon plastic play equipment, unnaturally bright against the dark skies, sat before it. I started to think, *Perhaps we could roll out our sleeping bags inside those tubular slides without being noticed.* But then I spotted it—a modest-sized canvas tent, something that might be used for a festival, with its walls rolled down to the ground. "Look, hon," I said to Scott, pointing at the tent. "Let's go!"

"You think we can get in there?" Scott asked.

"Oh, we'll get in," I assured him.

We whisked through the wet grass as fast as we could and, upon reaching it, peeked through one of its corners to see six picnic tables. Without a second thought, I unhooked a tent wall at a corner of the structure and we both squeezed inside.

"Oh, thank God." I said dropping my pack with a thud onto one of the picnic tables.

"Holy shit, it's dry! Everything is dry in here!" Scott exclaimed, thrusting off his pack and throwing back his hood. "This rain is like ice," he said, taking off his gloves and rubbing his hands together.

"I know, I'm freezing, and it's only going to get colder tonight."

Scott was already pulling out his phone to check the temps. "Says it's now supposed to get down to thirty-two degrees tonight," Scott said, looking up from his phone, his face filled with dread. "Do you think we'll be warm enough?"

I hesitated. I wanted to tell him, "Of course we will be, luv, don't worry." But I honestly wasn't so sure. If we had the right gear, like the two sleeping bags we'd sent back with my father that were rated to colder temperatures, we'd be fine, but our setup was subpar. "I think so. I mean, I don't know. I know we won't be comfortable, but we did okay at thirty-six degrees the other night."

"Yeah, but we hadn't walked all day in the rain that day." He motioned to his wet feet and bare legs. As much as we had wanted to put on long pants, we knew we couldn't afford to get them wet. We needed every article of clothing to keep us warm tonight.

"I know, hon, I know," I answered. "Let's at least do lunch for now."

"Sounds good," Scott replied, already munching on a handful of nuts.

While we ate, reveling in our shelter, I racked my brain for a solution.

"We could camp here," I suggested.

Scott looked around, sitting up straighter than before. "Hey, that's a thought. Do you think we might stay warmer in here? I mean, we're dry, we're out of the wind."

"Maybe. But we'd be running the risk of getting caught here. I imagine they patrol in the evening."

"Hmph," he said, slumping into his seat. "Yeah, they probably do, but really, what's the likelihood they're going to come looking in this tent?"

"True."

"How many miles have we gone?"

I looked at our damp guidebook pages, counted them up and let out a deep sigh. "Seven."

"We've only hiked seven miles?" Scott snapped.

"Yeah, because of all our stops I guess."

"That's it. We should hike on," Scott replied, laying his hand on the table with such command he reminded me of a judge with a gavel.

"Yeah?" I asked. He was clearly as miserable as me. I was shocked that, after all this, he was still so adamant about putting in a full day.

"Yeah, I mean, we probably won't be much warmer in here and if we've only done seven miles we may as well hike on and get our body temperature back up."

Better him than me deciding to push on. I didn't want to be the one responsible for turning us to hiker popsicles with the wrong call. He knew all the factors as well as I did and if he thought we could do it, then we would do it.

"Okay babe, then that's what we we'll do."

While we smeared peanut butter on tortillas, I got to thinking. I'd surrendered responsibility and placed my trust in him time and time again on this hike. And much to my own surprise I found peace in that. Whether the question was where to camp for the night or how much food to pack or which way to turn on the trail, it was so nice to not have to call all the shots. I was able to trust him out here only because my trust in him extended well beyond this hike, and although this ability to trust had become my new norm, I still found it immensely settling. I'd always been of the mind that I could do it all myself. Throughout my adult years my father would often tell others, usually when explaining why I chose this hike or that job, that I was "fiercely independent," and I'd prided myself on this. I believe I even used this self-reliance to justify relationships with men who didn't equally share the burdens, or who were in general unreliable. I didn't *need* a man to help me or guide my way. There are however—and I still believe in this firmly—not many men to which one should entrust such responsibility. Many perceive the privilege as entitlement and abuse the power. However, Scott showed me from the start that he wanted to share my weights and that his actions were not couched in his self-interest, but what was best for me, for us. What a welcome relief to not face life's forks in the road, hardships, or in this case, cold nights in the wilderness alone.

And so, upon finishing lunch, we packed our gear, bundled up, and emerged from our shelter into the brisk wind and mist. I shoved a yarrow leaf in my mouth and passed Scott a leaf too. He wouldn't balk at this plant, one that he already knew well from his time with elders. As I chewed the leaf, releasing its bitter flavor, my taste buds tingled and my mouth watered. Yarrow is also a sialagogue, meaning it will cause one to salivate. Whatever. A small price to pay for the warmth I soon felt creeping into my extremities. We walked another mile through swampy fields and reached the New York Power Authority's Blenheim-Gilboa complex. Here, hydroelectric technology provides large-scale energy storage and supplies electricity to the region. The complex also boasts the Lansing Manor Visitor's Center. When we stepped inside the visitor center, we were blasted by hot air, warming our cold skin and drying our sinuses. Electric heat—now that was *something*!

We got to chatting with an older man who acted as a host and tour guide. Although soft-spoken at first, he was soon bubbling with questions. Where had we started and where were we going? Where did we camp at night and how did we get food and water? In answering his many questions, my wheels started turning and I already knew that Scott's had as well. *Maybe this man could help us get somewhere warm.* We described in detail the cold night we'd had a couple nights ago and the trying time we'd had walking in the rain all day and our poor gear. We expressed our woe at sleeping in the even colder weather tonight and *just so happened* to mention that we wished there was a way we could get a hotel room.

"Oh yes, it is supposed to get very cold tonight," he said, wrinkling his brow.

"Yep, supposed to go down to freezing," I added.

"Hmm, you need a ride to a hotel?" he asked, seemingly deep in thought.

"We sure do. We considered hitching but it's a long shot out here and you never know who's going to pick you up," Scott replied.

"Well I'm about to close up here—" he started.

"Oh! Really?" I interjected, already so very grateful.

"But I'm afraid my car is too small."

"Oh," I said, pausing then and waiting for the rest of his statement. Surely, he'd say that if we didn't mind being squished, he'd give us a lift.

"Well, good luck you two. It's going to be a cold night," he said, going back to shuffling some papers behind a desk.

"Oh, okay, thanks," Scott said, turning for the door; I stood there dumbstruck a moment longer before following suit.

Once outside, I announced to Scott, "I would have ridden in the trunk."

"Me too. I would have stood on the fucking bumper."

Over our next four miles we hiked in temps that were thankfully now at the promised high of forty-five degrees. We filled up on water from a creek and walked a quiet road through the valley, passing rolling fields so green they nearly glowed, towers of carefully stacked, enormous blond hay bales, tractors with tires taller than me, and big old red barns. All the while the rain held off. Finally dipping back into the forest, we followed a rocky, overgrown woods road through blackberry brambles, twining grape vines with shredding bark, and tall oak trees. We were tired and these woods were thick with vegetation, so when we spotted a semiflat spot alongside the tract, we called it home.

We stripped off our wet clothing before crawling inside our tent and then hastily pulled on all the warm dry clothing we had and got tucked inside our sleeping bags for the night. It was already six-thirty and nightfall would be coming soon. It was important we get as warm as possible before the temps really started to drop for the night. And so, from our snug cocoon, we cooked in the vestibule and then ate dinner with the tent doors zipped shut to hold in our body heat and steam. By the time we were done, we were delightfully warm, and if it weren't for the fact that we could see our own breath inside the tent, we would've almost forgotten about the dire predictions. Not a bird or insect chirped from the dark forest, for even they had nestled in for the night. We wrapped our bodies around each other, pulled our bags tight around us, and fell into slumber.

Sometime after midnight, I awoke feeling like someone had beaten my body with a hammer. All my bones ached, and my joints felt so stiff it was painful to move them. My sleeping pad was no defense against the cold earth beneath us. I rolled over to alleviate the pressure on my hip bone and left shoulder, and as I did, Scott too rolled over with a deep groan, wincing. Apparently, he felt the same. It was just so cold. I felt as if I could feel every mile we had walked on this trek. Every single one. We awoke roughly every hour to roll over. And so, together we rotated, like a rotisserie chicken, throughout the night. When one of us rolled over to reduce the pain, then the other rolled over to regain the other's warmth. I hoped I didn't start to shiver because I knew if I did, I wouldn't be able to stop. I tried with all my might to convince myself I didn't have to pee. I didn't want to let any of our body heat escape the tent upon opening the door, but soon I had no choice. I strapped on my headlamp and crawled outside, its bright beam reflecting off frost that lay like a sparkling blanket atop the leaf litter. My breath billowed from my mouth. I peed as quick as I could and retreated to the tent to huddle close to Scott. I checked the time on my watch; it was five in the morning. The bands of tension that wrapped around my joints released their grip. The sun would soon rise and we would hike again, which would undoubtedly be warmer than lying here in this icebox.

CHAPTER THREE

When I opened my eyes and saw our sleeping bag cast
in the dim morning light, I unzipped the tent door to find a forest floor still shimmering with frost. I pulled out our cook pots, instant coffee, and the remaining
yarrow leaves. Scott remained fast asleep until he finally stirred to the sound of
my pouring hot water into our mugs. Sitting there, sipping yarrow-infused coffee,
our faces bathed in its steam, we peered at each other bleary-eyed and full of
relief. "I'm so happy it's morning," I told Scott, letting out a big sigh.

"Me too. I'm just so happy I'm drinking this hot cup of coffee."

"That too." I took a sip and could feel its warmth travel all the way down
my throat and into my belly.

"Tastes a little funny though," Scott said, making a face.

"Yarrow leaves."

"Good God, is nothing sacred?" Scott said holding up his cup of coffee.

"You know, I was a little worried last night," I told him, looking into
my mug.

"Yeah, me too. But I knew we would be okay," he said with a smile. "And
why's that?"

"Because, baby, you're hot. You're so hot, you could melt all this stuff!"
he declared, motioning to the frozen world around us. This is a line by Steve

Martin from *My Blue Heaven*, and he loved quoting it. I was glad he still had a sense of humor.

Miserable or not, we had survived the night, and that was all that really mattered. The temp on Scott's phone read just one degree above freezing; the temperature was rising. We slurped down some oatmeal and although half-tempted to lay back down in our sleeping bags, cuddling in the gradually warming of the earth, we instead pulled on our still wet shoes from the day before and got to hiking.

Our feet squishing in our shoes, we passed into Eminence State Forest, the former site of one of the first settlements in the Schoharie Valley. At one time, this forest had provided valuable resources—lumber, potash, charcoal, and bark for tanning—which to these settlers meant income. In addition to harvesting from the forest, settlers took to farming, growing hops, tobacco, and wheat. A sawmill, gristmill, and a good many homes were established on this land and its inhabitants eked out a living there until its resources were virtually depleted. In the 1930s, under the New York State Reforestation Law, the state gradually purchased this barren abandoned land and, over time, has returned it to a more balanced state. However, remnants of the past persisted everywhere we looked. Stone walls lined the trail, and we stumbled upon several foundations, their doorways crumbled, floors carpeted with leaves, and skinny trees growing inside them like planters. We imagined what these homes had looked like. Where inside these small spaces would the bed have been, and the kitchen, the bathroom? On second thought, likely they hadn't had indoor plumbing. More intricately built stone structures, those that had once been part of the mill, stood sturdy, keeping watchful eye along the stream that once fed them. These had a presence all their own, perhaps imbued with the energy of those who had once frequented this place long ago. It was as if we were discovering a lost civilization for the first time.

The trail was at times steep and rocky but still a far cry from that which we'd traversed in the Catskills. We rejoiced in this repeatedly, even as we tore through web after sparkling web on this trail. Yesterday's difficulties seemed so very far away. This time and place were ours and the trail was good.

"What the fuck?" I blurted, suddenly feeling the weight in my pack shift to one shoulder. I held my pack up from behind with one hand and examined myself. That's when I saw it, my shoulder strap hanging by a thread.

Scott was walking back towards me. "What's up?"

"My strap just broke!"

"What do you mean your strap broke?" Scott asked, bewildered, although he too was now examining the broken strap.

I shrugged off my pack angrily and looked at where the thick nylon ribbon ran through the buckle that was then stitched onto the padded shoulder strap. This entire thick ribbon had torn, not at the stitching but through the fabric of the pack itself.

"Shit," he said, now seeing clearly what I saw.

I wanted to scream. I wanted to cry. And I would do both but first I would get angry and rifle through my pack for a thread and needle. I wrenched out every item, hunting for that little Ziploc of emergency items I never used. Finding it, I huffed and sweated and cursed, pushing the needle back and forth through the thick ribbon and then the flimsy nylon of the shoulder strap. Twenty minutes later . . . I had sewn the strap back on. "It had better work," I mumbled. Scott, who had been sitting patiently, assured me that it would hold. I hoisted the pack back on. For a few sweet seconds it held . . .then dropped like dead weight. It had torn and worse now than before.

"God dammit." I threw the pack off again.

I stood staring at it. It was my partner and it had betrayed me.

"What the hell am I going to do? I can't hike with that thing." I said motioning to my pack. For so many years this pack had traveled with me on countless trails, carrying all that I needed reliably. It was as if it had a soul of its own. I was angry for it giving up on me and strangely mad at myself for deeming it worthless so readily.

"Hey, wait," Scott said then, reaching for a compression strap on the side of his pack. He had been missing a buckle on his pack from the day he'd bought it. It wasn't an integral part of the backpack, so rather than deal with getting it straightened out with the company, we'd secured the strap with a heavy-duty safety pin.

"Yes! That might work!" I grabbed it from him, nearly taking his hand with it.

I pushed the pin through the ribbon and padding of the pack, hoping that it would remain secure. Scott remained quiet, allowing me to work in my fury and knowing that anything he said could trigger my wrath.

"There," I said, standing up and putting the pack on. "There! It's holding!" I announced with giddy relief. I took a few steps and the safety pin popped open.

I threw the pack off violently and dropped to my knees in the dirt. I felt my face grow hot and my eyes well with tears until I could no longer see the ground before me.

"Come on babe, we'll fix it," Scott said. I could hear him rolling over the pack that I'd thrown beside me.

"You can't fix it. Just leave it be," I said meanly.

I knew I looked like a child throwing a temper tantrum, and I didn't care. But, then I did. My face grew hotter, not from anger but from embarrassment. Scott didn't deserve my anger. But I was just so frustrated. Why this? Why now? We'd come so far and now I'd have to either navigate getting another pack or hike in pain with a pack falling off me the rest of the way. Gear can make or break a hike, and dammit, I didn't want anything to break this.

"Hey," he said, coming over to me now.

I didn't want him to see me crying. Sure, I had cried countless times in front of him before, but I was supposed to be the experienced hiker, ready for any obstacle, not some enraged woman crying in the woods over a backpack.

I looked up at him with tears streaming down my face.

"Hey, you," he said, wiping away my tears. "It's okay. We'll get it figured out."

I wanted to resist him. I didn't need comforting. I was fine. But when he kissed my forehead and pulled me in close to him, I knew that this was all I needed. I let myself be held and cared for and loved. Whether my behavior was warranted or irrational, it didn't matter. And he didn't care either. All that he wanted to do was make me feel better. I buried my face in his shoulder and leaned into him.

"Baby. Don't worry. I will figure it out. Can I please look at it?" he asked calmly.

"Yes," I mumbled back. "I'm sorry. It's just this is the last thing we need right now. I know we don't have much longer left, but I can't hike with one shoulder strap."

He took his time and worked the safety pin through, this time angling it at a different direction and closer to the edge of the shoulder pad. "Try this," he said, holding up the pack for me to put on now. I slipped it on and furtively bounced a couple times on my toes, then paced back and forth on the trail. It appeared to be holding. I felt a small smile stretching across my face as I looked to Scott sheepishly.

"It's holding," I stated.

"Yes, I see that," he replied, with an expression that said *I told you so.*

"I'm sorry, honey. Thank you," I said, giving him a hug. "I guess I freaked out."

"It's okay. I get it. I'm just glad that we were able to fix it. But just so you know, you don't have to yell at me when I'm trying to help you," he said, holding me, his arms wrapped around the backpack, too.

"I know. I love you." I still felt like a child.

"I love you, too. It's okay. I love you no matter what," he said, and I knew that he meant it because no matter what argument we'd had in our time together, in the end we always came back to this. No matter what . . . I love you. We didn't arrive at the Rossman Hill Lean-to until two o'clock in the afternoon, having done just six and a half miles according to the guide. It was unlikely we'd make it another seven miles as planned. Apparently, the backpack crisis had taken a good deal longer than we'd thought. We broke for lunch, and with clouds that rolled in painting the sky gray, we felt the cold seeping back into our bones. I longed for our unseasonably warm temperatures, but it seemed they were done. Fall had definitely arrived.

After lunch we came to a large pond with a long promenade. The sun burned through the clouds, shining bright atop the water. We dropped our packs and laid on the warm wooden dock, our faces turned towards the sky, and despite the cold persistent wind, for just a few minutes we were warm. We had visions of sunbathing for the afternoon, but we instead returned to the trail and in a couple of miles we exited the woods into a sunny meadow, where the tall drying grass now scratched at our bare legs. Once through the meadow, we reached a road that would lead us into the tiny hamlet of West Fulton. In the abundant late afternoon sun, we took another break on the roadside, sharing an instant coffee and a smoke before hitting the pavement again.

"What do you think we might find here?" I asked teasingly, enjoying the ease of the flat surface beneath my feet and the way the pavement reflected heat against my skin.

"A whole lotta nothing."

"How about a pizzeria?" I posited. "Oh, wouldn't that be wonderful!"

I knew he was right. The guidebook listed no services in West Fulton, and we could tell by the map that it was tiny. But hey, a girl can dream.

"Yeah, maybe it'll be next to the Chinese buffet," Scott said with a smirk.

"Or maybe the diner or, or the Indian restaurant!" I was really pushing it now. We'd be lucky if there were a damn gas station in this town.

We approached a corner in the center of "downtown" West Fulton. So far all I could see were two churches, a tiny park, and a humble two-story white building. But wait, laughter trickled from therein. As we neared, I noticed an old-fashioned shop sign hanging outside a side door that read "Panther Creek," an artistically sketched outline of a panther's face above it.

"Wait a second, hon, what's this? Maybe it's a tavern!" I gasped. The laughter was louder now, and I could hear folks chatting.

"Nah, I doubt it," Scott said, barely looking up.

"But, do you hear that laughter? There's people!" I said again.

Just as we rounded the corner, a woman's voice called out, "Hey hikers! Where are you going? Are you hungry?"

In unison we spun around in a snap and saw a folding table filled with food, a grill, and roughly ten friendly faces standing on a tiny square of lawn.

"Well, sure!" I answered without second's hesitation and made a beeline in their direction. Scott followed suit.

A sweet-looking gray-haired woman thrust paper plates into our hands.

"Welcome travelers! Where are you going! I hope you can join us in our hall!" said a man with short dark hair who stood proudly before us, his arms outstretched, with a beer in one hand and a smoke in the other. He seemed to be in charge.

Suddenly I hesitated; memories resurfaced of instances in which overzealous fundamental Christians had lured me and other desperate hikers into their clutches with free food. In these instances, yes, one got fed, but part of the deal was enduring a painfully long lecture about how their way was the one true way and yours would only lead into the fires of hell. I looked to Scott; was he picking up on these vibes?

"We're, uh, headed towards the Adirondacks," Scott mumbled.

"Oh! The Long Path!" the man proclaimed. "So, you started in New York City?"

I nodded.

"That's amazing!" gasped a middle-aged woman with long curly hair standing next to him.

"You guys know about it?" Scott asked now looking around at the crowd, whose eyes were all on us.

"Sure, we do! We go hiking on it all the time," the man replied.

"Yeah, the trail is just a couple miles from my house!" another older woman chimed in. "Just over that mountain there!"

"I'm a Department of Environmental Conservation ranger, I'm on the trail a lot," a man added who sat in a folding chair.

"That's so cool. Not too many people we've met actually know that the trail goes through their town," I clarified, feeling a little more relaxed, the creepy religious zealot feeling beginning to fade some. "So, what are y'all doing here, I mean what is the gathering for?" It seemed only fair that I ask some questions of my own.

"We just love to eat!" piped in a mustached man who sat with a plate of food on his lap.

"Ha! Yes, we do love to eat! But we're an arts community. We have these meals regularly. Sometimes they're potlucks like this, or turkey dinners, or pancake breakfasts. We're always working to bring people together in this little town. It's a special place. West Fulton may be small, but there are so many wonderful people here," the man in charge explained.

Ah. Artists, not religious zealots. Now I could eat.

"Let me give you two a tour of our hall!" the man said then.

Well, almost.

Before we knew it, we'd dropped our packs and were following him inside the two-story white building. We first passed through a spacious kitchen with a wooden table spread with condiments, pots and pans, and the like. Clearly this space saw its share of use. He then led us up a narrow staircase to the upper level, which opened into a large room with hardwood floors, two walls lined with windows, and a stage. We learned that this building had most recently served as a Methodist church but before that had been used as a public hall for town meetings. Our impromptu tour guide was named Gregory, and he and his wife, Cornelia, were now its owners. They had been working on fixing the place up for the last eight years and besides their meals, they also hosted plays and about ten concerts a year. Gregory even invited us to come perform after we finished the trail.

"You guys have got to see this," Gregory said, reaching up and pulling a cord beside the stage.

Suddenly a large canvas banner nearly the width of the stage unfurled, awash with colorful logos and slogans.

"These are the names of the all the original businesses that once flourished here in West Fulton. I mean, look at this!"

It was astounding indeed. West Fulton had, at one time, been a full-fledged town offering every service one might need. It also appeared that many of the business owners had done double duty, as we saw the same names repeatedly. The funeral director could also do home repair and the plumber could also trim your beard. I mean, why not? There may have never been a lot of people in West Fulton, but it seemed together they all chipped in, creating a lively community. "Come on, though, I've kept you guys enough. You need to eat!" he announced, turning and leading us from the hall back down the stairs.

"Did he release you finally?" the woman with the curly hair joked, and I assumed this must be Cornelia by the sly look that she threw him. "Let these two hikers eat!"

And so we did. We piled our plates high with grilled potatoes, beets, sweet corn on the cob lathered with butter, chips, and homemade salsa. And in between ravenous bites, we learned the name of every single person there. We spent a good deal of time talking plants with a couple that own a nursery and then with the DEC ranger, sharing our tales of very large porcupines and the bear encounter from the other night. In the span of our hour's worth of conversation, we were offered numerous places to camp; we could pop our tent on the lawn, on the nursery owner's lawn four miles up the hill, or even in the town park. "Oh, the town won't care a bit!" Gregory claimed. We seriously considered our invites. But still, there were miles to do and with the sun dipping ever closer to the surrounding mountaintops, we decided we had better get moving. That is, after a group photo with the folks of Panther Creek Arts.

"You two come back and play a show for us!" Gregory said, patting Scott on the shoulder and passing him his card. "And be safe. You're almost there," he said, looking us both in the eyes with a wistful look that said he understood our desire to *journey*.

We departed to a chorus of "Good luck!" and "Have fun!" and as we climbed a steep grassy hill in the dusky light out of town we chuckled the whole way. How this group had illuminated our day simply by being gracious and friendly. It was so good to feel like "normal" people at an afternoon picnic and to get to know so many kind and interesting people that we otherwise would never had crossed paths with. True trail magic. We would surely return to play a show.

CHAPTER FOUR

"It's supposed to be just as cold tomorrow night," Scott announced, after scrolling through the weather on his phone.

We sat there in the early morning light, clothed in every shred of clothing we had and wrapped in our sleeping bag, grateful to have survived another cold night. Our evening had closed with hiking up seemingly endless freshly logged tracts, and we'd almost lost our way due to all the trees that had been felled. The DEC ranger had warned us of this industry on the mountain but there was no alternate route. By the light of our headlamps, we'd set up camp near a tiny stream as the temps dropped. As the night had progressed, the ground beneath us only grew colder, gradually drawing the heat from our bodies. I wrapped my hands around my coffee mug wishing I could cuddle my entire body around it. I looked over the day's mileage.

"Oh my God, hon."

"Oh shit. What?" Scott asked.

"I overestimated how many miles it was to Middleburgh."

"*Overestimated*? Well that's a first!" Scott shot back.

"No, I mean really overestimated. We could reach Middleburgh by three o'clock in the afternoon!" I declared, thrusting the guidebook pages at him.

"For real? Is there a chance we could sleep inside somewhere, where it's warm?" he asked, putting down his coffee, his face flushing with the mere thought.

"Mmm, well—"

"You're kidding me!" Scott interjected.

"Hold on a second. It's complicated."

"I don't care how complicated, or how much the cab fare costs, we're doing it."

"There's a bus that offers public transportation to a town ten miles away. Remember Andy telling us about that? Supposedly there's a hotel there. But I don't know anything about the bus route."

"We'll figure it out. Come on, don't you want to sleep inside? It's been freezing!"

"Of course I do, hon, I can't even feel my fingers right now."

We'd been graced with a miracle. If we could navigate this bus route, we were guaranteed warmth. This hotel, like the one in Windham, had been so far from the trail it hadn't made sense to plan on it, but given the extreme temperatures we'd been enduring, it was well worth the trouble. In just one week's time, we'd gone from being so unbearably hot that we feared heat stroke to so cold we feared hypothermia. I studied the directions to see just what kind of mileage we could do in the miles following Middleburgh.

"My God."

"Oh shit. Now what?" Scott asked, setting his cup of coffee down with a plunk.

"If we keep this pace up, we'll have just four more days of hiking."

Scott went quiet for a moment, then declared, "That's reason for celebration! Middleburgh, here we come!" He raised his coffee proudly like a frothy mug of beer.

We did some Google work and found that there was an inexpensive motel in a little town called Cobleskill. But our miracles didn't stop there . . . beside it sat a Pizza Hut. Suddenly I felt the heat returning to my fingertips, and my muscles yearned to move. We were motivated.

The path led us steeply up and down snowmobile trails, summiting countless unnamed knobs void of views; still, the miles seemed effortless. By noon, the sun shone bright and warm, so that we could finally peel off our many layers. We glided through the woods, the trees towering overhead, when suddenly we were thrust onto busy Route 30.

Mack trucks and cars whizzed past dangerously close as we walked against traffic between the painted white line and the steep embankment on a narrow strip of pavement. Just when I thought I could bare the rumbling roadway no longer; we rounded a wide bend and saw it . . . a looming rock promontory. Vromon's Nose sat like a giant, a monolith out of place amidst the flat farmlands that spread out, expansive, on the opposite side of the roadway. When we reached its base, we faced a skinny trail that went straight up.

"This is going to be fun," Scott announced.

"Yeah, probably not, but the guidebook says its only 0.2 miles to the top," I assured him.

He rolled his eyes at me and took off in the lead.

We climbed on loose scree up zig-zagging trail that proved to be one of the steepest on our entire hike. Two-tenths of a mile never felt so long, but when we literally clawed our way onto a more gradual sloping trail and then walked the short way to the summit, we were well rewarded. Hand in hand, we walked cautiously across the flat rock cliff crisscrossed with fissures to its edge. We stood speechless. A green valley spread out like a blanket below us, patchworked with fields of crops, their borders clearly delineated by clean straight lines. Winding roads snaked between gleaming silos, red barns, and tiny clusters of homes that sat farther in the distance. "This is what we hike for," I said to Scott, looking at his weary face in the sunlight. His beard was thick, his golden curls spilled out from his headband, his tan was further darkened by dirt, and his eyes were reflective. He looked different than he had before we'd left—smooth-shaven and showered and well rested—yet this version of his face now seemed like the only one I had ever really known, and he radiated happiness. He kissed me and added, "No, this is what we hike for."

We followed the flat rock of the cliff's edge across the ridgetop and stopped for lunch, basking in the warmth of the afternoon sun. I called the hotel in the nearby town of Cobleskill—they had rooms—we were good.

Reaching Middleburgh by two o'clock, we found a bustling town lined with sidewalks and stores. We grabbed a soda from the nearest gas station and set ourselves to the task of finding out how to catch the bus. Reportedly the library had bus schedules and so we walked until we spotted it. Once inside we did indeed find a schedule posted on the wall with many times and stops, going all the way to Albany, but interpreting it was proving impossible. I went up to the counter and chatted with the librarian and another woman who joined in to try and help and together we deciphered that the next bus would arrive at four o'clock and arrive in Cobleskill at five forty-five. The ten-mile ride would take nearly two hours. Our hearts sank. Middleburgh was indeed an adorable small town laid out for strolling but we wanted nothing more to do with strolling. We wanted to be showered and fed and warm and lying naked in our hotel bed with the heat blasting. We couldn't bear the thought of waiting another two hours just to ride another two hours in a moving vehicle. That was more time than we had spent in an automobile, even collectively, on our entire trip. The librarian graciously invited us to hang in the library until the bus came, but instead we thanked her and dragged ourselves out to a bench where we could have a smoke and wallow.

There we sat slumped on a wooden bench, as I gave strangers sad faces in hopes that someone might offer us a ride. Scott Googled away on his phone looking for a local cab company but came up with nothing. I had just suggested we pop in the local watering hole across the street and ask if anyone was going that way when all of a sudden, on the corner, a bus pulled up. We looked at each other and then back to the bus and watched as a man stepped inside. I jumped from my seat and ran up to its door just as it closed. Feverishly, I pounded on its glass surface.

The driver sneered at me silently and then opened the door.

"Are you going to Cobleskill?"

"Yes," he replied coldly.

"Can you wait one second? Our bags are back on that bench," I asked in the sweetest tone I could.

"Yeah, but hurry up, I got places to be," he shot back.

I turned and darted back to Scott and we scurried, fast as we could, dragging our packs and trekking poles. "Watch them pokers. It's a new bus and I don't want you messing it up," scolded the bus driver as we squeezed our way down the aisle to our seats. We tumbled into our seat, wedged our backpacks atop our laps, and placed our hiking sticks handles down on the ground with tips up so they wouldn't scratch the floor. Twenty minutes later we were standing in front of a dropoff in front of the Cobleskill Price Chopper. Turns out we had misinterpreted the schedule. *Thank God.* Scanning our surroundings, apparently, we'd been delivered to hiker heaven. Our hotel was just up the nearby hill, the Pizza Hut was across the parking lot, the laundromat was next door, and an AutoZone beside where we could get fuel for our stoves sat on the corner. We were happy as could be.

That night, we celebrated in the way only two people who've been deprived the pleasures of civilization would appreciate. At Pizza Hut we gorged ourselves on plates of cheap salad mix drowned in ranch dressing and prepackaged macaroni salad and sliced peaches likely scooped from a ten-pound can. After that we indulged in a large cheese pizza dripping with grease and cold bubbly Sprite served in bottomless plastic cups. For dessert we picked up a box of chocolate-chocolate-chip cookies, each one the size of our heads, and swilled whiskey cocktails back at the motel room. Like two beached whales, we managed to make love and afterwards, instead of postcoital cigarettes, turned to leftover pizza. We drifted off around midnight while watching bad sitcoms on television, the empty box still at the foot of the bed and the heat pumping hardily through the radiator.

We awoke feeling chipper, proof that the hiker metabolism is indeed a remarkable thing. After hoofing it to Price Chopper for coffee and bagels and to resupply for our final days on the trail, we returned to our room to leisurely pack up and lounge about—something we'd not yet allowed ourselves to do with a town stay. We had the bright idea to call the bus service rather than trying to interpret it for ourselves and learned that it would be headed our way in about a half hour. We would arrive in Middleburgh just after noon. Perfect.

When the bus door cranked open, we were greeted by the same cranky bus driver as yesterday, but this time rather than scolding us, he merely eyed us silently upon boarding. The driver made stops at Wal-Mart and Save-a-Lot and we were soon surrounded with the aging population of Middleburgh and they *all* talked about that new bus!

"What a bus, Joe! I couldn't believe it when I sat in those seats yesterday, hmm, maybe that was the day before last, can't remember," the white-haired man trailed off and then exclaimed, "She's a beaut!"

"Yes, she is. I'll have her again tomorrow," the bus driver replied proudly.

I guess this explained Joe's concern the day before and although we were on an older bus today, we were still careful with our "pokers."

The day was bright and new as we stepped off the bus onto the curb. Today would be grand. The sun was shining, and the temperatures were predicted to rise into the sixties. We took a seat upon that same bench outside the library and it was hard to remember how deflated, desperate we had felt just yesterday. Late last night, we'd decided upon shorter miles for the day and so with no reason to rush, we settled in for a good long sit.

Those are big backpacks! Where are you going?" asked a burly man who looked like he was working construction nearby.

"You look like you're on a long trip! Where are you coming from?" asked another passerby, this time a middle-aged woman walking her dog.

Over the course of an hour, we got to know the townspeople of Middleburgh. And it seemed that each one, upon learning that we'd been hiking for a month's time on the Long Path, offered words of support or found a way to relate. Some shared a story about a family member or friend who hiked part of the Appalachian Trail and many mentioned having read *A Walk in the Woods* by Bill Bryson. More importantly, it seemed they sparked conversation not out of suspicion but curiosity. We thought back to the strangers that had passed us on the trail in the Palisades and warily avoided eye contact and the man at the firehouse near Harriman State Park who nearly had refused to open his door and then handled us with great caution. How differently we were approached by those we met in the southern portion of the trail compared to those here near its northern terminus. Quite simply, the farther north we went, the nicer people became, and ironically here in Middleburgh, I couldn't help but feel I'd stepped into a tiny mountain town, reminiscent of those I knew in North Carolina. These people shined with a country hospitality that reigned supreme over anywhere else we had yet visited on this trek. Their interest and warmth filled us up and had we not gotten hungry again, we could have sat there on that bench for the rest of the day.

We crossed the street and grabbed hearty sandwiches for small town prices at Mona's Café. As we devoured our creamy egg salad and tuna salad on toasted white bread, we noticed the numerous patrons chatting with each other from their respective tables and making conversation with the waitresses as well. It seemed as if everyone knew each other and from what we could overhear, the conversations were light and pleasant, about common things like grandchildren and sports or how things were going at "the shop." Unknowingly, we'd stepped into a little slice of Americana, and it was lovely.

The Helderberg Escarpment

PART EIGHT:

THE CAPITAL

DISTRICT

Partridgeberry

CHAPTER ONE

Sweat beaded on Scott's brow and I could feel the back of my shirt dampening with perspiration, as we climbed up, up, up. Why does it always have to be *up?* Painful as it is, a long hard climb out of town is typically the rule on long-distance trails. It is to be expected; towns sit in the valleys, not on the top of the mountains. But neither of us dared to utter a complaint aloud, for at least we weren't cold and we had *everything* we needed . . . well almost.

The only thing worse than a steep ascent with a fully resupplied backpack is a fully resupplied backpack laden with liters of water. So, we'd decided to pack only what we needed to reach a reliable well with a hand-pump that, according to the guide, could be found at a road-crossing. When we reached said well, all we found was a rusted pump with a broken handle covered in cobwebs. A dilapidated house, slowly being swallowed by the forest, sat across the street. This crappy pump probably hadn't been used since that place had been livable.

We were nearly out of water. The guidebook showed no stream crossings between where we stood and our nearby camp for the night. But if there was one residence on this road, err, *had been*, surely there had to be others. If we had to, we'd knock on someone's door. We hoofed it up the street and after rounding a bend, saw a large body of water surrounded by grass to our left. But as we excitedly pick up our pace and drew closer, my heart sunk. A beaver lodge sat prominently in its center.

Beaver fever. The runs. The trots. The shits. Call it what you want, but this water looked like a cesspool for that which is more properly called Giardia. Even with just a few days left on the trail, this wasn't a chance I was willing to take. Giardia is a protozoa transmitted by ingesting water contaminated with animal feces and is the number one reason why we sterilize our water with chlorine. However, even with purification, it seemed we were asking for it. Once infected—if you're lucky—it takes one to two weeks for the protozoa to multiply and flourish in your intestinal tract. Then the symptoms set in: severe diarrhea, bloating, gas that smells like rotten eggs. Symptoms worsen until treated with antibiotics or an herbal antidote, or your immune system fights it off, which can take months and lead to a host of other health problems. Without resolve, one can nearly waste away. Beavers are known carriers.

Just then, we spotted a jeep coming down the road. *Perhaps its driver would stop and ask us if we needed anything.*

He passed us without slowing. I spun 'round to throw up my arms, maybe he'd see me in his rearview, but before I could, I saw the red glow of his taillights. He was backing up!

With his elbow on the sill, the driver leaned his head out the window, "Okay, gonna be nosy! Y'all hiking the Long Path?"

"Yes!" I exclaimed, feeling already we had an ally.

"Trail doesn't go this way," the man said, "it goes through those woods up there." He motioned down the road from where we had come.

"We know. We're looking for water because the handpump up there was busted, and the pond here looks pretty murky."

He laughed. "That hand-pump hasn't worked for years!" Then he added, "Oh man, the pond? Trust me, you don't want to drink out of there!"

When he had finishing chuckling, he motioned to the back of his jeep.

"Hop in and come on up to the house. You two can fill up at my spigot."

Scott was already taking off his pack to throw in the back.

"Oh my God, thank you!" I exclaimed.

"Yeah, thanks man. Thank you so much!" Scott seconded.

"Of course, no problem guys!"

The Trail Gods had smiled upon us once again. Turned out this man lived right around the corner. In ten minutes, we'd filled our reserves and were back on the trail.

It was only five-thirty in the evening, the earliest yet, when we rolled into our campsite on Cotton Hill. Tucked into a cove of evergreens, birch, and oak and carpeted with a bed of deep green moss, we found the most well-kept lean-to we'd encountered the entire trip. A beautiful place to call home for the night. We dropped our packs and I began setting up our tent inside the lean-to for extra warmth, while Scott got to building a fire using dry wood that lay scattered around the fire ring. We prepared dinner by the light of the setting sun rather than our headlamps and reveled in sitting upon the flat hardwood of the lean-to floor. With hot food in hand and a little nip of whiskey, my heart ached with gratitude for the moment; nights such as these were in short number. We had roughly thirty-five miles left to go.

"I don't know that I'm ready for this to end," I said while gazing into the fire.

"I know I'm not."

"You're not?" Honestly, I was a little surprised by how quickly he'd fired back and with conviction.

"Well sure, in a way, I'm ready. I mean, when we reach the end of this thing, I'm going to be so proud of us! Hiking over 350 miles without stopping—that's one hell of a feat. But the next day, we're going to wake up in our bed back in the *real* world."

"I know. The real world that in so many ways seems less real than this one. Life is so much simpler out here. I mean it's hard, but—"

"Hell yeah, it is," Scott interjected.

"Ha! Yes, it is. But we worry only about the necessities and any day in which those basic needs are met is a good one. Any day that gifts us with a beautiful vista or a stretch of trail speckled with unusual plants, or hell, a shower, a mini mart, or a hotel room, it feels like manna from heaven." I stirred the pasty noodles in my pot, grateful they were warm and that I still had a few bites left.

"As it should. I take a lot for granted in our everyday life. I try not to, but I know I do," he said, scraping his bowl clean.

"I do too. It's hard not to when your basic needs are so easily met every day. Flip a switch and there's light, turn a handle and there's running water, turn the stove dial and there's flame."

"Toilet seats . . . I took those for granted!" Scott added.

"Ah! I know. I'm looking forward to that." We both chuckled and then sat in silence for a moment, listening to the soft rustling of leaves overhead and pine sap sizzling in the fire that unleashed sparks into the darkening sky.

"We spend our energy focusing on all these things that don't really matter. Day in and day out we work and get wrapped up in the little dramas that don't really qualify at all. So much of that crap is trivial."

"All of that seems so far away now," Scott said, now leaning back on his elbows and lighting a smoke.

"It does, but it's all happening right now. There's a whole world back home that is just the same as we when left it and when we did, we were just as much *in* it as everyone else."

"You're right, we were." Scott took a long drag off his smoke. "Well, we'll just have to hold onto this. Hold on tight to this presence. This awareness."

I stood up and put another couple of broken branches on the fire. "We will do our damnedest. This is us wholly and completely, with perspective and unencumbered by all that needless weight. And *us*, my God, you're right. We will have completed one hell of a feat, together." I slid close to him now so that we sat shoulder to shoulder, our legs dangling from the edge of the lean-to. I poured a little more whiskey in our camp mugs.

"What we've done is nothing short of miraculous. How many couples could spend over a month together, every hour of every day, climb up and down mountains—so many mountains—in scorching highs and frigid lows, work the logistics of miles and food and camp, not to mention endure each other's stink after having not showered in days, and all without a single fight?" Scott asked while looking at me, the firelight illuminating those warm eyes. I held back a smile.

"Well. I don't know about a single fight!" I knew I could think of a few.

He smiled. "Yeah, well, there's going to be times when we get frustrated and even angry, but we worked through that stuff together. We stuck to the trail and we stuck to us and we're stronger for it. I love you more now than I ever thought I could love anyone." He wiped a tear from his eye, and I felt mine welling up as well.

It was true. My love for Scott had already exceeded that which I thought possible. It was varied and deep and passionate, like a vine with a hundred different tendrils that twined this way and that around my heart; but now there was a blossom, nurtured by having ventured together into the unknown. Together, we navigated through the challenging times and persevered when we thought we might not. Together, we also witnessed beauty and grace and recognized the undeniable magic of our earthly existence. These experiences cultivated trust and appreciation for each other, but deeper than that, a mutual reverence. This was a partnership, a companionship I had never before known. "Every day we've been out here, I've loved you more and not just because you're here hiking this trail—I'd love you trail or no trail—but because every day you gave me your whole self and every day you lifted me up. I've never had that. And damn, baby, if we can make it through this, we can make it through anything." I wanted to convey to him all that I felt inside, but as always, it seemed insufficient.

"Even re-entry into the *real* world," Scott assured me, focusing those warm eyes on mine. "We *will* be the same people once we're home and back to work, and we *will* hike again. This is not our last hike." He laid on this side now and guided me to come close. I pressed my body against his and breathed deep, struck by how clean we both still smelled.

"It's not, right?" I still found it hard to believe that I truly had a partner that *wanted* to hike these long trails with me. Some tiny part of me still said *It's too good to be true.*

"Not by a long shot. There are so many more to hike! I'd hike all my days with you if I could," he said then and kissed me gently.

"Holy shit. My nose is warm. First morning in a week."

"First morning in a week what?" I asked groggily.

"That my nose doesn't feel like a cold grape."

He grabbed his phone and checked the temps—it was fifty-six degrees and temps would be climbing back into the high seventies today. Apparently, Mother Nature couldn't make up her mind, but hey, we'd take it. Not like we had a choice in the matter anyway.

By mid-morning we were climbing up, up, up a wooded mountainside. Sweat trickled down my stomach, my calves ached, and this pack felt like a leaden weight ever since we'd mended the strap. Clearly, it wasn't distributing the weight properly. Scott was quiet as he led the way, swatting at the gnats that had reawakened on this balmy morning. We'd climbed so many hills on this trek already, why did we have to climb this one? What was so special about it anyway?

There won't be many more of these hills to climb, said a voice from the recesses of my mind, from somewhere cool and calm, where the heat of my present frustration did not smolder.

That voice was right. In just a few days, at this time, I would be in my car on my way to work or maybe zipping around running errands and wishing with all my heart that I was hiking this damn mountain. The familiar dull pain of muscles well worked, the awareness of my lungs expanding with fresh air and tightening when empty, the feeling of this cold, sweat-drenched shirt against my hot skin, the sound of rocks grinding and leaves crunching beneath my feet, and the wide world all around me, a part of me. These were the moments that we needed to hold onto. We were almost to the top.

"Fuck! This ascent is killing me!" Scott hollered out. He stopped suddenly and spun around to look at me wide-eyed, his wet curls dripping sweat down his temples.

"God, I know babe," I blurted, and then paused a moment to catch my breath. "Just two more days." Still grasping my hiking poles, I held out my arms to either side. "This is it."

He peered back at me with a blank stare.

"Shit," he said with a shake of his head, his tone more bittersweet than angry and onward he climbed. I followed suit this time giving gratitude for every footfall.

We ascended and descended, ascended and descended, hit woods road and then road-walk. And on that road, we were delivered manna. Scott discovered them first—bright red juicy apples. They hung from craggy branches of trees long abandoned, tucked into vine-covered thickets and hidden on the edges of overgrown fields. But not all were created equal. The first I bit into was sour and hard, but the next we tried was juicy and sweet. Our stride morphed into a wander, stopping every 100 yards or so and to stop and sample the scarlet fruits, tossing those in the weeds that were too tart and devouring the most prize. When we found an especially tasty tree, we couldn't help but stash a few away in our backpacks for later. Scott's pack was bulging, and he slowed while chomping on an apple as we walked the steep uphill towards Partridge Run Plateau.

"Baby, are you really going to eat all those apples?" I asked, snickering.

"We can have them in our oatmeal in the morning," he replied innocently.

"We only have two more days of oatmeal left!" I reminded him.

"Yeah, well, you'll be happy I have them later. We can take them home if we want. A little piece of the Long Path."

"Okay, as long as you carry them!"

But I already had more than I needed in my backpack, too.

In Partridge Run Wildlife Management Area, we returned to the forest and were offered the reprieve of mostly level cross-country ski trails, overgrown with thorny weeds and, thanks to some nincompoop that had ridden his horse from one end clear to the other, pocked with deep ankle twisting holes. Mounds of poop littered the trail, too, and was now baking in the sun. I was raised with a horse; they are beautiful animals and a joy to ride . . . but not on a hiking trail when the soil is still soft from a heavy rain. And for God's sake, put a poop bag on that thing.

But these unpleasantries were in sharp contrast to the beauty that framed our path. Unruly fields were filled with wild carrot—its flowering tops dried and curved inward so that they looked little bird nests perched on slender spikes—and burdock that stood six feet tall sporting coin-sized spikey burrs. The roots of both these plants, before they have flowered, provide delicious food. Wild carrot is just that, a wild version of our domesticated carrot. Dig it up to find an ivory carrot-looking root. Burdock, which in Japan is called gobo, is a common vegetable, used in sautés and soups, and has long been valued as a fortifying herb, ingested as a tea, in traditional Chinese medicine. I managed to gather some wild carrot seeds to add a hint of parsley flavor to our bowl of noodles that night. When we shuffled over leaf-covered forest roads, spacious sunlit woods suddenly grew up around us and the oaks' outstretched branches created a canopy over our heads. We then wove our way between the towering trunks of Norway spruce and red pine that stood aligned in perfect rows, the forest so dense that our eyes struggled to adjust to the darkness therein. And all along, we took leisurely breaks and snacked and talked and snacked some more.

In our last few miles of the day, we passed pond after lake after pond, each more beautiful than the next. We walked a white gravel road that curved this way and that and we were careful to take the correct forks. Our feet were tired and aching. Throbbing, in fact. It was as if our feet now knew, too, that we neared the end of this trail. But we hiked on until we came to a creek that would be our last good water source for the day. Creeks are better options than ponds or lakes because they are moving and not stagnant. Its water flowed under the road through a cavernous metal pipe, clear and steady into a deep pool where the creek wound into a meadow.

Like baby fawns we struggled to carefully balance ourselves on the sharply angled rock that lined the embankment down to the water, each of us holding tight to our water bottles and bladders. Loose rock slid out from beneath our feet and larger rocks shifted like see-saws beneath our weight. We were just kneeling to dunk our bottles into the deep pool of ice-cold water before us when a loose rock slipped out from under Scott's foot, thrusting him calf-deep into the water and freeing up more loose rock where he'd been standing. He turned 'round and instinctively stepped out onto the first surface he saw—a nearly vertical flat-faced rock—he tried desperately to balance himself, but it only served as a slide. He stumbled and slammed his shins against the rock, sliding waist-deep into the creek. All the while, I stood there dumbly, as if watching a film play across a screen, helpless in stopping his cascade.

I dropped my water bottles and clambered up the rocks onto the grassy edge to meet Scott as he clawed up the embankment. I reached out my arms and he grabbed my wrists tightly, climbing a couple more steps. *Oh, please no, don't let him have broken something. Please,*

please, no. He let go of my hands and grasped at his shin with one hand while leaning on me with the other. Wincing, he limped a few steps forward and then collapsed on the ground. I must have looked aghast because he stated more calmly than I expected, "It's not broken. I just need to rest." His leg was bleeding, gashed open in two places, the flesh already starting to swell, puffy and red. I wanted to cry for him despite his stoicism. We were a mere three-quarters of a mile from camp, but he was soaked from the waist down. He'd hike the whole day tomorrow with, best case scenario, a badly bruised leg and knee. But he didn't shed a tear, so neither did I, and instead I just filled the water bottles. I suggested we set up camp here in the meadow for the night. "It's merely a flesh wound!" he declared with a wincing smirk, and insisted we make it to where we'd planned on camping, beside a small pond.

And so, hand in hand we walked, slowly, down the gravel road that led to the pond. Scott reiterated "Ah! It's a flesh wound!" more than once and we both remarked how thankful we were that it hadn't been worse and that we weren't bracing for freezing temps tonight. After what seemed like an excruciatingly long time, we arrived at a pond surrounded by tall green grasses. At its far end was a single white pine with its whorled boughs outspread and, beneath them, a shaded nook blanketed with dry, auburn-colored needles. This tree would provide just what we needed—shelter and medicine. So, while Scott changed into dry clothes, I got to boiling some water for pine needle tea.

I plucked bundles of green needles from a low-hanging bough. Needles of white pine are not attached to the tree twig individually but rather grouped in bundles of five. No other pine in the Northeast has five needles to a bundle, therefore it's one of the easiest pines to identify. White pine, like many other pines, is antibacterial, therefore helpful in preventing an infection. Once I had a handful, I steeped the needles for about ten minutes, then drenched a bandana in the tea, more accurately called an infusion, and patted his wounds clean. "Oh hon, I wish I could just take that fall away."

I knew I was babying him, but I couldn't help it. What a potentially tragic fall that could've been. Scott has had a bad knee for years. Periodically, at home or at work, for no good reason at all, it'd just give out and he'd find himself on the floor clutching it in pain. His remedy—pop it back into place with a firm jerk. That fall could have ended our hike right then and there. I also had the feeling he was a little bit humiliated, although he had no reason to be.

"Ah. It'll be fine. It just fucking hurts, and that water—holy shit—it was cold," he said with a shiver. I poured the rest of the infusion into our mugs and we reveled in its lemony flavor. Internally, white pine is also diaphoretic, therefore raising our body temperature slightly, and packed with Vitamin C. At this point in the hike, we could use all the nutrition we could get. Afterwards I settled in to cook dinner for the both of us, only to epically fail. Twice, his pot of noodles toppled over because it was poorly balanced, and likely I was more tired and hungry than I'd realized. And so, after losing one dinner to the ground, using up two rounds of fuel, and wasting a half liter of water, we eventually ate what we had and promptly passed out, an owl hooting in the darkness.

CHAPTER TWO

Our eyelids flew open to the sound of gunshots. *Boom!*
Boom! Boom! Boom! Boom! Signs we'd seen along the road on the way into camp
last night were riddled with bullet holes. If this guy was hunting, he was a shit
shot, likely this was target practice.

"Great," Scott said groggily and pushed himself up to sit.

"I guess it's time for breakfast," I declared, rubbing the sleep from my eyes.

We started the day's miles with an easy walk down leaf-strewn gravel roads
that soon turned to dirt through open successional forests. The pale gray bark
of passing trees matched the overcast sky, while at the same time the yellowing
leaves seemed to only grow brighter, luminescent, as we walked beneath their
outstretched branches. We walked along the edge of a wooded escarpment on
land that likely had been farmed, evidenced by the smooth soil beneath us and
the winding rock wall that ran beside us. Through the trees we could see Gifford
Hollow below.

Descending to the valley, we swooshed and stumbled our way through a
farm field thick with tall grasses. The green-gray seedpods of milkweed, dried
and split, revealed tufts of silk and the rusty-colored plumes of ripe dock seeds
punctuated the sepia-tone landscape. We could see at the far end of the field the
pitched roof of a lean-to and the perfect place for a break. As we grew closer, we

found plastic lawn chairs and a bench with real backs that we could lean against. These were arranged thoughtfully around a brick firepit in front. Around back were stacks of firewood just waiting to be burned by a grateful hiker. Inside the lean-to was a register.

Welcome to the lean-to. Hope you enjoy it as much as we do. Please sign your name and let us know where you are from.

The lean-to had been built by Adam Forti, as an Eagle Scout project for hikers' use, with the permission of the private landowner, John Valachovic. The firepit had been built by Eagle Scout Joe Staubach. I paged through the journal and discovered numerous updates from John and Boy Scout Troop 1079, which continued to maintain it:

6/10 Weed-whacked grass today and sprayed bee's nest—hope this finally gets 'em!

7/6 My son and I chopped some more firewood today. It's around back.

8/19 Left some reading material for the hikers.

Interspersed between these entries were entries from many hikers who had passed through and in turn taken a rest at this little oasis. This lean-to was a testament to the care and generosity we humans may impart to one another, strangers that we may never meet. We all would do good to follow the lead of Troop 1079 and this landowner, John, and in addition, treat each other in the real world a little more like we do on the trail.

After a solid reprieve, we hoisted our packs again, hiked along a level trail through the nearby farm fields and then up and over steep winding country road where we followed the trail into Cole Hill State Forest. The forest here felt gentle and bright as we skimmed the edge of a wooded escarpment and lunched in a heap of leaves with a view through the trees of a far-off ridge. Afterwards we vacillated between dark groves of eastern hemlock, where the air smelled of rich damp dirt, and then spruce, where the scent of resin wafted on the breeze and the needles, dry and crisp, crunched beneath our feet. We emerged on a country road in what seemed an instant and were startled with what we saw on the horizon. A jagged grey silhouette pressed against a perfectly blue sky—the

Blackhead range reduced to a viewpoint far in the distance. How had we already come so far from those rugged peaks? Reflecting now, it felt like nearly all of the hike had taken place in the Catskills, its challenges and grandeur eclipsing that which came before and after. We knew that land so well now. No longer would we look out from our cherished spot on Acra Point and wonder what secrets those mountains held in the distance. Instead we would remember what it was like to walk through them, for a period of time, to be a part of them, and in that way, they would always be a part of us.

We returned to the woods, bumping along rutted ATV trails that wove through private woods full of trees plastered with "No Trespassing" signs for what felt like a very long time. Though the woods around us seemed wide, this thin line of trail felt like the only place we were permitted to tread. The ATV tracks eventually decreased as we wandered through ankle-deep leaves over many a rock and root. Where would we possibly put up our tent for the evening? When the trail wasn't sharply sloping left or right, it was overgrown with thorny Japanese barberry shrubs and catbrier and still the "No Trespassing" signs persisted. It was looking like our last campsite wouldn't be desirable one, if we found one at all. We filled up our water bladders for the evening from Fox Creek, a slender ribbon of water in a rocky bed. Looking uphill, I traced its path best I could, and saw that it appeared to meander along the base of a pasture before flowing downhill to us. Visions of tiny protozoa reproducing in my intestinal tract filled my head. *Ah, screw it. By the time those buggers get me I will be back in civilization.* I dunked my water bottle and watched as the sediment swirled inside the plastic vessel.

"This water is murky," said Scott.

"Yeah, well the fact that it's flowing out of a pasture doesn't help," I answered with resignation.

"A pasture?" He looked uphill now at the tract of muddy ground. "Ah, shit. We're going to drink this?"

"What choice do we have? I don't know of another water source coming up and we have to make camp somewhere." I was growing frustrated. I didn't want to, but I couldn't help it. It just didn't seem fair that we had to struggle so on our last night.

"Yeah, somewhere. There's POSTED signs everywhere. I guess we'll just have to be stealthy."

"And hope an ATV doesn't roll up on us," I added.

"This sucks."

"*Sure does.* I had a very different vision of our last night out here."

"Me too, babe." He paused and took a deep breath. "We'll find a good spot somewhere, just have to go a little farther." He had a way of doing that. He could be grumpy as hell, but if my mood started to decline, he'd turn it around, knowing it wouldn't help matters if we both felt sorry for ourselves.

Our water bladders sloshing with what I guessed might be manure water, we hiked on, crossed a road, and followed a grassy trail between two hedgerows only to pop out on yet another road. To our left sat a modest-sized, historic-looking farmhouse in pristine condition. It was lovely with its crisp white paint and black shutters, a wide porch framed with flowers, and a manicured green lawn.

"Look at that place, it's beautiful."

"Sure is," Scott replied with an edge in his voice that suggested he was thinking the same as me.

"Be nice if *they* put us up for the night," I said sarcastically.

"Sure would," he answered.

We trudged up the paved road and saw an old man in blue overalls walking slowly but surely toward his mailbox. We paused, both thinking to say hi, after all, it was clear we'd just followed the trail through his property. But he didn't lift his gaze, and anxious as we were to find camp, we carried on.

"Well hi there!" the man suddenly called out to us.

We halted and turned around to see him looking back at us, one hand firmly grasping his walking stick.

"Hello there!" we called back in unison and Scott put his hand up, gesturing a friendly country wave. The man started walking towards us then. Each step was focused, but steady. We started toward him and we met at the end of his driveway. And there he stood, just standing there, grasping his wooden walking stick and smiling. His stature seemed to broaden, strengthen as he took in the sight of us. He radiated.

"You two are part of a very small group!" he spoke then, his eyes bright and shining.

"Excuse me?" I asked.

"Well you two are hiking the Long Path, aren't you?" he asked.

This man was himself part of a very small group himself, that very small group of people who knew of the Long Path, especially out here, where the trail reduced to a patchwork of parcels between roads, not frequently utilized for recreational hiking.

"Well, yes we are," I said, studying his face now.

"Then you two *are* part of a very small group!" he said proudly.

"This is our last night on the trail," Scott declared.

"Well, where did you start?" the man asked.

"Manhattan," Scott replied.

Just then the old man's eyes grew even brighter. He took a step back.

"New York City? You started at the beginning?"

"Sure did," I answered.

"You two are thru-hikers then. An even *smaller* group!"

Turned out this man was ninety-two-year-old Mr. Wilsey, a longtime resident of this area. Upon learning his name, I recalled that we'd crossed Willsie Road earlier in the day. Generations of his family had lived here, and he had raised his own family here. We learned that he'd been instrumental in creating the trail corridor we'd walked for the afternoon.

"After I discovered the trail, I went knocking on my neighbors' doors. I told them that this trail was valuable. This trail was something special. We *had* to allow it to pass through our property," Mr. Wilsey explained, his very presence imbued with energy. He pointed in the direction of where his neighbors lived.

If it hadn't been for him, we'd have been walking roads all the way to John Boyd Thacher State Park. A narrow corridor or not, at least we'd been in the company of trees and dirt rather than pavement.

As we chatted, a boy rode by on his bike passed and waved, "Hi, Mr. Wilsey!"

Mr. Wilsey waved back, then turned to us and said, "I don't remember his name, but he's such a nice boy. So helpful when I need a hand."

A few minutes later, a woman jogged by. "Hi there!" she called out to Mr. Wilsey and continued up the road.

Mr. Wilsey waved back, then turned to us, "She might be my niece. Not sure." He said, scratching his brow. It seemed everyone knew Mr. Wilsey and he knew everyone, even if he couldn't quite remember names and relations. However, he did remember hikers. He told us about a woman who he'd helped shuttle so that she could hike several small sections in the area. He explained that she'd been from Manhattan, and years later when 9/11 struck, he'd worried about her so. Thankfully, he got in touch with her; she'd been in Italy during that time.

"Some people hike pieces of this trail but not many hike the whole thing," he said motioning with his hiking stick. "That's a long ways. I didn't start hiking until I later in life. But when I did, I fell in love with it. A relative got this walking stick for me in Arizona, it's made from saguaro cactus. I can't go very far now, but I still like to use it," he said, passing it to us to admire.

We talked for a solid hour, mostly about the trail and its route and the experiences we'd had, like Grandpa Porcupine and the bear in the night, and the hot spells and cold spells and the lack of water.

"We had such a problem with water. Before we started the trail, it'd been so rainy where we lived that we assumed the streams would be running. Did it rain much here over the summer?" I asked.

"Hmm . . . this summer . . . don't remember," he said shaking his head. "So, this is your last night, you say?"

"Yeah, can't believe it," Scott said.

"Where are you going to camp?" he asked.

"We thought we'd hike on a few miles, see if we can find some public land up ahead," Scott replied.

"Well, I can put you up in the master bedroom!" he said, gesturing to that lovely little farmhouse we'd both admired.

Scott and I looked at each other. This was a serious offer to weigh. We may have been bemoaning our circumstances just an hour earlier, but a real true home seemed awfully luxurious for our last night on the trail, but then again, the company of Mr. Wilsey, that was hard turn down.

"Oh, my goodness. Thank you, Mr. Wilsey, but I think we want to spend our last night in the open air. That's so kind of you though," I explained.

"Well if you two have a problem, you come back here, and I'll put you up!" he said again. We continued to chat, and I got to thinking about this expanse of farmland. He'd already told us that he owned all the surrounding land, but only because it paid to for the corn that he could grow, not because he cared much for "owning a bunch of stuff."

"Hey, say, I know something that we would take you up on," I started. I felt a little rude asking, but already I felt Mr. Wilsey was a friend.

"What's that?"

"A spot in your fields to put our tent?"

Without a second's hesitation, he exclaimed, "Of course!"

Mr. Wilsey explained that he had told the trail conference they should put a lean-to in one of his fields because the view from the top of the hill was one of the best around. We thanked him for his generosity and revealed how nervous we'd been about finding a spot to camp given all of the POSTED signs. "I never saw any reason in posting signs. I can't see the end of my property anyway, so what does it matter?" he explained. He even went further to tell us about a family some years back that would come every year and camp up on his hill. "Same time every year they'd put up their tent right behind that bush-row! Didn't even know their names. But they never caused any problems, so I saw no point in bothering them."

Just as Mr. Wilsey instructed, for the best view we set up camp amidst the red clover on the other side of the corn at the top of the hill. He'd even supplied us with fresh water. I prepared dinner, and as we slurped noodles seasoned with the fresh parsley-like flavor of wild carrot seeds, we let our gaze settle on the blond haybales squat in the green grass below, the low ridge mottled in autumn hues, and the sharp angle of Vroman's Nose, blue in the far distance; the setting sun bled purple, blue, and blood orange throughout the clouds, providing a water-color backdrop. That night a full moon rose just as it had on our first night on the trail, and from our illuminated perch we could see a single twinkling light from Mr. Wilsey's lovely old farmhouse below. The air was cool, filled with a chorus of chirping crickets, and the night was peaceful; several times we were visited by a deer that, startled by our presence, gave a huff, and a barred owl that hooted, *hoo, hoo, too-HOO, hoo, hoo, too-HOO-aw,* keeping vigil from the forest's edge.

CHAPTER THREE

A rooster's shrill crow tore through my dreams and I
awoke to find our tent bathed in early morning light that dyed its walls the color
of egg yolks. I unzipped a door and looked out at Mr. Wilsey's fields blanketed
in dew, the skies a soft blue masked in a thin layer of clouds; I wanted today to
last forever. I looked over at Scott, who still lightly snored, his body curled up
against mine. I wanted to be with this slumbering man forever and in this very
tent would be just fine. My heart ached. I didn't want to reach the end. Maybe
we never had to leave this tent. If I was real quiet, he'd sleep through the day and
forget that there was a trail to hike at all. But when I carefully rolled over to face
Scott, so close that I could feel his gentle breath on my skin, he stirred.

We began the morning as we usually did—with oatmeal—but today we
added the sliced apples that we'd gathered from the roadside. The apples were
hard and mostly sour but still they tasted like found treasure. I looked at the day's
mileage and for the first time did not consider it relative to how many miles we'd
have to do tomorrow or the next day or the day after that. In just ten and a half
miles, we would be done.

By the time we finished breakfast, the hard, fast caffeine jolt of instant black
coffee was coursing through our veins, and despite our reluctance to reach journey's end, we were eager to see the end of this trail. For over thirty days we had

envisioned it. And so, we packed up our gear, broke down camp, swished through the clovers and then shouldered through ears of sweet corn. By the time we hit the road, our feet were sodden and our shirts and shorts as damp as the fields, at one with our landscape. We walked roads largely level and free of traffic and so the miles rolled by fast. Idyllic farmland framed our path and although the red orbs of the apple trees beckoned, we continued onward without stopping. Our packs were still full of the apples that we'd picked two days ago; once home, would we still desire these fruits that were as hard as baseballs? We followed the aqua blazes into the dark woods of John Boyd Thacher State Park by way of a snaking trail. From this point forward we would walk a true trail to the end.

"I can't believe we're here," Scott said, lighting a smoke and taking a seat atop a rounded rock by a wooden post marking the trail.

I dropped my pack, plunked down atop it, and lit a smoke too. We needed a moment to take this in.

I took a couple drags, long and slow, and peered around at the forest that seemed to only grow darker. "It's surreal," I announced to our silence. The light cast through the trees had disappeared, and I began to wonder if it were really as dark as it seemed. I blinked my eyes, hoping they would adjust.

Then it started to drizzle.

"I thought it wasn't supposed to rain until this afternoon?" Scott directed his question to me, as if I somehow had an explanation.

"It wasn't supposed to," I replied, staring dumbly up at the treetops, tiny drops speckling my face. *How could it rain on our last day?* As the drops continued, light but steady, my disbelief turned to anger. *This wasn't how I envisioned it. It wasn't fair. Not fair at all.* I took another drag of my cigarette, cupping it now to keep it from getting wet. I could see Scott doing the same. "At least it's just a drizzle," Scott said. He had a point. It could be worse, and if there's anything that the trail has taught me, it is that we humans are not in control. If the right factors come together to make rain, by God, it will rain. We finished our smokes, loaded up our packs, and continued down the trail. All of one hundred yards, when a sound like a *whoosh!* stopped us dead in our tracks. The rain was coming from behind us, that *whoosh* growing in volume. In a fever, we dropped our packs and rummaged, retrieving our rain jackets and pack covers. We were still struggling to get them on when the rain started to pummel the leaves overhead so hard it sounded like pebbles on tin.

"These weathermen don't know shit!" Scott yelled over the din. The rain fell so hard that it flattened the brim of his hood.

"What the fuck!" I growled through my teeth. I sounded like a child, I knew that, but I felt like one, too, one that deserved a gold star. Dammit, we'd done our best job, we'd hiked nearly every mile of this trail and we deserved a reward for our efforts. So many times over the last month I'd pictured this day, and always, each time, we were cast against a panorama of blue skies and plentiful sun.

We clomped on down the wide, leaf-covered trail without speaking. Rain poured off my hood like that from a rooftop missing a gutter, splashing drops that caught on my eyelids and then streamed down my face in rivulets. I stopped fighting it. I don't know how, except that I didn't have much choice. I licked my lips and tasted the rainwater, clean and cold and continual. The leaves, red- and orange- and plum-colored, glowed. My face was wet, my hair, my hands, and with every step I splashed water on my bare calves. Wet leaves, in thick stacks, stuck to the tips of Scott's hiking poles and, like patches, decorated the back of his rain jacket. Suddenly, I almost walked right into him. He'd stopped and seemed to be gazing ahead on the trail. I stood beside him and narrowed my eyes to see through the rain what he might be seeing. He turned then to look at me, and his eyes, too, glowed blue and bright like that of chicory. It struck me then, perhaps we too could be nourished by this rainfall if we only let it seep in. Tonight, we would be dry and warm and with all the comforts of home. Now, we were here on the trail, in a rainstorm.

"So be it," Scott declared with a little smile.

"So fucking be it," I answered.

The rain had lessened, downgrading from torrents to weeping buckets, when we turned sharply left into a picnic area and strode across its soggy lawn to a spacious pavilion. Beneath its shelter, we stripped off our raingear and pulled on thermals and hats, then wrapped ourselves back up on our jackets to protect against the wind that had picked up. We sat here for a long while, eating cheese doodles that turned soggy in our pruned fingers. Fake cheese–covered nuggets never tasted so good. Eventually the clouds emptied themselves and the only rain that fell was that from the treetops. I looked at my watch to see that we'd sat here for nearly an hour. Time to get walking.

When we reached a road crossing, we found a parking lot, a stone wall running its length, beyond it, a veil of grey. The wind whipped as we left the shelter of the forest and hit pavement. We climbed atop the flat slate surface of the rock wall and came to stand. Just then, as if by order of the Trail Gods, the wind gusted hard, rolling away the clouds, revealing splotches of the faraway mountains. As our eyes adjusted to the spectrum of grays on the horizon, we spied the Green Mountains of Vermont, those mountains which I vividly remembered hiking on the Appalachian Trail in weather not all that different from today. It had taken me eleven days to traverse them and every single day it had rained. When I had reached their summits, I'd been equally entranced by their beauty, but alone in the heavy fog. There were now so many mountains I'd hiked over the years, so many peaks atop which I'd stood in awe and some that I'd returned to so many times I knew them as well as I knew myself. But never, until this journey, had I known what it was to stand beside the man I loved and share that beauty, to be with another who would now move forward with the knowledge of this place, identical to mine own, a shared memory.

"Look at the way that strip of fog just hangs there in the valley," Scott said then, pointing to a thick ribbon of clouds far in the distance.

Clouds will settle in a valley, over water. It dawned on me then just what that ribbon might indicate.

"That could be the Mohawk River, which would mean, just beyond that is the start of the Adirondack Mountains."

"That's them. That's definitely them. The Adirondacks," Scott said, pointing to the strip of brownish black that stood stark against the light grey of the sky. "We did it," he declared.

I grasped his hand that had finally warmed after the rain.

"I love you, baby."

"I love you so damn much," he said then, squeezing my hand tight.

From where we stood, perched on the edge of the Helderberg Escarpment, we could see a proud pavilion-like structure that shared our cliff, approximately a mile away. Judging from the guidebook, this was likely part of the visitor's center; it sat just a handful of miles from the trail's end.

After a short walk through the woods, we indeed popped out at that pavilion and then followed the edge of the escarpment to the attraction at the end of an expansive parking lot. There we stood in its shadow; this was no average visitor's center but rather a multi-million-dollar ecofriendly facility. Despite its creators' efforts to align this building with nature, it seemed out of place and in futile competition with the ecological beauty surrounding it. This structure only confirmed my suspicions, which had arisen at the Sam's Point Visitor Center: we humans have developed a sorry preference to visit nature from within the comfort of completely unnatural confines. We're encouraged to gawk rather than interact, unintentionally maintaining separation. Nonetheless, we strode inside and proudly announced to the woman at the front desk that we were completing the Long Path today. Her reaction was delayed, and I had the feeling she hadn't the slightest clue what I was talking about; still, she soon smiled brightly at us and handed us chocolates wrapped up in foil to look like eyeballs.

Wow. That's right. Back in the real world, Halloween was on its way. Any notion of the holidays had been far from our minds. Today was our holiday and all that mattered was that we were standing in this spot, just south of the Adirondacks, which, before now, we'd seen only on the map. So be it. Chocolate eyeballs now seemed a perfectly celebratory offering, a sort of gold star, as did using a real bathroom, and so, by her directions, we headed downstairs. Here, we found an array of taxidermy displayed in panoramas behind walls of glass; the same kind of animals that we had seen and heard and smelled, and lived amongst, during the last month. There was also a mock cave with a button that, when pushed, played a recording of water dripping down its sides. It couldn't compare to the sound of fat drops drip-drapping off moss-covered rocks into shallow shadowy puddles, not to mention the feeling of the cool air these moist cliffs encase on warm skin, and best of all, the taste of that mineral-rich water. We grabbed a couple of maps outlining the park and eyed the leather couches surrounding a coffee table. It was awfully tempting. All the world seemed to call to us to rest here awhile . . . after all it was warm and dry. But instead we exchanged a knowing look and scurried back up the stairs. We would be warm and dry tonight.

"Your Mom called!" exclaimed the woman from behind the front desk.

"Pardon?" I turned and said. Surely, I hadn't heard her right.

"She called for directions, said your Dad was on his way and worried about finding his way to you," she explained.

Apparently, it doesn't matter how old you are, Mom will always be Mom and, just the same, Dad will always be Dad. My father may have a cell phone, but the only numbers he has programmed are immediate family and these are the only numbers he calls. Therefore, it's usually my mother who makes the necessary phone calls to retrieve directions and the like, which she then relays to my father. Forget Googling—my father also refuses to use a computer because he claims he can't understand them (that and they're an ideal way for the government to track you), but he's a pro when it comes to operating one of our modern televisions with three different remotes. Nonetheless, Dad, adventurous as he is, has more than once delivered me to or retrieved me from a trailhead in the middle of nowhere. Today he would do just that at the northern terminus of the Long Path.

We thanked the woman at the front desk, pocketed a few more eyeballs, and retreated to the Adirondack-style chairs sheltered under a roof outside the front door. We dug out our tin pots and alcohol stoves and fired them up for coffee, then threw on our puffy jackets, tugged on our knit caps and reclined in our wooden chairs like the Long Path king and queen atop their thrones. For lunch we dined on the last of our hard cheese and English muffins, sipped instant black coffee—deliciously luxurious in the middle of the day—and unwrapped eyeballs for dessert. A victorious feast. I spread out the park map which offered an up-close look at the remainder of our route and, with my finger, traced a bold white line to Old Stage Road, where the Long Path emblems ran out. We had just five miles left.

With much reluctance, an hour later, we got to hiking. By now the sun peeked through pockets in the sky's thick clouds and we walked along the edge of the Helderberg Escarpment, which carved around the valley like a half-moon keeping sentinel. One of the most fossiliferous regions in the country, the escarpment safeguards a geologic history, telling a story of this land dating back hundreds of millions of years. From beneath our feet, walls of smooth rock dropped steeply into a chasm below. The foundation of John Boyd Thacher State Park, essentially a chunk of porous limestone, is continually shaped by underground waterways, rainfall, and time. This rock atop which we stood housed a maze of caves that spread like subway tunnels beneath a city, but with much less order. As we turned away from the escarpment and into the woods, we soon got up close and personal with this erosion. *This section of the Long Path through Thacher Park has geological significance, with many fissures in the limestone rock, some of which are covered with leaves. Please use caution when hiking on the Long Path and other trails within Thacher Park*, read a sign nailed to a tree near the entrance of the woods.

Shallow gashes scarred the leaf-strewn forest floor to either side of us, and to prevent a wandering hiker's fall, orange netting encircled deep hollows that revealed tangles of roots and rocks and chunks of soil. As we hiked on, remaining on our narrow trail, we allowed our gaze to widen; it soon became apparent that the very ground atop which we tread was essentially fissured into plates and chunks. Now and again, we'd spot a crater beside a large rock and we'd have to stop and peer inside, but there was no seeing bottom, it seemed a portal to the belly of the earth itself. How different it would have been to grow up in this region, exploring the forest. Back in our neck of the woods, the forest had always offered solace. I would sometimes imagine my legs as roots that stretched deep into the soil, and there I would stand immovable, grounded and strong. But here one could not trust in that immutable solidity of earth, not when the very ground beneath your feet is uncertain.

Scott stopped to tape up a couple toes that had finally rubbed raw from walking in wet socks and shoes since his fall in the stream. He laughed as he tore the surgical tape between his teeth.

"What's so funny?" I asked.

"It's a little ironic, don't you think? This is my first blister of the whole hike."

"I guess even our feet know it's time to surrender."

The miles passed in a blur. We teased each other relentlessly about falling into a fissure or being swallowed up by a sinkhole, we sang every song we knew about walking hundreds of miles, and even pretended as if we were on our own survival reality show.

"With just a few miles to go will Scott and Heather make it to the end?!" I chided Scott in a TV announcer voice. We had to make light of the enormity of reaching our journey's end. Had we not, we both would've been sobbing.

One mile from the end, we followed a short side trail to a vista called High Point, the highest point along the Helderberg Escarpment. We took a good long break here, snacking and smoking, gazing into the wide valley toward the city of Albany and at the horizon, where we could see the pronounced peak of Mount Killington in the Green Mountains. Atop a cold, flat rock, Scott cradled me as the sun poured down upon us, warming our bare arms and legs, which were now brown like the dirt and ornamented in scrapes and scabbed bug bites. Again, I was struck by how utterly different I felt now than during those days in rainy Vermont, another lifetime ago.

"Thank you, baby." I broke the silence. This, a sorry summary for all my gratitude. My chest cavity felt filled with so much heart it might explode.

"Are you kidding? I should be the one thanking you. This has been one of the most amazing journeys of my life," he said, holding me tighter, pressing his cheek against mine, his thick beard scratchy against my dry skin. Our bodies might be weathered but in all that weathering we were changed, comfortable in life's inevitable uncertainty and no longer anxious about what might come next.

"Me too, luv. I never thought I'd find a man who'd *want* to go on these crazy hikes with me."

"Nor did I think I'd find a woman who loved the wander, the unknown. We found each other. Thank God."

I felt his warm tears now trickling down my cheek and soon, my own. Tears of happiness, of victory, but also tears for the journey's end. They blurred my vision, smudging the thin white clouds that curled across the sky, and it was as if we were surrounded, wrapped up in pale blue. When the wind, light and warm, turned crisp and cool, we knew we had rested long enough.

Walking our last mile through the reds and oranges and purples of the autumn forest, I let myself see, feel, be, every bristly spiral of lycopodium and fan-like spray of cinquefoil leaflets. Red partridgeberries glowed like little lights, slyly showing us the way through the leaves at my feet. And then, just as I'd feared it might, my heart grew so large that it felt like a mushroom cloud ballooned in my chest, cracking my sternum and blasting open my ribcage. I was vulnerable, exposed. But I had no fear. I let the wind blow through me, and as it did all that love I'd been feeling was no longer directed to Scott, to the trail, to the little red partridgeberries; it was diffused and my reluctance to finish evaporated like dew on a hot rock. There was so much more to look forward to, so many more miles to hike and vistas to admire, sour mountain ash berries to nibble and stinging wood nettle leaves to precariously pluck, soaking rainstorms to endure and rocky cliffs to sunbathe atop, bags of orange-dusted Cheetos to eat and ice-cold sodas to slurp, and for the first time, I knew, through all this, I'd have my love by my side.

The trail led us into an expansive field filled with tall golden grasses where the sun shone so bright that I had to squint, buzzing insects whizzing by my ears. Then, just as suddenly, we were carried into the darkness of the woods, and my eyes struggled to adjust yet again. The air was cool and still and smelled of damp earth. When we reached a metal gate that marked the boundary between woods and road, we could see on its other side the smooth, crushed gravel of the parking area just off Old Stage Road.

We whooped and hollered, we were children elated, enlivened by the very ground atop which we stood. No longer were we doing it, we had done it. Our excitement obliterated the ordinariness of this no-name parking lot in upstate New York where no plaque marked the trail's end. Hell, there wasn't even a Long Path emblem on a tree. From the looks of things, it mattered to no one but us that we'd walked this thin line of trail 358 miles to reach this spot on the map. But generally, I think that's the way it works anyway, at least when one lives a life that is defined as meaningful on their own terms. Daily occurrences in and of themselves are typically not significant and we often mistake our milestones for the mundane when in the moment. It's not until we reflect that we discover the significance of a series of occurrences or singular events. Our experiences are what we make of them and what they make of us and the meaning that we find in them. We wouldn't yet know what effects might ripple out from our shared experience out here on the trail, but what we did know for certain was that we'd discovered each other over and over again, mile by mile, day by day, and night after night.

After we'd reached a frenzy and finally exhausted ourselves, we plopped down on the gravel and offered up some tobacco to the Trail Gods for seeing us through to the end. There may have been moments in which we felt victorious, but overall, we'd been humbled, graced with the opportunity, patience, and endurance to walk this path, and throughout we'd received so many gifts—beauty, clarity of mind, strength, and, above all, love.

Just then my father's pickup truck came barreling down the road and turned a sharp right into the parking lot, his tires skidding on the gravel.

"Hey! Hey!" he said as he hopped out. "A long time since Nyack! You two look great!" He gave us each a big hug. He grabbed our packs, wincing under their weight and threw them in the back of the truck with a grunt.

"I brought you guys something," he declared then, barely able to conceal a grin.

He reached in the cab of the truck and retrieved a wooden board from the backseat. It had been painted white, accented with tiny evergreen trees and shellacked. In dark green lettering it read: *Long Path Official End-to-End.*

"I brought a hammer and nail, too. You can't finish a trail without a sign at the end!"

One night we had called my parents from a hotel room and lamented that we'd find no sign marking the trail's end. Before we'd started our hike I'd casually mentioned taking our picture at the end of our hike by the finish sign to Andy, to which he replied over the receiver with a chuckle, "What sign? There's no sign."

I had paused, phone in hand, looking dumbly at Scott who sat beside me. "Well, how will we know when we've reached the end?" I asked.

"Just stop walking when you reach Old Stage Road. We're in the process of blazing and building a trail all the way to the Adirondacks proper, but it's not really trail yet. Old Stage Road—that's the official trail's end."

Just stop walking. Yeah, okay, we were like two well-greased wheels that had been set in motion. We'd be lucky if we didn't walk through the parking lot, into the Adirondacks, and clear to Canada. Turns out my parents thought we deserved a sign, too, one that conveyed not only STOP! but YOU DID IT! So, together, they had handmade one.

Scott carefully held the sign in place while my father nailed it to a slender tree that stood tall behind a thicket of overgrown blackberry vines. Somewhere along the way, Scott had found one of those metal Long Path emblems, a disk that had been nailed to a tree to mark the trail, in a patch of moss. He'd planned on keeping it for sentimental value, but now he'd dug it out of his pack and wedged it between the sign and tree trunk. Numerous finish photos ensued and before we knew it, there was nothing left to do but go home. But before hopping into the truck, I walked across the gravel to the edge of the parking lot and peered down the road; two consecutive telephone poles stood, each blazed in aqua along the roadside. It was true that we had reached the official end, but I knew then, our long path was just beginning.

THE END

Reaching the trail's end in John Boyd Thacher State Park.

ACKNOWLEDGEMENTS

Writing a book, I have learned, is a lot like hiking a long-distance trail. The dream begins as your own and although your hike may be solo, by no means will you attain that dream without the help and support of those you meet along the way.

Thank you to my love, Scott, for your ceaseless encouragement, enthusiasm, and support in all my endeavors. You helped to carry my load, both figuratively and literally, and bolstered my confidence when I feared I wouldn't make it. You are my rock. With your love, I know I will always reach the next summit.

To my parents, Doug and Pam, thank you for fostering in me a love for the outdoors, providing me the security to seek the big adventures, and your unwavering belief in all I do. Mom, your patience and ability to listen is profound and your love ever felt. House the Cat, you've not only helped to scare away the bears but made each mile we've hiked together more special than they'd ever be alone. You both have always supported me in my less-than-typical aspirations.

Aunt Debby, thank you for your continual support in my writing endeavors and reminding me not to sweat the small stuff. Thanks to your expertise and assistance over the years, I have written my *third* book.

To my sister, Linnea, who was the writer first. You inspired me to put pen to paper.

Thank you to Andy Garrison, for sharing your wisdom about the Long Path. Your generosity in providing logistical insight, enthusiasm, and support not only made our hike a successful one but made this book possible. Your passion for this trail is contagious. And my goodness, you sure answered a lot of questions.

Thank you to Bob Ross for your support in the Long Path and your generosity in helping this book come to fruition.

Thank you to Ken Posner, for your belief in the Long Path and your belief in this book. You provided support not only on the trail, but well after our hike was accomplished. You offered your experience and kindness without hesitation. That is a rare quality.

To Emeline Posner, thank you for your expertise and thoughtfulness in editing. The care and consideration with which you handled this book made the work a joy. You helped to craft my thoughts into words.

To Star Left, I am so glad we met on that country road years ago. Thank you for your assistance and companionship throughout our hike. You always gave us something to look forward to. Thank you for your friendship. It's good to know there's another weirdo out there like me.

Thank you to the many people we met along the way who offered water, food, words of support, and friendly conversation. You are the people that make a long hike special and a testament to the kindness of strangers. Never doubt that the smallest gesture makes a big impact.

Thank you to the blog readers, Facebook followers, and friends and family back home that rallied us on and joined us in spirit. You shared in our journey and made it an adventure.

Lastly, thank you to the New York–New Jersey Trail Conference and its volunteers for making this trail a reality and working to preserve the Long Path for perpetuity.

ABOUT THE AUTHOR

Heather "The Botanical Hiker" Houskeeper is an herb-alist and long-distance hiker. She has thru-hiked the Appalachian Trail, Mountains to Sea Trail, Long Path, and Florida Trail, and is the first person to have hiked the Finger Lakes Trail and its six branches in one continuous trek. She holds a bachelor's degree in philosophy from Warren Wilson College and a certificate in herbal medicine, botany, plant identification, and medicine making from the Chestnut School of Herbal Medicine. As a lifelong student of Nature, she utilizes the trails that crisscross her meadows, thread through her forests, and climb her mountains as pathways to deeper learning.

In her profession as The Botanical Hiker, Heather guides others into the natural world through seminars, workshops, and plant walks, striving to deepen their relationship with the natural world and its botanical inhabitants. She is the author of two books about edible and medicinal plants, and the Wild Food columnist for *Dirt Magazine*. This is her first narrative book.

She resides in Milford, Pennsylvania, with her partner, Scott, coonhound, Amos, and a whole mess of wildflowers.

To learn more about The Botanical Hiker, visit her website at www. TheBotanicalHiker.com. Join her on Facebook at www.Facebook.com/ TheBotanicalHiker and on her blog at www.TheBotanicalHiker.blogspot.com.

12 - Setßm provisions
285 - Yarrow - 254
277 - A walk in the woods - Bill Bryson
middleburgh
288 - wild carrot, Burdock
289 - white Pine - Pine needle T